Reading Islam

Social, Economic and Political Studies of the Middle East and Asia

FOUNDING EDITOR: C.A.O. VAN NIEUWENHUIJZE

Editor

Dale F. Eickelman

Advisory Board

Ruth Mandel (*University College London*)
Bettina Gräf (*Ludwig-Maximilians-Universität*)

VOLUME 123

The titles published in this series are listed at *brill.com/seps*

Reading Islam

Life and Politics of Brotherhood in Modern Turkey

By

Fabio Vicini

BRILL

LEIDEN | BOSTON

Cover illustration: Image drawn from Giorgio Tentolini's artistic work "Namaz."

Library of Congress Cataloging-in-Publication Data

Names: Vicini, Fabio, 1981- author.
Title: Reading Islam : life and politics of brotherhood in modern Turkey / by Fabio Vicini.
Description: Leiden ; Boston : Brill, [2020] | Series: Social, economic and political studies of the Middle East and Asia, 1385-3376 ; volume 123 | Includes bibliographical references and index.
Identifiers: LCCN 2019037124 (print) | LCCN 2019037125 (ebook) | ISBN 9789004409316 (hardback) | ISBN 9789004413757 (ebook)
Subjects: LCSH: Muslims--Turkey--Istanbul--Intellectual life--21st century. | Muslims--Religious life--Turkey--Istanbul. | Gülen Hizmet Movement. | Weşanên Nûbihar. Rêza Rîsaleyên Nur--Reading. | Islamic learning and scholarship--Turkey--Istanbul--History--21st century. | Islamic renewal--Turkey. | Islam and politics--Turkey. | Islam--Social aspects--Turkey.
Classification: LCC BP63.T82 I788 2020 (print) | LCC BP63.T82 (ebook) | DDC 297.094961/8--dc23
LC record available at https://lccn.loc.gov/2019037124
LC ebook record available at https://lccn.loc.gov/2019037125

Typeface for the Latin, Greek, and Cyrillic scripts: "Brill". See and download: brill.com/brill-typeface.

ISSN 1385-3376
ISBN 978-90-04-40931-6 (hardback)
ISBN 978-90-04-41375-7 (e-book)

Copyright 2020 by Koninklijke Brill NV, Leiden, The Netherlands.
Koninklijke Brill NV incorporates the imprints Brill, Brill Hes & De Graaf, Brill Nijhoff, Brill Rodopi, Brill Sense, Hotei Publishing, mentis Verlag, Verlag Ferdinand Schöningh and Wilhelm Fink Verlag.
All rights reserved. No part of this publication may be reproduced, translated, stored in a retrieval system, or transmitted in any form or by any means, electronic, mechanical, photocopying, recording or otherwise, without prior written permission from the publisher.
Authorization to photocopy items for internal or personal use is granted by Koninklijke Brill NV provided that the appropriate fees are paid directly to The Copyright Clearance Center, 222 Rosewood Drive, Suite 910, Danvers, MA 01923, USA. Fees are subject to change.

This book is printed on acid-free paper and produced in a sustainable manner.

Printed by Printforce, the Netherlands

For Asya

Contents

Acknowledgments IX
Note on Transliteration and Turkish Pronunciation XI

Introduction: Reading Islam in Modern Times 1
1. Reading is Transcending 3
2. Accommodating Modernity 7
3. Thinking Islam 11
4. A Revival of Muslim Civility 17
5. Fieldwork in Two Concealed Communities 22
6. Before and after July 15 27
7. Outline of the Book 31

1 Outreaches of Religious Service 33
1. Reading the *Risale* 36
2. Reforming Society through Educational Service 39
3. From *Hizmet* to Individual Duty 45
4. Modernity and the Displacement of Islamic Ethics 50
5. The Islamic Revival, Urban Life and Community 56

2 Living the Brotherhood 63
1. Daily Life in the Houses 64
2. Discipline and Prayer 69
3. Time and Prayer 72
4. Living by Example 74
5. Brotherhood between Pedagogy and Authority 79
6. Brotherhood between Civility and Corporate Personality 84
7. Virtues of Mutuality 87
8. Living Sincerity 92

3 Reading, Reflection and the Search for Transcendence 97
1. Appealing to the Imagination 101
2. Iterative Reading 105
3. Reading as Cultural Practice 109
4. Genealogies of Reflection 115
5. Toward a Sufi Cosmology 119

6   Reflecting on Death   124

4 Putting Islam to Work   132
  1   Education, the Nation and the Islamic "Ethos"   134
  2   Accessing Quality Education   141
  3   Modern Times, Docile Methods   145
  4   From *Jihad* to Reforming Society   148
  5   Life and Tutoring in the Gülen Housings   151
  6   Romanticizing Prophethood   155
  7   Learning by Example   158
  8   Embodying Responsibility   162

5 Politics of Brotherhood   169
  1   "You'll Be of Service to This Country"   171
  2   The Nur Self's Spaces of Will and Freedom   173
  3   The Relativity of the Good: On the Modern Liberal Conception of the Self   177
  4   Being an Aware and Responsible Muslim   183
  5   On Brotherhood and Moral Reasoning   188

Conclusion   198

References   207
Index   230

Acknowledgments

This book is the outcome of several years of research, fieldwork, and writing, and would not have been possible without the support and contribution of a number of interlocutors, colleagues, friends, and family. I would first like to express my deepest gratitude to Armando Salvatore. With intellectual rigor and philosophical erudition, but also by example, Armando has been a fundamental reference point for me, as a scholar and a person, during these years. Those who are familiar with his work will recognize the influence of his thinking across most of this book, and there are no adequate words to express my gratitude. I also owe special thanks to Michelangelo Guida and Setrag Manoukian, both of whom have played a crucial role in my intellectual initiation. Michelangelo has extended to me most of what I know about Turkey's society and politics and has encouraged me to explore the religious-conservative camp with scrutiny and dedication. As a colleague and a friend, he has always expressed the greatest generosity to me, and I am indebted to him for this. To Setrag, I am particularly grateful for having introduced me to seminal debates in the anthropology of Islam and the Middle East several years ago during my graduate studies at the University of Milano-Bicocca, and for his encouragement and advice during these years.

Besides, I have particularly benefitted from conversations with Paola Abenante regarding the anthropology of Islam, Sufism, and the place of "modernity" in the exploration of this complex field; Kim Shively and Martin van Bruinessen on the trajectory of Islamic movements in Turkey, and the sociopolitical transformations of the last decade and a half; and Nada Moumtaz about the question of continuity and change in Islamic tradition. I am also grateful to all my other colleagues whose engagement with my work have contributed to giving this book its final shape: Fida Adely, Hatsuki Aishima, Schirin Amir-Moazami, Ercüment Asıl, Philipp Bruckmayr, Estella Carpi, James Seale-Collazo, Feray Coşkun, Kristina Dohrn, Dietrich Jung, Jakob Krais, Önder Küçükural, Gennaro Gervasio, Oğuzhan Göksel, William Holt, Kasper Mathiesen, Shireen Mirza, Paulo Pinto, Francesco Piraino, Emin Poljarevic, Dietrich Reetz, Samuli Schielke, Mark Sedgwick, Kirstine Sinclair, Abdulkader Tayob, Mara Tedesco, Caroline Tee, and Berna Zengin Arslan.

The research project that lies at the heart of this book was initially conceived at the Istituto Italiano di Scienze Umane in Siena (now Istituto di Scienze Umane e Sociali, Scuola Normale Superiore, Florence and Pisa). I owe special thanks to people from the Centro AMA, particularly to Maurizio Bettini and Simone Beta for their support and help. A particular thank you also goes to

Leonardo Piasere, who has encouraged and advised me at critical moments of my fieldwork; to Claudia Mattalucci for her guidance and friendship; and to Ugo Fabietti, who sadly has left us too soon.

I would also like to thank the Berlin Graduate School Muslim Cultures and Societies (BGSMCS) and *Zentrum Moderner Orient* (ZMO) for having provided me with a fellowship at the beginning of the writing of this work. I am also grateful to the organizers and participants of the 2012 UCSIA Summer School, Antwerp. In particular, I would like to thank Robert Hefner, Grace Yukich, Nancy A. Khalil, and Pooyan Tamimi Arab, for suggestions and criticism. This project was completed at Istanbul 29 Mayis University, where apart from people already mentioned above, I would like to thank Emrah Safa Gürkan and Özgür Ünal Eriş for their sympathetic support and friendship.

I am particularly indebted to the series editor at *Brill*, Dale F. Eickelman, for his encouragement and support at different stages of the process, as well as to my in-house editor Nienke Brienen-Moolenaar for her assistance with the completion of this book. I am also grateful for the valuable suggestions and comments made by the anonymous reviewers for *Brill*. I would also like to express my gratitude to James Disley for assisting me with editing a preliminary version of the manuscript.

Needless to say, this book would have not been possible without the help, patience, and humanity of the people I worked with in Istanbul, whose names I have not mentioned in order to protect their privacy. A thank you goes to the elder brothers and students of the communities that I researched who trusted me and dedicated their time to me.

Finally, this work would have never been possible without the support of my family, in particular my mother and father. Last but not least, my deepest gratitude and affection goes to Entela, the person who has probably taught me most about humanity. Without her encouragement and her unshakable belief in me and my work, this book would never have become a reality. Thank you for having chosen to take this long journey with me.

Note on Transliteration and Turkish Pronunciation

I have generally opted for using the Ottoman and Turkish versions of words in the Latin script of Modern Turkish when the text deals primarily with Ottoman and Turkish history and, relatedly, with the two communities under study (i.e., *ulema* in place of *ulama*, *vakıf* in place of *wafq*). Contrarily, when talking more generally about the broader Islamic tradition, Arabic terms have been preferred to Turkish ones (i.e., *tafakkur* instead of the Turkish *tefekkür*, *dhikr* instead of *zikr*, *sunna* instead of *sünnet*, *fiqh* instead of *fıkıh*). Words of Arabic and Persian origin have been transliterated following a highly simplified transliteration system, without using diacritics apart from the ʿ*ayn* and the *hamza* of the words Qurʾan and *shariʿa* and *daʿwa* respectively. Also, the names of Islamic works and scholars have been reported without diacritics. Turkish words have been reported in their modern Latin script form, without diacritics apart from those that are normally present in modern Turkish writing (ö, ü, ğ, ç). For simplification, I have pluralized Turkish and Arabic words using an "s" (i.e., *ulema*s in place of *ulemalar*, *abi*s in place of *abiler*). Names of places like Istanbul have been rendered in their commonly used English forms. All dates are expressed in CE.

Modern Turkish is written in Latin script, but it contains several letters that are not present in the English alphabet, which are pronounced as follows:

Ç, ç   "ch" as in "chart"
ğ   lengthens the sound of the vowel preceeding it; when between two vowels it is not pronounced
I, ı   the sound of the "a" as pronounced in "along"
Ö, ö   same as the sound of "u" in "turn"
Ş, ş   "sh" as in "shine"
Ü, ü   "u" as in "cube"

Introduction: Reading Islam in Modern Times

The evening reading had finished more than an hour before. After eating the bits of fruit and drinking the several glasses of tea that typically followed community meetings, the group of roughly twenty students who had attended the lesson had departed. Rather than returning to his room to study for the upcoming exams, Selim—a student at the Faculty of Law at Istanbul University in his early twenties—kindly agreed to stay with me to answer my questions, as we continued to sip from our tea glasses. Despite his young age, Selim had been entrusted with the duty of looking after a group of university students that he lived with in a house that was affiliated with the *Suffa* community, one of the many groups composing the constellation of the Nur movement. Like other such communities, people at *Suffa* follow the teachings of Said Nursi (1877–1960), a late Ottoman Muslim reformer who inspired what probably is the most important reformist-oriented Islamic revivalist movement of modern Turkey. As the highest guide present in the house, Selim was clarifying for my benefit the seminal importance of Nursi for generations of Muslims who had grown up in the country after the foundation of the Turkish Republic in 1923. To illustrate how their approach to Islam differed from that of previous generations of Muslims, he clarified:

> Muslims must worship, right? It is a requirement of Islam. But if you told me 100 or 150 years ago, 'We've got to perform the daily prayer because,' let's say, 'if we don't, hell will be waiting for us,' this would suffice and people would go on and do their prayers. This is because there was not even the slightest hint of a question in their minds. But today if you tell someone: 'Go and do the prayer,' he's going to ask, 'What for?' This is the age of reason. This is the age of science (*fen*). In the olden days, people never questioned anything… but today, we've got to have reasons for why we must worship.

These words reflect the general conviction of people at *Suffa* and in the Nur movement at large, that today it is no longer the time for Muslims to be content with believing and complying with the main requirements of faith obsequiously. Today is the time of thinking and hence of knowing *why* one has to be a good Muslim.

The novel view that contemporary Muslims should aspire to an informed way of living Islam is dependent on the altered epistemological conditions of modernity, which have indelibly changed the way even the least engaged

Muslim entertains thoughts about religious truths and obligations. Beginning in the nineteenth century, Muslim scholars and practitioners have been confronted with the question of why exactly they believe in and practice Islam. Ever since it has indeed become crucial for them to be able to reply to all questions and doubts concerning their faith in ways they had hitherto never done, a condition that has been famously named the "objectification" of Muslim consciousness (Eickelman and Piscatori 1996, 37–38). Such a stress on the reasons behind one's faith has a powerful reverberation in view of the specific focus that people at the *Suffa* community have on reading as a central formative practice.

The same can be said for the Gülen community—today best known in Turkey by the acronym FETÖ, Fethullah Gülen's Terrorist Organization (*Fetullahçı Terör Örgütü*)—the other offshoot of the Nur movement *Reading Islam* explores.[1] Despite its self-representation, especially abroad, as a Sufi movement, this community also maintains a reform-inspired attitude. Since my earliest encounters back in 2005 with members of the community in Istanbul, I have been struck by the importance that they bestowed upon persistently reading not only the texts of both Said Nursi and their leader Fethullah Gülen (b. 1936/8) but also books about modern science—while the Qur'an and other classics of the Islamic tradition were mostly ignored. The fact that they spent most of their time reading these kinds of texts was highlighted by young men I was speaking with as a sign *per se* of a distinction between their way of living Islam and that of other Muslims both in Turkey and elsewhere. What surprised me most was not that they did not pay as much attention to the classic Islamic canon as I would expect. Rather, it was the fact that reading was upheld as a defining characteristic in their concept of a correct Muslim life. To me, such an attitude suggested the existence of a visceral relationship between the reformed branch of Turkish Islam to which these two communities belong and a particular idea of modern times as times of scrutiny and knowledge.

By presenting an account of the place reading and, more generally, intellectual practice occupy in the life of new generations of piously educated Muslims in today's Turkey, *Reading Islam* jolts the self-assuredness lying behind common assumptions that see Islam and Muslim life as unsuited to reflection and intellectual discernment (Ahmad 2017). For Selim and the other young men I met in the field, engaging with fundamental ontological questions about their place in existence and their responsibility as human beings living in the

---

1 In the book I will refer to it as Gülen community (*Gülen cemaati*) because this is how the group was generally named by outsiders when I conducted my study, although, as it will be shown, the community preferred to define itself as *hizmet*.

modern world is an integral part of the way they lead a Muslim life. For them, collectively reading and discussing Islamic texts is conducive to responding to questions that appear more and more pressing today, when an era of hedonism and areligiosity has come to predominate. This does not mean that I will attempt to link directly the reading of Islamic texts with the use of critical reason. As it will be shown extensively, within both the *Suffa* and the Gülen communities reading was associated with a path aimed at achieving spiritual awareness and that retained a clear disciplinary character. Also, the fact that reading the *Risale* was for my interlocutors a way to "re-enchant" their worldview seems to suggest an even sharper contrast between their practices and modern understandings of intellectual engagement. However, contrary to scholarly accounts that would exclude *a priori* religiously-grounded forms of reflection from proper intellectual practice, *Reading Islam* illustrates how, for these young men, reading and reflection are part of the way they cultivate themselves as informed Muslims.

1   Reading is Transcending

Taking into account meditative practice in Islam, and in religion more generally, implies to engage in an enterprise aimed at exploring intellectual practice beyond what are usually considered its proper limits. Notoriously, since the Enlightenment, attempts at relating human existence to an otherworldly domain have been implicitly accused of high doses of irrationalism. In this eminently Western tradition, indeed, intellective speculation has been conceived as something that had to remain confined within the limits of this world. The human search for knowledge was equated to the search for the inherent truths, that is, to the exploration of worldly phenomena and causal relations among them. If a transcendent principle had been included into such a heuristic framework, it would imply a negation of the very project for modern knowledge which was based on the rational and scientific scrutiny of human and natural life. As a consequence, over time philosophy came to be regarded as a discipline concerned with the rational exploration of human life, while metaphysics developed into a field that was no longer related, as it was in ancient times, to transcendence and the cultivation of an ethical conduct (Hadot 2004). Relatedly, when the humanities and the social sciences emerged as two separate domains of knowledge in the nineteenth century, they were in turn both conceived as distinct from theology. Therefore, the place of transcendent reality in human life in general, and in reflective practice in particular, has been generally omitted from scholarly investigations in the social sciences because it is considered either logically or methodologically inappropriate (Milbank 2006 [1990]; Kahn 2016).

Jeffrey L. Kosky (2004) has interestingly identified the origins of the exclusion of transcendence from scholarly inquiry in the emergence of a philosophy of immanence declaring the "death of God." Relying on Hegel's critique of coeval philosophers like Kant and Fichte, Kosky traces the genealogy of this tradition back to Martin Lutero. He argues that as the Protestant priest attempted to allow the ordinary believer to access a more intimate relation with God, he paradoxically ended up secluding religious experience to the private inner domain. While transcendence was before conceived as being part of the worldly order of things, Protestantism banished the idea of the infinite (and hence of God himself) from the sphere of human heuristic speculation. Although this move was probably motivated by the noble intent of preserving the image of God from mingling with worldly matters, it instituted an "unbridgeable separation" between finite human existence and transcendence. As a result, God has been definitively severed from the field of tangible and knowledgeable objects and projected into an unreachable domain that the religious practitioners can only yearn for (Kosky 2004, 14). One of the consequences of this process was the foundation of the "subjective standpoint" that according to Kosky is so central in modern philosophical views, including those of Kant and Fichte. Such views consolidated during the Enlightenment, which "absolutized the distinction between the finite and infinite, man and God," in ways that man was seen as determined by finitude and as incapable of elevating himself to the eternal and absolute (Kosky 2004, 16).[2]

In their critique of the foundation of modern philosophy, several authors have lately begun rehabilitating transcendence as a tangible ground of epistemological, ethical, aesthetic, and political realization (Taylor 1989, 2004; Milbank 2004, 2006 [1990]; Schwartz 2004; Zizek 2004). The same is happening, though slowly and partially, in the field of anthropology. Given the long-standing interest for the presence of spirits, gods, and saints in human life, this

---

2 From an aesthetic perspective, John Milbank (2004), an advocate for the need of reintegrating theology into the social sciences, has described these transformations as God's seclusion into the field of the sublime, intended as an unreachable aesthetic ideal. For Milbank it is not accidental if the concept of the sublime became so dominant within post-Enlightenment aesthetic theory. This fact was the other face of a parallel process by which the idea of transcendence was re-articulated in a fashion that made it detached from worldly reality and, consequently, from aesthetic experience. As far as in this new formulation of transcendence, God was confined to a transcendent and unreachable sphere, so He was also forcibly excluded from the human experience of beauty, which became, instead, the object of the *subjective* sensibility of human taste. It follows that in modern times the locus of aesthetic experience was confined to the inner sensibility of the spectator and no longer seen as a manifestation of God's majesty.

field of the social sciences should be better equipped than any other to address the issue of transcendence. Despite this special affinity with non-worldly matters, however, anthropologists have for long avoided engaging in a serious debate with theology (Milbank 2006 [1990]; Robbins 2006; Kahn 2016). Interestingly enough, this inclination has not undergone a change of course even despite the increasing recent focus of the discipline on the ethics of everyday life. Rather, this new trend of research has generated an opposite result (Robbins 2016; cf. Lambek 2010; Laidlaw 2014).[3] Only recently, some authors from within the fields of anthropology and the sociology of religion—and of Christianity in particular—have begun pointing out how difficult it is for the discipline to liberate itself from the restraints imposed on it by what I would call an immanent "secular" perspective on religious phenomena (see Robbins 2006; Kahn 2011; Fountain and Lau 2013; Bialecki 2014, 2018; Vicini 2017; Lemons 2018).

The anthropology of Islam has lately dedicated comparatively more attention to self-fashioning processes than to the role played by transcendent entities in the cultivation of Muslim life. Largely influenced by the work of the late Foucault (Foucault 1997a, b, c), key studies in the field have indeed highlighted how Muslims fashion themselves as pious subjects by complying with a set of disciplinary practices through which they embody key Islamic virtues (Mahmood 2005; Hirschkind 2006; Silverstein 2011). While at its core this scholarship contains a critique of the secular modern foundations of the social sciences and philosophy which is similar to the one that I have traced above—especially when it comes to the conceptualization of religion (Asad 1993, 2003)—it has remained quite indifferent to the way the encounter with the divine shapes pedagogical processes. Only more recently, some scholars have started to point to the place of non-human agency and teleological imaginaries in Muslim forms of commitment to an ethical life (Meyer 2008; Mittermaier 2011; Abenante 2013; Abenante and Vicini 2017). Opting for such an approach does not imply that self-formation has to be removed entirely from the analysis. Rather, it means to address disciplinary practice in combination with other modes of religiosity that are instead "acted upon" Muslim subjects. In this light, this scholarship has questioned whether the paradigm of self-cultivation may not

---

3 As put harshly by Robbins (2016, 770), in important works exploring the ethos of the everyday: "Religion—with its supposed habits of distanced reflection, love of explicitly formulated rules and values, and tendency to speak in imperative tones—is only necessary for those who somehow cannot work out their ethical lives in the comfortable immanence of the everyday. A harshly lit realm of imposing, codified demands, [...] the transcendent appears from the ordinary point of view as an agent of rough justice at best, and a source of profound alienation from truly ethical human living at worst."

have prevented us from engaging with other "modes of religiosity" that foreground—rather than background—the "metaphysical Elsewhere," the otherworldly (Mittermaier 2012).[4]

Reading Islam joins the footsteps of these works in calling for major attention to human relations with transcendence and suggesting that such a focus helps formulate a view of Muslim life that goes beyond secular liberal representations of the "autonomous self" more radically than the "Asadian school" is able to do. However, this new trend has generally explored transcendence as an indefinite "outside" made up of dreams, hopes, and a sense of destiny which can intervene in this world to influence the course of things. Instead, this book explores the way transcendence is invoked by Muslims as an outward referent that sustains their exercises of meditative speculation and related forms of ethical reasoning. Centered on the reading of key Islamic texts, indeed, meditative practices within the *Suffa* and the Gülen communities are based on a sort of systematization of transcendence into an eidetic framework that is made more tangible through the observation of basic natural phenomena. In this light, thinking of their existence in relation to God was for my interlocutors conducive to framing their life in a broader perspective and motivating themselves to engage in society in particular ways.

By exploring these aspects *Reading Islam* delineates a perspective that differs in significant ways from the common understanding of intellectual endeavor. For this reason, an objection might be anticipated that the forms of reflection practiced by these young men are different from how the use of reflective capacities is normally conceived today. Indeed, it might be added that while it is nobody's intention to deny that religious forms of commitment may include practices of reflective meditation, precisely because they point to a transcendent order of things, these forms of intellectual engagement are, to state it plainly, not fully rational. Yet this is exactly the kind of assumption that *Reading Islam* wishes to unravel. The fact that certain forms of intellectual practice are considered legitimate and reasonable whereas others are checked at the gate depends on the dominion that secular liberal views that tend to see reasoning as a process eminently related with the inherent world still have within both common and scholarly understandings of intellectual engagement. It is because of this conceptual separation of reason from religious

---

4 Partly inspired by this new trend, some recent studies on destiny and fortune have also been important in recognizing the role of transcendence in everyday life (Gaibazzi 2015; Menin 2015; Elliot 2016; Schielke 2019). However, differently from *Reading Islam*, this scholarship describes ethnographically the life of ordinary Muslims who are *not* committed to the cultivation of a pious life.

practice, of immanent from transcendent thinking, that religious life in general, and Muslim life in particular, ends up being generally portrayed as coercive rather than as a possible wellspring of intellectual engagement contributing to deliberative processes.

2   Accommodating Modernity

Investigating reading practices in Islam also involves taking into account the lines of continuity and rupture in the way today's Muslims approach their tradition compared to past approaches. The study of authoritative texts has traditionally occupied a central place in Islam as it has represented the way knowledge has been passed through generations of scholars. In the past, knowledge transmission was based on the memorization and recitation of the written corpus of the Islamic tradition—mainly the Qur'an and the traditions of the Prophet Muhammad (*sunna*), but also the manuals of Islamic jurisprudence (*fiqh*)—in the presence of a master descending from a chain of authorized scholars (Eickelman 1978; Messick 1993). As illustrated by a vast body of anthropological scholarship investigating the link between Islam and modernization processes, however, the diffusion of universal schooling, new technologies, and the general mass-mediation of religion in the last one hundred years have reconfigured the ways in which knowledge is transmitted in Muslim-majority countries (Eickelman 1992; Messick 1993; Starrett 1995; Eickelman and Anderson 2003; Hirschkind 2006; Silverstein 2011; Spadola 2014). Compared to the past, today's Muslims are presented with a much broader repertoire of possibilities for access to Islamic knowledge (which goes from vernacular texts to the internet), whereas conventional pedagogical paths have survived at the margins and often at the cost of significant reshaping.

The central place that reading practices of vernacular texts have for people in the *Suffa* and the Gülen communities is the outcome of these transformations and the index of the convergence of the Nur movement toward a modernist view of knowledge that prompts direct scrutiny and access to the sources. As narrated by Nursi in his biography, from a very young age he had shown a certain unwillingness to comply with the study program of traditional Muslim colleges (*madrasa*). Rather than spending hours pondering a few Qur'anic commentaries and books on *fiqh*, Nursi was reportedly eager to grasp the core teachings of all the available texts in the shortest possible time (Vahide 2005, 10–11). It was in line with such a modernist inclination to learning that Nursi opted for espousing a direct writing style in his *magnum opus*. The *Risale-i Nur* (the Epistles of Light) is a 14-volume commentary (*tafsir*) on the

Qur'an originally dictated in Ottoman language by Nursi to his students, which was later transliterated in vernacular Turkish with the goal of making it as accessible as possible to ordinary Muslims. Since the 1950s the printing of the text favored its capillary diffusion among an emerging public of newly literate Muslims who were settling in the major Turkish cities at the time. In a Habermasian fashion, it is indeed possible to affirm that the higher level of accessibility of the *Risale* compared to other Islamic texts available at the time was decisive for its penetration among the masses and ultimately marked the movement's innovative character (Eickelman 2003).

Considering the limited access that Muslims had to Islamic texts only half a century ago, the role of printing in the diffusion of the *Risale* cannot indeed be underestimated. Rather than taking the outcome of these transformations for granted, however, *Reading Islam* aims to scrutinize the unpredictable outcomes that are disclosed by the grafting of new technologies and epistemological views to long-standing Muslim paths of knowledge and related practices of intellectual discernment. In this regard, it will be shown how beneath reading practices of the *Risale* long-standing Islamic cosmological views continue to persist refashioned in new and original ways. This does not mean to deny the impact that new technologies have had on contemporary paths to Islamic knowledge, but to stick to an informed analysis of texts, and of the reasoning practices attached to them, as revealed by ethnographic inquiry, so as to show how old practices are reframed today under a new light. An approach that excessively emphasized the role of the written medium in the analysis of meditative practices in Islam would indeed risk conflating the image of these Muslims with that of the bourgeois solitary reader of newspapers and novels that has been so aptly described by Benedict Anderson (1991 [1983]) in his study of modern nationalism. But this image does not do justice to the Islamic repertoires of thought and action that survive underneath Muslims' reliance on new methods and technologies for accessing knowledge.

Relatedly, in the book the relationship between modernity and Islam is tackled through a genealogical approach that looks at how key Islamic concepts and practices have been reinterpreted over time as Muslims had to face new conceptual and epistemological challenges. In this vein, modernity and Islam are not seen as two opposed and incompatible poles, as it has often been implied in sociological and political studies of the past. Also, the elegant posture of postmodern approaches emphasizing the constructed and hence contingent nature of distinctions such as "traditional" and "modern" is not espoused here—if not just to point to how also the Nur movement has absorbed, though only superficially, the puritan rhetoric of nineteenth-century Islamic reformist discourse depicting Sufism as backward and "unmodern" (Sirriyeh

1999; Bruinessen 2009). Similarly, I am not overly concerned with modernity as a self-attributed category by which some groups of people differentiate themselves from all the others. On the one hand, this aspect will be stressed: since my interlocutors were eager to set themselves apart from many other contemporary Islamic movements they can probably be thought of as being the expression of an "authenticated Islam" (Deeb 2006). However, on the other, the use of modernity as an emic category tells us little about the complex processes of accommodation and adjustment that authoritative interpreters of the Islamic tradition such as Nursi had to accomplish in order to provide ordinary Muslims with a convincing reply to new questions about the suitability of religion in a disenchanted modern world.

Reading Islam approaches modernity, first of all, as an epistemological condition. In his early writings, Michel Foucault (1972, 1980) used the notion of episteme to define the dominant regime of truth of an epoch, a concept he later abandoned in favor of the more power-dependent notion of "discursive formation." The episteme circumscribes those sets of unspoken principles and rules that in each epoch determine whether one fact can be considered true or not, or to say it with the same language of modern episteme, scientifically valid or not. In Foucault's words, the episteme is "the 'apparatus' which makes possible the separation, not of the true from the false, but of what may be characterized as scientific" from that which may not in a certain epoch (Foucault 1980, 197).[5] In normal conditions, shifts in episteme require a long time to occur unless, similar to what happened in the late Ottoman Empire beginning around the second half of the nineteenth century, a domain of knowledge is disrupted and forced to adapt to a new one (in this case foreign) and end up being dominated by a different episteme. As it will be illustrated, the strain that modernist discourses on reason and human agency have put on Islamic tradition is correlated to the enforcement of the institutional changes in education and the judiciary brought about by increasing foreign pressure. These changes were paralleled by the emergence of a modern public sphere in which people were asked to debate issues related to the well-being of the nation in public; a process that, as we will see in Chapter 1, determined the reduction of Islam to an ideological banner (Habermas 1989; Salvatore 2001a).

---

5 Similar to the notion of paradigm that Thomas Kuhn (1962) developed for the natural sciences, in Foucault's account the assumptions upon which knowledge is constructed in a certain epoch appear as self-evident and unquestionable. Only once a shift in the episteme takes place is it possible to realize how relative the vision that that particular perspective had projected on reality was. For an exploration of epistemic shifts on the interpretation of Islamic law in modern Egypt see Nakissa (2014).

Following Western powers' encroachment on their lands, Muslims were obliged to come to terms with new domains of power and related forms of knowledge. In this regard, they had to face what Alasdair MacIntyre has called an *epistemological crisis*, that is, an event marking the emergence of new questions which cause the "dissolution of historically founded certitudes" and threaten the integrity of the tradition as a whole (MacIntyre 1988, 361–362; Cornell 2010). Moments of crisis can be generated either by processes internal to a tradition and its society or by the encounter with a new and alien tradition. In either case, these crises spur the practitioners of a tradition to reinterpret their repertoires of knowledge and draw from them solutions to hitherto unsolved problems. Applied to our case, the *Risale-i Nur* was Said Nursi's response to the epistemological crisis generated by the encounter with Western forms of knowledge. Let us recall Selim's words above and notice the prominent position that the mind takes in his explanation of how a contemporary Muslim should be able to explain his faith in God. Or think of how my interlocutors highlighted reading as a key formative practice of our times for cultivating themselves as informed Muslims able to live in a modern world.

As I will illustrate in the following chapters, the modernist emphasis that my interlocutors put on thought and reflection has also affected their understanding of what significant Islamic practice is and of how it should be approached. For instance, they believe that only through reading can they achieve the kind of religious awareness that the *Risale* envisaged for them, whereas this would not be possible by only disciplining themselves to a regime of Islamic conduct. Peering beneath the surface, however, Nursi's criticism of some aspects of modern civilization, such as excessive faith in the use of human rational faculties, persists. In this regard, in the following chapters, I will explore how and to what extent a real and definitive epistemic rupture has taken place in the views of my interlocutors. I will ask whether it is not more suitable to talk in terms of a changed emphasis and point out how such a switch in accent conceals more complex and less easily decodable shifts within Islamic practice. Investigating these changes requires placing Muslim reading practices in a perspective of *longue durée* that investigates them in terms of both proximity and continuity with regard to a longstanding Islamic tradition of intellectual endeavor. To this end, Muslim forms of intellectual speculation will be read on the background of a cosmological framework that my interlocutors drew upon a Sufi heuristic tradition, which cannot be easily reconciled with post-Enlightenment rationalist epistemology.

3   Thinking Islam

An account of the patterns of continuity and rupture within Muslim formative practice has to be grounded on a solid formulation of Islam as a tradition offering intellectual and practical repertoires that Muslims draw upon to think of their place and role in the world as human beings. Common representations of Islamic tradition that reduce it to *shari'a* (seen as a compendium of strict, predefined, and unchangeable prescriptions) do not do justice either to the historical complexity of the legal tradition of Muslim societies (Salvatore 2007; Hallaq 2009), or to how Muslims rely on it to make sense of their life. These depictions reproduce a view of Islam as excessively rigid, which is more a projection of Western fears than a reality (see Euben 2001). They also tend to overlook the role that Islam has historically played in providing Muslims with a discourse for self-betterment and for articulating their human relations in society. One of the aspects that will emerge in the discussion is that by reading religious texts my interlocutors engaged with a set of ontological questions about the meaning of their existence and life and speculated on how they could develop themselves into "full" human beings.

Since the publication of Talal Asad's (1986) seminal essay on the anthropology of Islam, the notion of tradition has been at the center of some of the most important works on the topic. The idea that Islam would best be understood as a "discursive tradition" has provided the discipline with a useful tool to overcome the deadlock between the two main threads of inquiry that were dominant at the time. While some studies tended to emphasize the cultural specificity, and hence incommensurability, of multiple "local" historical manifestations of Islam (el-Zein 1977), others mainly thought of Islam as a blueprint with some definitive and seemingly unifying traits that are unadaptable to change (Geertz 1968; Gellner 1983). By suggesting a focus on processes of interpretation, argumentation and authorization around key texts of the Islamic tradition such as the Qur'an and the *sunna*, Asad advanced the idea that although Islam has a core of fundamental texts that are shared by Muslim practitioners around the world, it is at the same time a malleable and evolving corpus that can be interpreted differently on the basis of the specific historical developments and power formations that structure the articulation of knowledge in each particular context. Asad's contribution was particularly innovative in terms of breaking the monopoly of the Western-centered perspective on Islamic religious practice, and his work was an inspiration for an entire new generation of scholars (e.g. Bowen 1993; Lambek 1993; Messick 1993; Starrett 1998; Hefner 2000; Mahmood 2005; Deeb 2006; Hirschkind 2006; Silverstein 2011).

Yet the idea of discursive tradition has recently been questioned for putting too much emphasis on the coherence of Islamic discourse and so presenting an understanding of Muslim life which is unable to go beyond the contours of religious commitment. Some critics have highlighted the ambivalences and inconsistencies that people who try to comply with the prescriptions of the Islamic tradition may endure (Schielke 2007, 2009; Schielke and Debevec 2012), or made the plain point that not all Muslims are pious people, so that there may be "too much Islam in the anthropology of Islam" (Schielke 2010, 2). Others have instead highlighted the risk these approaches run of mono-thematizing Muslim life, ending up reproducing a sort of post-orientalist reification of Islamic culture (Soares and Osella 2010). In sum, these critics agree that not all Muslims are necessarily committed to a project of pious moral reform. Even when they are, they may simply not be able to comply with its requirements, either because they are moved by multiple and contradictory systems of values, or because their agency is restricted by other social or economic factors.

These arguments have their ground in the "ethical turn," a recent set of anthropological studies exploring how people make ethical choices in concrete everyday experience, and especially at extraordinary, critical junctures of their life (Fassin 2014; see also Lambek 2000; Laidlaw 2002, 2014; Zigon 2009; Faubion 2011). In turn, this new anthropological trend has taken inspiration from a group of philosophers known as the "virtue ethicists" (e.g. Anscombe 1958; MacIntyre 1984 [1981]; Williams 2011 [1985]; Taylor 1989). Emerged against the formalist approaches to ethics that were dominant in continental moral philosophy in the second half of the twentieth century, these thinkers argued for a return to the ethics of Ancient Greek philosophers, and to the views of Aristotle in particular. Following the lead of these works, the "ethical turn" in anthropology has combined an attention to processes of moral cultivation with an ethnographic exploration of the conundrums people face when they make their moral decisions. One common and important point of this trend (which explores what otherwise are quite different social and cultural contexts) is the idea that moral deliberation mainly consists of a process of critical reflection intended as the intellectual capacity of solving complex dilemmas. Yet this is also the point on which these authors depart most radically from the perspective of the virtue ethicists. In their view, indeed, the exercise of ethical deliberation cannot rest on a set of embodied dispositions enshrined in tradition. Rather, solving complex dilemmas implies the subjective capacity of rationally sorting out the most appropriate moral option among those available. In this vein, this anthropological scholarship understands ethics as an exercise that is *per se* at odds with the preordained set of dispositions that traditions enshrine. On this same basis, these authors have criticized Alasdair MacIntyre's (1984

[1981], 1988, 1991) formulation of tradition and, *via* him, Asad's understanding of Islam as a discursive tradition (Laidlaw 2014; see especially Fassin 2014, but also Pandian 2008).

In particular, according to James Laidlaw (2014), MacIntyre and the anthropological scholarship he has inspired *via* Talal Asad (in particular Mahmood 2005) tend to neglect the fact that individuals' moral choices are always determined by a plurality of irreconcilable values, so that when making moral decisions people very often have to juggle conflicting ethical claims. Laidlaw especially blames MacIntyre's *After Virtue* (1984 [1981]) for reading Aristotle through a communitarian lens that, in his view, obscures the central place that ethical deliberation had in the Aristotelian account of the virtues by replacing it with normative principles like authority and tradition. In particular, he ascribes this inclination to MacIntyre's reliance on Aristotle's "craft metaphor" to describe the process by which people learn the virtues, namely, in the same way apprentices do as they learn their skills through constant practice in context. By extending this metaphor too far into the ethical domain, Laidlaw argues, MacIntyre ends up reducing Aristotelian ethics to the embodiment of virtuous dispositions through "practice," with the result that intellectual processes of moral deliberation are overshadowed in his account (on this see also Coleman 1994).[6]

Laidlaw and others' invitation to consider the place of intellectual deliberation in ethics sheds light on some of the possible limitations of mainstream studies in the anthropology of Islam. It is true, indeed, that although the scholarship inspired by Asad has never excluded reflection from the domain of Muslim disciplinary practice, it has tended to highlight the importance of reiteration within religious practice at the expense of intellectual engagement. As pointed out above, the studies of Mahmood and others have been inclined to depict ethical formation as a self-enclosed and self-fulfilling process in which connection with a transcendent order does not play a central role. On this point, I am in agreement with Laidlaw when he argues that Asad and his school have excessively highlighted disciplinary processes to the detriment of consciousness and reflective processes. As a result, though unwittingly, they have offered an account of Islamic life that is closer to Bourdieu's idea of *habitus* than they would acknowledge (Laidlaw 2014, 75). As it has been observed from

---

6 In reality MacIntyre has always stressed that for Aristotle "intellectual virtues" (the exercise of *phronesis*) were as important as "virtues of character" in the process of learning how to behave ethically within the *polis* (MacIntyre 1984 [1981], 154 ff.). However, it is true that in his account of Aristotle most of the learning processes pass through living practice in the community, which limits the understanding of Islamic education in general, and intellectual practices dealt with in this book in particular.

a more articulated sociological perspective, what makes Bourdieu's formulation of the Aristotelian notion of *habitus* redundant is the fact that in the description of the French sociologist the *habitus* lacks any reference to a *telos*, namely to a set of ethical concerns and principles constituting the axis of a tradition, which operate independently of the imperatives of impersonal social structures (Salvatore 2007, 88–98). Similarly, it is the lack of reference to a narrative that goes beyond the contingency represented by religious prescriptions that makes these anthropological accounts of Muslim life look self-referential. This is particularly evident in the work of Mahmood. Even if she has notably argued that in Bourdieu the *habitus* appears as a mere reflex of social structures (Mahmood 2005, 139), in her ethnography of the women of the mosque movement in Egypt the *telos* of ethical action is eclipsed and her women's commitment to a path of moral reform is mainly presented as the reflex of their *will* to conform to authoritative religious discourse.

While I agree with part of the critique that Laidlaw and others move, there is, however, an important aspect that the exponents of the "ethical turn" in anthropology seem to overlook. This is the ontological nature of ethical discourses and the fact that they are embedded into traditions. I found problematic the way the idea of tradition is discarded in this trend in the name of what I would define a more or less explicitly formulated sort of moral universalism. This is what these authors end up doing, I believe, by putting the individual as such—that is, dispossessed of the background of ethical narratives that compose a tradition—at the center of the stage of moral deliberation. By foregrounding the plurality of moral options individuals are confronted with in practical situations of their lives, indeed, these scholars seem to disregard the plain anthropological fact that human beings as such are educated within specific traditions of ethical practice. By advancing an idea of human beings as the space of intersection of conflicting moral impulses, they project modern secular conceptions of the self on Muslim life. This perspective resonates with the view of the rationally autonomous self of Kantian genealogy who, as a "subject" of his own, is capable of deliberating independently of how he has been, and continues to be, shaped by history, that is by a tradition of ethical engagement to which she belongs (see also Chapter 5 on this point).

This issue has been thoroughly addressed by Talal Asad in his critique of how a secular liberal view of subjectivity *as* agency continues to permeate important fields of the social sciences, anthropology included (Asad 1993, 13–19; 2003, 67–99). Although Laidlaw and others would probably agree with Asad's critique, their view of moral deliberation as delinked from a notion of tradition conceals a similar view of human subjectivity underneath. As stated by more recent critics of this trend, "by reiterating human creativity against the weight of norms" this scholarship has ended up "highlighting the universally shared conditions of the human subject" (Fadil and Fernando 2015, 61; cf. Deeb 2015), thus tacitly reproducing secular liberal views of the self *as* agent, which contradict alternative Muslim formulations. On a philosophical ground, some respectful critics of Laidlaw have observed how his theory of "moral pluralism" (the idea that a pluralism of values permeates our moral choices in concrete life) contradicts the theories of many virtue ethicists; not only MacIntyre but also authors who have inspired him such as Bernard Williams (2011 [1985]) (Mattingly 2014, 477–478). As specified by Mattingly (2014), Laidlaw advances the view of a "fragmented self" that is constantly traversed by a plurality of contradictory moral inputs. By so doing, he misses one of the most important points raised by Williams and other virtue ethicists: that to think of themselves as ethical people, human beings need a coherent view of the self which can be achieved only if life is integrated into a similarly coherent view provided by a tradition. It is only by reconciling their life narrative with a tradition that people can become ethical selves.

This aspect is especially true for people committed to a specific religious program as those explored in *Reading Islam*. The present work has indeed the comparative advantage of not having to deal with people facing moral dilemmas and fundamental life choices. It is an ethnographic account of two enclosed Islamic communities in which people are "willing" to comply with the set of practices and disciplines that dominate their religious spaces. Although in the last chapter I will deal with ethical concerns that arise in the mind of my interlocutors regarding the responsibility they felt to be their own for engaging in society to promote their communities' mission of revitalization of religion, these aspects are never tackled in terms of moral deliberation in this work. Rather, moralizing religious discourses are analyzed for how effectively they provide my interlocutors with refreshed perspectives on how to understand their place and role as Muslims in the contemporary era. From this perspective, my inclination to rely on the notion of tradition is *also* the natural development of the particular environment within which my research took place. Certainly, a permanent tension exists between discourse and practice, between ideals of ethical conduct and the contingency of human life, and this was also true for my interlocutors, many of whom were not always as disciplined as they were supposed to be. Simply, *Reading Islam* will be addressing questions that are not related to the exploration of such conflicting moral claims.

But in response to both the "ethical turn" and the important trend of anthropological studies on Islam led by the work of Talal Asad, *Reading Islam* questions power-dependent views that tend to outline a normative understanding of religious tradition, namely as a force imposing ethical standards on people.[7] In *Reading Islam*, tradition is understood as a set of intellectual repertoires through which Muslims constitute themselves ontologically as persons committed to a specific program of ethical formation and engagement in society. The book accounts for how the Islamic tradition has been reformulated, starting from the key sources of the two communities under study—mainly within the *Risale-i Nur*, and only subsequently in Gülen's books—and then interpreted and enacted by my interlocutors. In this regard, tradition is thought of for the capacity it has—through texts as well as through the interpretations that are derived from the reading of these texts—of providing people with coherent ideas about the human self, its nature and development in relation to both transcendent and mundane principles, including views on personal freedom, responsibility and participation in society. As such, it is seen as providing the necessary set of narratives that ethical selves need as they relate themselves to a transcendent principle by means of specific religious imaginaries.

As famously stated by Samuli Schielke (2010), there may be too much Islam in the anthropology of Islam. Yet what I find more striking is the way transcendence, God, and the ethical narratives offered by tradition have long been ignored in the anthropology of Islam as well as in the study of religion.[8] In this regard, *Reading Islam* calls for reconciliation with a theologically informed perspective that sheds light on how human ethical programs are grounded in concrete narratives about the afterworld, transcendence, and the place of humanity in the cosmos. It is based on these premises that, by reflecting on religious texts, my interlocutors had access to a new and broader horizon of sense from those offered by the dominant discourses in society. Reading Islamic texts offered them an avenue for transcending their own contingent existence and

---

7   Other critiques have highlighted how Asad's conceptualization of Islam as a discursive tradition possesses a marked prescriptive character insofar as it would be mainly concerned with singling out the historical and social power dynamics through which correct Islamic practice is authorized (Ahmed 2016, 270–274; see also Anjum 2007; Marranci 2008). While this critique has mainly been directed to the central place that orthodoxy and orthopraxy occupy in Asad's formulation of Islam as tradition in its totality—a view that I do not necessarily agree with—instead, my main concern is with the effects that this emphasis on prescription has for the way we understand how Islam is lived by its practitioners. Asad's emphasis on the power of discourse in delimiting the set of practices to which Muslims have to discipline themselves to does indeed set limits to our capacity to include Muslims' forms of reflection and discernment in the account of what is valuable Islamic practice, as if living a Muslim life would only consist of following up authoritative prescriptions rather than of engaging with an intellectual tradition.

8   Samuli Schielke has himself more recently observed how God has been rather absent in anthropological explorations of Islam and proposed to ethnographically explore the impact of "the power of God" on Muslims' lives (Schielke 2019).

finding quiescence in a renewed awareness of God and in a comprehension of His broader design. Such awareness was then translated into concrete forms of action in society that were similarly placed within a higher project of social transformation.

4 A Revival of Muslim Civility

The *Suffa* and the Gülen communities are two manifestations of a broader Islamic revival that started in the 1980s and later expanded in the 2000s under the administration of the Justice and Development Party (*Adalet ve Kalkınma Partisi*, AKP). Apart from some limited exceptions (e.g. Mardin 1989; Tapper and Tapper 1991; White 2002; Yavuz 2003a), the academic literature on Turkey has long ignored the resilience of religious movements in the country. This was in part the result of the impact of modernization theories of the 1950s and 1960s which sanctioned that, differently from other Muslim countries, Turkey was destined to follow in the footsteps of the West (Lerner 1958; Lewis 1968 [1961]; for a critique see Kasaba 1997). Sharing many of their views with secular Turkish elites, these scholars saw Islam as backward, as a dross of the Ottoman epoch that was destined to disappear soon from the country's social fiber. Accordingly, Muslim forms of solidarity were considered irrelevant for understanding sociopolitical change in the middle-to-long term (see Mardin 1997). Only with the emergence of Islamically-inspired parties and their success in the 1990s has a new interest emerged in the literature. In this case, however, the scholarship has generally focused on the political aspects of the phenomenon. Rarely have scholars attempted to shed light on the deeper religious motivations, views, and organizational forms that animated the Islamic revival in the country.[9]

Despite the efforts made by the Republican elites after 1923 to diminish the relevance of Islam, religious groups—including both more conventional Sufi brotherhoods and new networks gathering around local Muslim preachers—continued to enjoy large support among the masses, especially in the countryside. Even if outlawed, they survived underground and reorganized themselves in new associative forms that came to be called *cemaat*s (religious

---

9 The attention has been generally confined to Islamically-inspired political parties or public manifestations of Islamic identity as the veil issue in the late 1990s (e.g. Göle 1996; Saktanber 2002a; Yavuz 2003a; Çınar 2005; Shively 2005; Delibaş 2014). Only lately, and in rare occasions, have scholars explored the bottom-up social dynamics that underlie more apparent public manifestations of Islam (e.g. White 2002).

communities). In this form, they could operate in society in a more cohesive and compact way by drawing money from their religiously conservative constituency and reinvesting them in the education sector. By offering accommodation and scholarships to students from a conservative background, they were in time able to raise a Muslim counterpublic which could finally challenge the political order put in place by the secular elites in the country (see Chapter 1). Among other such communities, those affiliated to the Nur movement distinguished themselves for upholding a view of religious education that should integrate the teaching of modern secular subjects and especially science. Nursi thought that beside poverty and disunity, ignorance was one of the three main hindrances along the path to the civil advancement and modernization of the country. For this reason, he advocated not only the compatibility but also the complementarity of scientific and religious knowledge, and suggested that people ought to be educated accordingly in both modern scientific subjects and Islamic ethics (Vahide 2005, 61, 87). To a mass of Muslims who under the early years of Turkish Republic had felt culturally dispossessed by what they perceived as an aggressive top-down project of state-led secularization, Nursi offered the attractive possibility that another modernization, which was not at odds with Islamic teachings, was possible.

In line with such an educational mission, both the *Suffa* and the Gülen communities have for long offered cheap accommodation and scholarships to students coming to Istanbul or other major Turkish cities to attend quality high-schools and universities. Beside their education at school, students would receive proper religious upbringing within the houses and dormitories of these two communities. These places functioned as laboratories where these new generations of Muslims were educated to the intrinsic values of these communities and possibly turned into trustworthy adherents in the long run. Well known for the presence of its schools in the four corners of the world, the Gülen community is the one that has implemented this project in the most systematic, effective, and strategic way compared to any other religious group in the country. By investing hugely in the private education sector over the last four decades, it has been able to influence several generations of people who have later taken relevant positions in society, including state institutions, thus rebalancing the grasp on power that the secularists had benefited from since 1923. According to specific community ideals, once graduated from university, students raised in this community were expected to operate in society as lay Muslims supporting the group either ideologically by promoting its message, or economically by financing its activities. As such, they would also represent the living proof of the compatibility of religious inspiration and modern life, and served as an example to younger members. A saying of the Prophet (*hadis,* in Arabic *hadith*) that was often mentioned by Gülen and quoted to me by students of the community is a fine illustration of this community's reformist project: "The way you are is the way you will be governed" (*nasılsanız öyle yönetilirsiniz*). It is not by imposing sociopolitical change from above that they hoped to transform society; it is rather from below and by educating people in the ideals of the community.

Given the way the values taught within the *Suffa* and the Gülen communities are later translated into Muslim forms of engagement in society, it is evident that their impact on the configuration of religion and politics in Turkey has gone far beyond their declared apolitical character. As part of the broader Islamic revival, in the last thirty years they have contributed to the bottom-up process of social reform that has allowed Islamic contents to regain prominence in the public sphere and paved the way for the success of Islamically-inspired parties such as the Welfare Party (*Refah Partisi*) before and the AKP more recently. From this standpoint, together with other Islamic groups, the *Suffa* and the Gülen communities have taken part in a silent revolution which has generated deep transformations and power shifts in Turkish society. Accordingly, following Gramsci, some authors have linked the political success of Islamic groups to their capacity to establish an effective counter-hegemonic culture in the country (Tuğal 2009). Similarly, recent studies on the Gülen community have pointed to the group's ability to operate in a neoliberal economic environment and intercept the educational needs of a newly emerging class of conservative people as some of the main reasons of its success (Hendrick 2013; Tee 2016; Walton 2017). Relatedly, they have generally argued that the community's heavy investment in education responds to an overall strategy aimed at gaining influence in society, rather than being oriented by a sincere commitment to educational ideals (Hendrick 2013; Tee 2016). As it will be illustrated in Chapter 4, the Gülen community has always tried to draw as many people as possible to its ranks, and it has elaborated a specific pedagogy to achieve this goal. In this regard, it is possible to speculate that there lies a precise political calculation by its chief members beyond their claims that the community is dedicated to "serve society" (*hizmet etmek*). This hypothesis would also be in line with the numerous allegations accusing the Gülen community of having used the thousands of members it had infiltrated in the police and the military to mastermind the coup attempt of July 15, 2016 (see below).[10]

---

10 These events and the implications that its aftermath had for the community will be briefly mentioned at several junctures of this work, yet they will be addressed more specifically in the final part of this introduction.

Although *Reading Islam* shares some of the arguments expressed in these works, it takes another radically different approach to understanding the resilience of Islamic forces such as those exemplified by the *Suffa* and the Gülen communities. The mentioned literature on the Islamic revival in Turkey has indeed tended to depict the latter as a sort of reflex response to deeper (and hence implicitly more significant) economic transformations and to neoliberalization in particular. It also essentially presents us with an image of Islam as the main ideological tool in the hands of religious and political elites engaged in a battle for cultural hegemony against their opponents. While this perspective certainly tells an important part of the story, by focusing on macro-structural transformations, it falls short in explaining the religious ideals, motivations, and imaginaries that lie behind people's decision to join Islamic groups. In this regard, these studies seem unable to explain the reasons why the perspective offered by Islamic communities has been appealing to so many people. Besides, while they are successful in showing the oft-forgotten connection that exists between interest and religious behavior, they do so at the cost of projecting a secular liberal perspective that understands human action as mainly guided by means-to-end calculations on religious behavior, without giving proper consideration to the place of human ethos within it. In counterpoint to these approaches, *Reading Islam* sheds light on the way long-standing, yet reconfigured, Islamic ideals shape Muslim life while at the same time functioning as motors of social engagement and transformation in modern Turkey. This is not intended to belittle the sociopolitical impact of the two communities under study and of Gülen's in particular. Nor does the book mean to underestimate the contribution that neo-Gramscian theories can offer to an understanding of the transformation of Turkish and other Muslim-majority societies in the last three decades (LeVine and Salvatore 2009). Rather, it is a matter of bolstering a sociological analysis that explores the worldviews that animate Islamic groups and give shape to their forms of civic engagement without disregarding the importance of structural transformations.

Within this framework, one of the goals of *Reading Islam* is to shed light on how the *Suffa* and the Gülen communities have contributed to the reactivation of long-standing Muslim forms of civility and solidarity in the context of the transformations of Turkish society of the last thirty years. In relation to this topic, Walton (2017) has rightly pointed to the existence of a "civil society effect" driving Turkish religious actors in the last decades to reset their stances in harmony with global discourses emphasizing human rights and participation in civil society. Nonetheless, *Reading Islam* is not entirely satisfied by such a perspective. Similar to the studies mentioned above, this approach entails the risk of interpreting the Islamic revival as the reflex of broader global processes and not as the outcome of an original Islamic civilizational impulse. The intent is not to belittle the impact of structural transformations on the way public claims for religion have been made in Turkey in the last three decades. Nor am I skeptical "over the possibility of syntheses between Islam and civil society" (Walton 2017, 23)—although it should be kept in mind that the inner mechanisms regulating Islamic forms of civic engagement can be different from, and sometimes conflicting with, those of secular civic associations. Rather, *Reading Islam* reads contemporary forms of Muslim life and social engagement that underpin the activities of the *Suffa* and the Gülen communities in a line of continuity with longstanding "inner" Islamic civilizational trajectories and only then sheds light on how these ways of living a Muslim life have been reorganized in new contexts, yet without entirely losing their original impetus.

One of the tenets of this book is that, although in modern times key Islamic motives have been grafted to broader dynamics, they have continued to maintain their original anchor in the set of Muslim imaginaries and ideals provided by the Islamic tradition about how to live a rightful life and to establish a just society. In this vein, the logic that underlies forms of civic engagement within the *Suffa* and the Gülen communities is essentially oriented by principles that go "beyond secular reason" as they remain entangled with a sense of transcendence that exceeds the contingency of individual interest and worldly life— and that hence are not guided by purely means-to-ends calculations. For this reason, investigating non-secular forms of social action requires revisiting the secular assumptions that still undergird main directions in the social sciences (Asad 2003; Milbank 2006 [1990]). A scholarly enterprise that is aimed at liberating the social sciences from the restraints imposed on them by immanentist "secular" approaches to human behavior that still dominate the field must be based on an attempt at going beyond conventional ways of reading sociopolitical action as means oriented to ends.

In search of an alternative direction, *Reading Islam* follows new sociological works on Islam in suggesting that an assessment of the endurance and resilience of religious traditions should stand on a comprehension of how such traditions continue to provide their practitioners with alternative ways of inhabiting the world—despite claims of an impending secularization of society. As suggested by Armando Salvatore (2016), the Islamic tradition has historically articulated the two main variables that shape human societies, namely knowledge and power, by providing religious practitioners with mold and meta-institutional patterns for thinking social cohesion and mobilization. Differently from modern secular models that are based on state-centered and hierarchical ways of organizing society, Muslim models of "civility" have traditionally been more flexible and based on under-institutionalized kinds of social bonds, thus allowing for a more egalitarian articulation of the knowledge-power equation. The forms of Muslim cohesion and mobilization—as well as the pedagogies that are embedded into them—that are promoted within the *Suffa* and the Gülen communities are the expression of a historically specific reinterpretation of these Islamic patterns. Although they have been in part bent to accommodate the pressure exercised on them by more rigid institutional models that have been brought in as a result of modernization processes, these patterns—and in particular that of the brotherhood as both an organizational form and a source for moral reasoning—continue to be rooted in a longstanding project of Muslim civility.

As such, the project that my interlocutors advocated precedes that of secular modernity and remains in large part alternative to it. As formative intellectual practices and related ideals of civic engagement promoted by the *Suffa* and the Gülen communities predate the times when any idea of a clear opposition between society and the state, the religious and the secular (at least in terms of how these latter dichotomies have been formulated within the discourse of liberal political modernity) emerged, they also exceed these distinctions in ways that have to be explored before sentencing their extinction under pressing strictly political or economic dynamics. It follows that a tension exists between these alternative projects and those promoted by the defenders of secular modernity. Further, a conflict persists within the same objectives of these communities, which are dictated by the double, inner and other-worldly, orientation of their programs. This tension will be specifically addressed in the following chapters, but especially in Chapter 5 and in the conclusion in relation to the evolution of the sociopolitical field in Turkey in the last few years.

5   Fieldwork in Two Concealed Communities

The anthropological enterprise is of necessity dependent on the researcher's possibility of entering social spaces and establishing human contacts that, as an outsider, he should not be supposed to access. This has generally implied a high degree of suspiciousness on the part of interlocutors in the field, particularly when research is conducted in the Middle East. It is not an accident if one of the most often told anecdotes by anthropologists working in the region is how they have been, more or less jokingly, labeled as spies. This was also the case with the present research. In 2010 the presence and influence that Islamic movements had gained in society in the previous fifteen years was still perceived as a shocking social change, especially by people coming from a secular background. Not only was I researching a politically hot topic, but I was doing fieldwork within communities whose secrecy made them a subject of suspicion for their potential subversive goals. Indeed, there were already widespread speculations about the attempts that were made by affiliates of the Gülen community to infiltrate state institutions, especially the police force and the judiciary; an aspect that made my research sound even odder to those whom I illustrated it.[11]

Making my fieldwork even more peculiar was my decision to spend several months within the facilities of these two communities, living side by side with male students who were being socialized into their lifestyle and vision. My access to the Gülen community in Istanbul was made possible by contacts with elder brothers of the community that I had met in 2005 in Milan for some interviews I conducted for my M.A. thesis research. Given the pyramidal structure of the community's global network, when I returned to Istanbul in 2009 to ask for permission to conduct my research I was told that, in line with internal rules, I should talk to members of the network operating in my country of origin—under whose jurisdiction I apparently was assigned in their organogram. Members of the community in Italy were able to put me in contact with a high-level member in Istanbul, who in turn introduced me to Selman, the brother who was responsible for overseeing the community's educational activities in the neighborhood of Şişli. Selman, in turn, introduced me to Kamil, as I will call him, a twenty-three-year-old student of engineering at Boğaziçi University. Kamil had met the community in his village of origin some years before, while he was finishing high-school.[12] Raised in the province of Kayseri, like many students staying in the houses of the Nur network, he came from a provincial family of humble means. Kamil was the guide responsible for the student house where I spent almost six months living with a group of another twelve boys divided between university students (between nineteen and twenty-three years of age) regularly residing there, and high-school students

---

11   The community's penetration into the state apparatus was first exposed in the aftermath of the 28 February 1997 so-called "postmodern coup," when the extracts of a tape recording in which Gülen apparently suggested his followers to infiltrate in the "arteries of the state" were broadcast on national TV. More recently, accusations were moved by the journalist Ahmet Şık in his book *İmamın Ordusu* (The Imam's Army) which became a well-known publication especially after the detention of the journalist between March 2011 and March 2012 as part of the investigations related to the "Ergenekon" trial, which led also to the confiscation of the page proofs of the book.

12   All the names and places of origin of the people mentioned in this study are fictitious. This choice abides by ethical rules of the anthropological enterprise. It also follows an open request of the students, who feared that they might misrepresent the view of their community. Meanwhile, the request was justified by reference to the high level of secrecy surrounding the two communities.

(between fifteen and seventeen years of age) only staying over during weekends. Kamil is the person who introduced me to the community and accompanied me to visit other houses and dormitories located in the surrounding area. I continued to visit him later when he moved to a nearby dormitory to look after a group of around ten high-school students. But overall, Kamil is the person I spent most of my nights with, chatting about Islam, Said Nursi, and his life and plans as a student and a committed Muslim.[13]

It was again Kamil who, in order to satisfy my pressing questions on theological issues and Said Nursi, of whom he was a great admirer, brought me to one of the reading meetings that were held at the *Suffa* foundation (*Suffa vakfı*), the official name of the *Suffa* community. Access to this community was smoother as I personally addressed the director of the foundation at one of the meetings without the need of any reference—if not the few words one young student spent to introduce me. I was thus allowed to stay at *Sarıgüzel* (beautiful yellow), the nickname of a house managed by the community in Fatih, notoriously the most religious neighborhood in the city, where many Islamist organizations and associations are also located. Here I spent three months living with six university students, attending reading meetings, and having exchanges with students and elder brothers living in this and two other student houses located nearby.

While students in both communities were suspicious about my real identity and intentions, the fact that I had been allowed by elder brothers to stay reassured them and facilitated our exchanges. All my interlocutors were informed about my status as a researcher. They knew that my goal was to learn about their community's pedagogies and ways of living Islam, and they generally accepted me well as a Christian and hence, like them, a believer in one and the same God. Even if this often led to long disquisitions about the fallacy of Christianity with respect to Islam and to several attempts by them at converting me, our differences did not prevent dialogue between us. The process was also facilitated by the sympathy that Turks generally feel for foreigners, especially for those coming from the Mediterranean region, toward whom they feel particularly close in terms of culture and manners. Additionally, in line with specific sociability rules of the communities that will later become familiar to the reader, given my older age, the students addressed me with respect. At the same time, however, the fact that I was only a few years older prevented the conversation from being hampered by excessive deference.

---

13 Furthermore, for the sake of comparison, in the last month of the fieldwork I resided for some days a week in another house of this community in the neighborhood of Fatih.

Even if I never converted to Islam, I was indeed called and known by them as "Fabio *abi*," a designation that implied their subordinate status, but also their proximity, toward me.[14]

As most of my interlocutors were university students, they generally had no particular difficulty in understanding my role as a researcher.[15] With particular regard to the Gülen community, because it was the object of many books and conferences, my presence was not only tolerated but also acknowledged as valuable. My interest in their educational mission was read either as the mark of the community's relevance or at least looked on with the hope that I might represent them in a positive way once I had written my book. Within both communities then, the fact that I had decided to research their activities was also seen as a sign of the reliability of the knowledge contained in the *Risale-i Nur*. Alternatively, it was interpreted as a mark of destiny, that is, of God's will, because through my research I could contribute to making Nursi's message accessible to a foreign public. The conviction that our encounter must have been determined by divine providence (*tevafuk*) was strengthened by the story of how I found out about the existence of the Nur movement in the first place, something I was often asked about during my fieldwork. This happened in summer 2004 in a petrol station in the vicinity of Gaziantep on my way back from a road trip to the Eastern Anatolia Region, when an unknown man wearing a robe handed me a booklet containing the English translation of a portion of the *Risale*.

My choice of living in the student facilities was motivated by the belief that they offered the best perspective from which to observe how students were introduced to the Nur teachings and educated into mature Muslims committed to their community mission. However, it did not simply reflect a sort of inquisitorial attitude based on a positivist view of the research process as

---

14   The term *ağabey*, here rendered in its abbreviated and colloquial form *abi*, means "elder brother" and it is used both within family relations and in everyday interactions to address males of an older age. The term is used also within Islamic communities in Turkey when younger and less experienced members address elder and more experienced brothers-in-religion. In this work, the substantive is added to the name of those students and adult brothers of the community that either for their age, community status, knowledge and experience, or a combination of these factors, were addressed as such by my young interlocutors.

15   The students generally came from pious and conservative families of Anatolian origin. They frequented some of the most prestigious public schools and universities of the country, a right they had gained thanks to their high performance in the annual national examination (see Chapter 4).

centered on "observing" with one's eyes. Living in the houses was, for me, a whole life experience which inevitably led me to realize how important daily interactions were for the unfolding of pedagogical and socialization processes within the two communities. Also, texts were not just read collectively but they were actualized in concrete attitudes and interactive forms that shaped community life along the bonds of religious brotherhood. Hence, for me to conform, though not always successfully, to the implicit rules that regulated the dynamics of community life was a way of grasping their significance (on this see in particular Chapter 2). For instance, after the first weeks, when I began to tire of the enclosed atmosphere of the house or regretted taking part in what for me were pointless conversations, I came to notice how students frowned at me for not conforming to their expectation for reciprocal interest and care. Similarly, only after some time I realized that when talking with elder and more authoritative brothers, I inadvertently bent my back, letting my shoulders sink and my arms fall on my legs, keeping my sight deflected from theirs, my eyebrows arched down, and my voice thin and low. These were all embodied attitudes of respect and deference that reflected my perceived, though still partial, assimilation of consolidated sociability forms of the two communities. From this standpoint, my experience of living within their houses allowed me to explore how Muslim life was, first of all, embodied through daily life and socialization in community spaces.

Given the centrality that reading practices take in this book for the exploration of Muslim forms of reflection, it may seem that I am espousing a perspective that pays major attention to written sources. Yet, in contrast, large parts of *Reading Islam* are dedicated to shedding light on how texts (both written and oral) were embedded in community life. Beyond scriptures, socialization within the enclosed space of the houses was a way for my interlocutors to live and embody the forms of solidarity and the ideals of civic engagement promoted by their communities. As an additional caveat, it is important to remark that although fieldwork was mainly conducted within student facilities, this does not imply that the book is simply a study of Islamic education. Adult members of the two communities regularly visited the students or came to the houses to attend reading meetings and the encounter between old and new generations of students of the *Risale* shaped paths of authority and guidance and permeated community life extensively. There was *not* a clear distinction between pedagogical techniques and community life in the houses: living together in community with fellow peers and elder brothers was the way of processing embodied texts by directly experiencing them through social practice.

6 Before and after July 15

It is important to remark that the present research took place in a radically different political situation from that of today. At the time, the Gülen community and the AKP administration were conducting a parallel battle against the grasp that the secularist forces had been maintaining over the institutions since the foundation of the Republic. In the spring of 2010, students affiliated with the Gülen community whom I was living with had been asked by their superiors to join the march in support of the forthcoming constitutional referendum on September 12. The referendum had been held by the AKP administration with the actual aim of undermining the power of the secularists. While talking politics was taboo in the houses, the newspaper *Zaman* and the TV channels of the community clearly supported the "yes" vote and denounced attempts by the secularist forces to plot against the AKP administration. For instance, *Zaman* had attacked the so-called E-memorandum in which the military had objected the election of AKP co-founder Abdullah Gül as President—who was eventually elected in August 2007 after the AKP won early elections (Villelabeitia 2009). Similarly, the same newspaper had supported the *Ergenekon* and *Balyoz* (Sledgehammer) trials, in which members of the secularist establishment, including retired generals and active army officers, judges, and academics were investigated for being members of a shadowy organization—the so-called "deep state" (*derin devlet*)—which was plotting a military intervention aimed at overthrowing the AKP-led government. These data add to today's widely shared opinion that the community and the AKP administration were on good terms at the time, as they shared the will to reduce the influence of the military in the country (Çakır and Sakallı 2014).

Despite their battles and interests possibly overlapping between around 2006 and 2011, however, the Gülen community and the AKP are two quite different manifestations of Turkish Islamism. They possess a different intellectual genealogy and express a very different vision about Turkish society and politics, especially with regard to foreign policy (Vicini 2014b). While some first skirmishes between these two forces date back to 2009 when they diverged on their reaction to the Gaza flotilla raid (Tanrıkulu 2014), it was the second overwhelming political victory of the AKP in 2011 that marked the beginning of the clash. According to rumors, the community claimed merit for the victory and accordingly asked for control of some key ministries. In response, an increasingly confident AKP administration considered pursuing its political project without having to compromise with the community. The tension increased in 2012 when, on February 7, prosecutors allegedly close to the

Gülen community unsuccessfully tried to summon Hakan Fidan, the head of the National Intelligence Organization, for conducting secret talks with the PKK on behalf of the AKP administration (Butler 2012). After that, the situation escalated quickly. The clash reached its apex in 2013.[16] In the summer of that year, Gülen first openly criticized the government's response to the Gezi protests, creating irritation in the administration (Birnbaum 2013). The most decisive moment, however, was a few months later, when in November a leaked draft of the law aiming to close down the *dershanes*—the most important revenue source for the community (see Chapter 4)—was published on *Zaman* (Çakır and Sakallı 2014). The community fired back between December 17 and 25 of the same year by leaking compromising wiretapped conversations revealing a potentially explosive corruption scandal involving prominent members of the executive, which led to the resignation of three members of the cabinet (BBC 2013). While Gülen denied any involvement in the scandal (Franks 2014), his followers were indicated as the only possible force able to intercept secret communications thanks to their infiltrated members in the National Intelligence Organization. These events marked a point of no return in the conflict after which any attempt at mediation was in vane (Koru 2016).

Since these events, fearing that the Gülen community could pose other security threats for the country, the Turkish government has been engaged in a large national operation aimed at cleansing the institutions, and particularly the police, military, National Intelligence Organization, and judiciary from affiliates of the community. In May 2016 the National Security Council officially sanctioned the introduction of the group in the list of terrorist organizations. It renamed it the Fethullah Gülen's Terrorist Organization (*Fetullahçı Terör Örgütü*), today best known through the acronym FETÖ, making people legally liable for allegiance or sympathy toward it. Afterwards, a wave of arrests, dismissals from public posts, and confiscations involved all the people who were allegedly affiliated with the organization. These operations took particular vigor following the coup attempt of July 15, 2016, in which members of the organization played a prominent role in organizing and staging the operation, according to police testimonies and court documents that have been filed to date (Yinanç 2017)—a stance agreed upon by a recent academic analysis of the role of the Gülen community in the coup attempt and how it may impact its survival (Yavuz and Balci 2018). With the publication of the last of a series of legislative decrees (*Kanun Hükmünde Kararname*) that were enacted under the state of emergency in the aftermath of the coup attempt, a total of around

---

16   Two books that well illustrate the intricacies and stages of the conflict between the Gülen community and the AKP administration are Çakır and Sakallı (2014) and Koru (2016).

125 thousand people considered close to the organization have been removed from their posts in the army, police, judiciary, and bureaucracy (*Yeni Şafak* 2018).

The series of arrests and investigations that followed July 15 have had a devastating effect on the financial and organizational structure of the community, especially at home, where all the schools, journals, foundations, media companies, and businesses having proven ties with the community have been closed and their properties confiscated (*Hürriyet Daily News* 2016). As of today, all the activities of the community, including the student houses in which I conducted part of my research, have been closed down. Although the community abroad has not been damaged so consistently, it is now involved in a battle for survival. The UK and the United States are most certainly the two major countries where the community has been able to establish a safe haven (Tee 2018). Yet even there they face pressures that Turkey is exerting on their administrations to close the community's schools and collaborate on the arrest of its members. These efforts include an explicit request to the US administration for extraditing Fethullah Gülen (Baker 2018) that has remained unattended for the moment. Currently, only a few countries such as Somalia and Azerbaijan have accommodated Turkey's appeal to close the activities of the community (Norton and Kasapoglu 2016).

The image of Gülen and his group is definitively compromised in Turkey and it looks very unlikely, if not impossible, that the community will one day regain credibility in the eyes of the people. The coup attempt caused the death of 248 persons among police forces, military personnel, and civilians, and since the events both the conservative and secularist strata have blamed the community as the culprit for what happened. The community has also undergone an internal critique by some prominent ex-members living abroad or having had to relocate there, mostly in the United States, following the coup attempt. Representing the intellectual circle of the community, these people have criticized the highest echelons of the group for deceiving the large cohort of sympathizers and members who continued to sustain it in good faith until the last days before the coup attempt, unaware that the community was hatching a conspiracy (*T24* 2016; Bacık 2018). The implication here is that the Gülen community has widely disregarded the expectation of many Turkish Muslims who believed it could be the bearer of an Islamically-inflected message of peace and brotherhood, able to cut across national borders and confessional divisions as longed for by its leader.

The coup attempt has also had other important consequences on the political situation at home, where the power balance has significantly turned in favor of the AKP administration. Reflecting a process that had already been ignited since the Gezi protests of summer 2013 (Vicini 2018), following the coup attempt the nationalist conservative block—mainly represented by the electorate of the Nationalist Movement Party (*Milliyetçi Hareket Partisi*, MHP)—has joined the religious conservatives in support of all the measures that the AKP administration has taken to clean the institutions from the gülenists. In a parallel move, the very large majority of Islamic groups in the country, including the *Suffa* foundation, have openly condemned the Gülen community and took the side of the current administration. In a long statement released after an internal consultation took place in the foundation's headquarters in Erzurum among its members, the *Suffa* community defined the coup attempt as a "bloody, treacherous and vile" act (*Suffa Vakfı* 2016). In addition, highly respected exponents of the Nur movement, such as Nursi's student Mehmet Fırıncı, blamed Gülen publicly for exploiting the teachings of Nursi and damaging the reputation of the entire movement (*Risale Haber* 2016).

The popularity of the AKP emerged clearly strengthened from the war with the community. The trust of the majority of the people in Recep Tayyip Erdoğan has been confirmed by the success obtained by its party in two successive electoral consultations: the 2017 Referendum sanctioning the passage from a Republican to a Presidential system, and the June 2018 general election, in which Erdoğan became the first elected president of Turkish history. In the process, following the cleansing of members of the community from the institutions, many public posts are now being filled by members of other Islamic communities and foundations, generally branches of the Naqshbandi order (*Birgün* 2017). New spaces of action are open for such groups in the education and media sectors. Interestingly, some Nur groups have even taken advantage of this new special relation between the institutions and religious groups to expand their activities in Turkey's South-East (Çepni 2018)—not coincidentally one of the places in which the Gülen community started its educational venture.

A full analysis of these recent transformations is beyond the scope of this book. What happened, however, does raise a few questions regarding some of the arguments presented here. If the community has been long involved in the cultivation of state power, what remains of the "civic" potential of its original impetus? As it will be discussed in Chapter 5, in Muslim history—and particularly within the Ottoman Empire—the social/civic domain has often overlapped with the institutional one, so that it has traditionally been difficult to establish a clear separation between the two (see also Vicini 2016). Forming a group of educated Muslims who may eventually enter important public institutions to challenge the domain of the secularists has always been a scope of these and other religious and non-religious groups in the country. Rather, the discriminating factor is whether this goal is pursued with sincere dedication to a religiously-grounded civilizing mission, or for the mere purpose of increasing one's influence and power. Relatedly, it will be speculated on how a process of excessive idealization of the community's mission by Gülen has probably hindered his community from becoming the bearer of an Islamically inflected, yet universalistic, message of peace and brotherhood it said it aimed to become. Yet the main goal of *Reading Islam* is not to elaborate on the contingent, often opaque, and hence unpredictable strategies of religious movements and their leaders. Instead, it is to explore the philosophical views, religious motivations, and imaginaries that have been mobilized by the *Suffa* and the Gülen communities and that have upheld the sense of participation of many common Muslims to their reformist project for so long.

7 Outline of the Book

Reading Islam moves progressively from an investigation of Muslim life, socialization, and reading practices of key texts within the shielded space of the housings of the two communities under study, to exploring how philosophical discussions conducted herein are linked to the way my interlocutors thought of their forms of participation in an Islamic project aimed at reforming society. Chapter 1 introduces the landscape of activities promoted by the *Suffa* and the Gülen communities. Their emergence is placed in a historical perspective that goes back to the time of the birth of the Turkish Republic and later framed in the set of sociopolitical transformations that brought about the Islamic revival of the 1980s. The chapter sheds light on how Said Nursi's revivalist message has been transmuted into new forms of Muslim organization (*cemaat*) and mobilization by reference to longstanding, yet reinterpreted, Islamic notions among which the ideal of *hizmet* (literally, "service") occupies a prominent position. Chapter 2 shifts the scene to the enclosed space of the students' houses of the *Suffa* and the Gülen communities, and illustrates how the organization of time and space, as well as the arrangement of moments of Muslim sociability according to shared principles of respect and reciprocity, permeate these places. Extracts from reading sections and daily life within these communities help to shed light on the way the environment of these places, as well as the forms of socialization they gave form to, were both conducive to the embodiment of specific key virtues of purity and sincerity of faith, which were in turn functional to the other main goal of fostering strong inter-subjective relations along the lines of religious brotherhood.

Chapter 3 explores in detail the reading practices of the *Risale-i Nur* within the *Suffa* community in light of related exercises of meditative reflection on nature and existence (*tefekkür*). It adopts a genealogical perspective to illustrate the signs of continuity and rupture this practice marks regarding longstanding forms of intellectual engagement within the Islamic, and particularly Sufi, tradition. Through an account of the role of imagination within *tefekkür*, the chapter links what may at first appear as a novelty of sort—namely, the unprecedented emphasis on the most rational form of meditation within the Islamic tradition—to a more "classic" Ibn Arabian cosmological framework. In parallel, the chapter advances the idea that an anthropology of reading, both in Islam and beyond, should divert part of its attention from the strictest technical aspects of the practice to more seriously consider how the material support provided by the texts is relied upon differently within different and culturally specific intellectual contexts.

Chapter 4 focuses specifically on the Gülen community to shed light on how a longstanding pedagogical practice upholding Islamic prophetic models of guidance and exemplariness (*temsiliyet*) is therein intertwined with modern Republican educational discourse and Western pedagogical theories. By combining the analysis of Gülen's first writings with the ethnographic description of their actualization in daily life within the student houses of this community, the chapter details the pedagogical strategy adopted by this community over time to draw a diverse, broad number of people to its ranks. Moreover, it illustrates how these same strategies rested on a strong sense of responsibility that elder students of the community had to embody in the process, with the consequence that their educational efforts emerge as the very same activity through which young members of the community shaped themselves as persons committed to the community's mission in the first place.

In Chapter 5, I finally build on previous discussions on reading and the place of reflection in Muslim life to explore the ideals of freedom and responsibility in relation to forms of civic engagement that are promoted within the *Suffa* and the Gülen communities. By illustrating the alternative genealogy of these views with regard to their modern secular counterparts, the chapter highlights how, by reference to transcendence, Muslim forms of civic engagement retain a specific Islamic potential for thinking of human relations and solidarity from a non-liberal perspective which yet possesses a universalistic inclination. However, the chapter concludes by pointing to the potential tensions that continue to exist between Islamic forms of civic engagement and the political order of the contemporary world, an aspect which has also been dramatically illustrated by the recent rifts within the religious conservative camp, to which I briefly return in the conclusion.

CHAPTER 1

Outreaches of Religious Service

Backstage at the opening of the 2010 Said Nursi Symposium, an electronic screen repeatedly flashed a sentence declaring that, until his death, the mission of Said Nursi was "to save the faith" (*imanı kurtarmak*).[1] Today's adherents of the Nur movement, including people at *Suffa*, claim that Nursi wrote the *Risale-i Nur* to counter the materialist and positivist ideologies that had spread in the late Ottoman Empire by reconciling the idea of faith with that of reason and modern science.[2] For this reason, they believe that Nursi was a renewer of Islam (*müceddit*), one of those Muslim guides who appear on the Earth once every century to refresh the Islamic message in accordance with the changing social, cultural, and historical conditions.[3] Accordingly, Nursi came into this world to reinterpret revelation in line with scientific discourse and save religion from the intellectual torpor into which it had fallen in the previous two centuries. Discontent with the state of Islam in late Ottoman times, he attacked both the old class of the scholars of Islam (*ulema*) and the Sufi leaders (*şeyh*), holding them responsible for the dire situation of Islam at that time. While he deplored the former for their collusion with state power and their inability to renew their teachings in terms of method and approach, he accused the latter of remaining attached to elitist disciplinary paths that were inaccessible to the vast majority of ordinary Muslims or, in the worst hypothesis, of supporting idolatry.[4]

---

1 The Said Nursi Symposium is an international meeting organized by a group of Nur foundations every year in which Muslim scholars from Turkey and other countries are invited to discuss topics related to Nursi's thought. The title of the 2010 Symposium was "The *Risale-i Nur*: Knowledge, Faith, Morality and the Future of Humankind."
2 The word *Nur* that denotes the movement is particularly fitting to refer to both the rationalist/enlightening and Islamic/ethical dimensions which are intertwined in Said Nursi's views. Usually translated as "light" in Islamic circles in Turkey, *nur* also carries the meaning of "spirit," intended as a sort of flash of inspiration that has both intellectual and spiritual connotations. Instead, adherents of the Nur movement deny that the term might refer either to Said Nursi himself or to the name of his village of origin in Eastern Anatolia, as some have claimed.
3 See Algar (2001). For the tradition of *müceddit* (in Arabic, *mujaddid*, "renewer [of the century]") in Islam, see Donzel (2011).
4 The conformity to Islam of some practices of devotion usually associated with Sufism, such as the cult of the saints and of their tombs, has been a long-debated issue by both orthodox and Sufi scholars since the times of Ibn Taymiyyah in the thirteenth century (Rahman 1979 [1966]). However, Sufism has been particularly questioned since the end of the nineteenth century following the impact of Western ideas and techniques of governance, with their

Sami *abi,* a thirty-year-old brother with a degree in psychology who was at the head of the *Suffa* foundation's office in the Edirnekapı neighborhood in Istanbul, expressed the situation that Said Nursi had to cope with in the late Ottoman Empire with the following words:

> At that time ignorance was widespread even among the Sufi leaders, scholars of Islam and masters (*hoca*). For example, they quoted one saying of the Prophet (*hadith*) to claim that the Earth was flat and had water flooding underneath. [...] But this *hadit* was *müteşabih*, that is, it used a simile to explain something. In the West, science (*bilim*) emerged from a strong clash with religion. For centuries knowledge had been in the Church's hands, and the Church also controlled education. It was not a coincidence that the greatest men of knowledge were also believers. [...] Yet [in Christianity] there was this solipsistic theory about the Earth and the idea that the world was flat. When people like Copernicus started to refute these theses, there was a clash and science and religion took two separate paths. Then the European states developed until they came knocking at the Ottoman Empire's door... And when the sultan talked with European scientists he made a big mistake: he told them that the Earth was flat. So they laughed in his face and thought that Islam must be the same as Christianity. Then, such ideas diffused in the country and people started thinking: 'We don't need religion anymore.' They started to have doubts about religion. It was in this way that materialism spread, as well as propaganda against religion. [...] The *şeyh*s, the *hoca*s, and the *ulema*s weren't able to find answers to the questions posed by science nor to European thought in general. They said things like the Earth being flat... But this was ignorance (*cahillik*). It was not Islam. At this moment and for these reasons the *üstad*[5] started writing the *Risale-i Nur*. [...] His goal was to save religion (*din*) from the anti-religious notions that were conveyed in parallel within the sciences (*fen*) and philosophy (*felsefe*). The *Risale* was written to save the faith.

---

emphasis on reason, on the one hand, and under the pressure of Islamic reformist scholars who defended a purist version of Islam, on the other (for a critique see Ewing (1997), Sirriyeh (1999), and Weismann (2011); see also Gilsenan (2005 [1982] ff.)). For this reason, apart from Nursi, many Sufis in Turkey also acknowledged that the Sufi lodges had to reform their methods to keep up with the times (Silverstein 2007).

5 Translatable into English as "master," this is one of the terms that, together with *Bediüzzaman* ("wonder of the time"), people in the Nur movement use to refer respectfully to Said Nursi.

According to Sami, Nursi's perceived impetus for revitalizing Islam has to be framed within the context of the rising prominence that positivist thought was gaining in the late Ottoman Empire, and which for the most part was appropriated by the secularist rhetoric in the first Republican period (1923–1948). Moved by the will of decoupling the implicit association of science and atheism within such a rhetoric, Nursi began writing the *Risale-i Nur* to offer a new synthesis that integrated scientific accounts of nature within an Islamic cosmology. His aim was to rebuff the doubts of the positivists and reassure ordinary Muslims with sound answers about the compatibility of science and religion. While in today's Turkey anti-religious attitudes are no longer dominant, it is in the frame of such ideological confrontation that the birth and early development of the Nur network must be approached.

In this chapter, the emergence of the Nur movement is placed in the context of the challenges that this and other Islamic groups had to endure following the foundation of the Republic in 1923. The establishment of a modern nation-state in place of the Empire was accompanied by a set of institutional reforms that led to the shrinking of the space left for religious expression in public space and implied a parallel twofold process. Indeed, Islam as an ethical system and knowledge tradition was overcome by new technically-oriented epistemologies highlighting reason-based empirical inquiry. As a consequence, the *ulema*s lost the control they had traditionally maintained over education. However, the new born Republic did not aim at the total erasure of religion from people's life. Rather, it opted for institutionalizing Islam through the foundation of the Directorate of Religious Affairs (*Diyanet İşleri Başkanlığı*). By so doing, the state began competing with resilient Islamic networks, which continued to provide rural communities with ethical guidance and social cohesion, for the appropriation of the banner of Islam as a legitimacy tool that served the goal of securing its grasp on society. Indeed, the state's aspiration to embody Islam's charismatic aura and transform it into a symbol of national unity validated through national education widened the gap separating the culture of the urbanized and more secular-oriented elites from that of the majority of the traditionally conservative people inhabiting the Anatolian region, who continued to remain attached to Islamic networks.

New Islamic actors like the *Suffa* and the Gülen communities emerged in the 1980s by thriving on such ousted but resilient networks, as they embraced new organizational forms and principles: community (*cemaat*) and religiously motivated service (*hizmet*), respectively. Taking advantage of a new political environment, these and other Islamic communities were successful in securing the integration of countrymen into the sociopolitical life of the nation and in offering their sons upward mobility opportunities. Thanks to their appeal to

Muslim forms of civility and solidarity, these communities were able to draw a growing public of pious people who were able, in time, to challenge the supremacy of their secular opponents. These new opportunities favored a slow, constant, and progressive process of transformation of society that brought to power a new conservative elite. The AKP's political success represents the most visible manifestation of such process.

1   Reading the *Risale*

Located near the Suleiman mosque, one of the largest complexes on the European shore of Istanbul, is one of the main centers of the *Suffa* foundation. The place was a guest-house and a *Risale-i Nur* reading center for hundreds of people in the neighborhood. Every Saturday night, groups of males flocked to the place to collectively read the *Risale*, a practice that they saw as conducive to the strengthening of their faith. Whereas more outwardly-focused offshoots of the Nur network, such as the Gülen community, have extended their activities in several fields beyond strictly religious activities (see Yavuz 2003a; Hendrick 2013), more conventional groups such as *Suffa* have remained primarily dedicated to the original purpose of promoting reading circles of the *Risale*. Among the few major factions in which the Nur movement is divided, the *Suffa* community belongs to "the readers" (*okuyucular*) because it espouses an approach that gives particular importance to the careful and attentive reading of this text.[6]

The *Suffa* foundation was established in Erzurum in 1982 by Osman Demirci and other former students of Said Nursi such as Mehmet Kırkıncı.[7] It expanded to Istanbul in the early 1990s. Today the foundation manages a dozen of places

---

6   Apart from the Gülen community, other main branches of the Nur movement include: the *yazıcılar* (writers) who think that the original scriptural form of the *Risale* in Arabic characters was the best form for disseminating the *Risale*; the *Yeni Asya* (New Asia) group, which split from the main network in the 1970s following the decision of issuing a newspaper, the still published *Yeni Asya*; and the *Med-Zehra* group, which instead emphasized Nursi's Kurdish ethnicity. This last group has in turn traditionally oscillated between a faction standing for multi-language education (in Turkish, Arabic, and overall Kurdish) of the *Risale*, to another promoting Kurdish nationalism organized around the magazine *Yeni Zemin* (Yavuz 2003a).

7   Demirci and, particularly, Kırkıncı are known to have been close to Fethullah Gülen, who was also from Erzurum. Allegedly, it was Kırkıncı who first introduced Gülen to the *Risale* (Erdoğan 2006 [1995]). This proximity also explains why, though differing in their approaches, people at the *Suffa* and the Gülen communities have similar views when it comes to the forms of civic engagement that they promote (see Chapter 5).

including cultural and educational centers, student dormitories and libraries. It also offers scholarships and organizes educational trips and seminars where it conveys the message of the *Risale* to students of different ages. Other promotion activities include the editing of an English version of the *Risale* and financial support offered to a website explaining the text. At the time of my research, *Suffa* was also active in recruiting students willing to undertake university studies in Turkey from abroad, especially from the Turkic Republics, including the Xinjiang Uyghur Autonomous Region in China, and Indonesia.

Muharram *abi* was the head of the Istanbul branch of *Suffa*. In the late 1980s, he was asked to leave his town of origin in northeastern Anatolia to open the first *Suffa* center in town. Around fifty years old, he is still an esteemed reader of the *Risale* and holds his lessons every Saturday night in the hall of the foundation. Usually wearing simple shirts and trousers, Muharram addresses his audience with severe tones. He alternates the rhythmic reading of the *Risale* with loud admonitions, but also with some jokes that make the attendees laugh out loud. Males of different ages and classes take part in these meetings: from university students to elderly men. Most of the attendees are workers, shopkeepers, and small businessmen, with a minority of employees, lawyers, and doctors. Although the majority of them have grown up in Istanbul, they all share an immigration background from some Anatolian province. None of the attendees would indeed say: "I am from Istanbul" (*İstanbul'luyum*). This is related to the importance that regional and ethnic identities still play for social relations in metropolitan contexts with a composite population. However, in the case of my interlocutors, it also depended on their reluctance to identify themselves with the culture of the city, as they preferred to highlight their proximity to the countryside and its cultural legacy.

People at *Suffa* held an ambivalent relationship with the countryside. On the one hand, they imagined Anatolia as a sort of enchanted place of the past where Muslims once lived their faith purely and naturally. This transpired when, with a certain degree of melancholy, they told me of their parents or grandparents who, having been raised there, did still have the opportunity of breathing a religious-cultural atmosphere close to that of Ottoman times. The fact they lacked proper education was thought to be a *plus*. Having only a limited knowledge of things, they believed and worshiped God with greater devotion and sincerity than today's people. However, given the prominence that modern lifestyles and related hedonistic and areligious ideologies have gained in the last decades, these people were seen as no longer fitting the context. For people at *Suffa* today, Islam can no longer be lived in the simple way their grandparents did. Rather, Muslims have to "understand" religious teachings and provide irrefutable answers to those questioning their beliefs.

In the eyes of my interlocutors, the *Risale* provides them with an innovative path to cultivating faith. Explanations of why and how they had begun attending Nur circles were generally accompanied by enthusiastic narrations of how the *Risale* had changed their life. They described their encounter with the community as a sort of liberating moment when a renewed sense of faith was instilled in them. These claims were generally accompanied by their disapproval of other Muslims in Turkey, whom they perceived as only superficially following Islamic conduct out of habit and without "knowing why." My interlocutors defined these people as "Muslims by imitation" (*taklidi müslümanlar*), echoing distinctions by nineteenth-century reformist scholars inviting believers to reject corrupt practices inherited by the previous generations (Rahman 1979 [1966], 197–198). In particular, they lamented that most ordinary Muslims today do not possess the necessary knowledge to explain the reasons behind basic Islamic beliefs and practices, which in their eyes should be a requisite for every educated Muslim.

On this point, consider the words of Nimet, a thirty-six-year-old brother who was responsible for one of the student dormitories *Suffa* managed in Şişli, a neighborhood on the European side of Istanbul. While he was giving me a spontaneous introduction to the community's goals at the students' summer camp where I first met him, he said:

> Before, when I was a young boy, my father would come to me and oblige me to perform the prayer... But then, when I was eighteen years old, I read the *Risale*... After reading the *Risale* I no longer needed somebody to remind me to perform the prayer. [...] Really, it has saved my faith. [...] Because then, when you read the *Risale*, you look at a piece of fruit, at an animal, at manhood... and you see that God protects everything. The *Risale* has explained the existence of God to me.

A full treatment of how reading the *Risale* impacts on my interlocutors' worldview and the implications this has for anthropological debates on Islam is adjourned until Chapter 3. Here, it suffices to note that reading this particular text was perceived by my interlocutors as a distinctive trait of their way of living Islam; a practice that was believed to be conducive to the attainment of a specific kind of religiously-grounded awareness. This distinctive trait acquired a particular relevance for new generations of students with a conservative background, like those I met at *Suffa*. More than others, they felt compelled to counter areligious discourse they were still presented with at school and to distance themselves from conventional ways of being a Muslim in Turkey. As an example, take the words of Bekim, a twenty-year-old university student from the province of Gümüşhane, in the Black sea region, living in a house managed by *Suffa*:

> Up to three years ago, when I was still in my village of origin I had been a Muslim, but only from an outside point of view. [...] Each Friday I went to the mosque to attend the weekly collective prayer just as my mother taught me. Yet I was a Muslim 'for show' only. [...] In reality I was empty inside and I did not know anything about Islam. [...] Since entering the community I have been learning something. Previously, I was only a Muslim by imitation...

The embarrassment Bekim feels upon remembering the time when he went to the Friday prayer just out of habit reveals the new kind of Muslim educated person that the *Suffa* community aims to cultivate. Enlightened by the *Risale*'s message, people like Bekim feel they are better equipped to live their faith in the context of modern society, where moral decay and decline in religious awareness are widespread. Against many ordinary Muslims who live Islam unwarily by simply mimicking an outer path, reading the *Risale* is perceived by people at *Suffa* as conducive to cultivating the status of "true Muslims" (*hakiki müslüman*): people whose commitment to faith is based on informed belief. As mentioned above, this inclination to "objectifying" Islam into a subject of knowledge that Muslims have to be able to articulate in intellectual terms is a common trait of this and other reform-oriented reinterpretations of the Islamic tradition (Eickelman and Piscatori 1996, 37–38). What is distinctive of *Suffa* are the means through which religious awareness is achieved, and the specific perspective on Muslim life that this opens. People of this community see reading the *Risale* as the necessary condition to educate themselves into religiously aware and educated Muslims ready to engage with modern society. For this reason, *Suffa* is mainly devoted to the dissemination of the *Risale* throughout society. Other dimensions such as entrepreneurship and dedication to the cause of *hizmet* received greater emphasis within the Gülen community.

2 Reforming Society through Educational Service

One night, at the beginning of my fieldwork, I paid a visit to Mustafa, a teacher that I had met back in 2005 during one of my first trips to Istanbul. Mustafa was now working at a private middle school linked to the Gülen community in Silivri, one of the remotest districts on the European side of the city. That night, to my surprise, he brought me to one of the community's decision-making meetings (*istişare*), at which community brothers met local businessmen to decide what activities to promote and raise money for in the neighborhood. When I was allowed to speak at the end of the meeting, I asked those present what it meant for them to conduct *hizmet*, an expression they had used to define their way of contributing to the activities of the community—and that, as I will show in a moment, is central in the self-definition of this community, although it had already been used by Nursi in the *Risale*.

Murat, one of the oldest businessmen present, with a stern look on his face replied: "First it means worshiping (*ibadet*)," that is to say, "gaining God's approval (*Allah'ın rızası*) and thus going to paradise." As he immediately added, *hizmet* means promoting initiatives that open paradise's doors further, because all the work they did was thought of as a contribution "to save people by bringing them closer to Islam," the main aim of *hizmet*. Then it was the turn of Abdurrahim, another businessman a few years younger, to take the word and state: "*Hizmet* means two things: doing something good like financing *hizmet* activities. [...] It also means shaping high-quality human beings," whom he defined as people abstaining from drugs and alcohol. Abdurrahim also stressed how the community aims to realize such a project by opening schools where teachers can educate their students in a friendly and sincere atmosphere. He concluded by adding that *hizmet* can be alternatively defined as "giving without expecting something back in return."[8]

In the statements of both businessmen, the word *hizmet* is used to refer to a broad civilizing mission aimed at creating a better society by educating new generations of pious Muslims. The two goals are strictly related in the minds of members of this community. As it will be discussed in Chapter 4, Gülen has repeatedly defined his project as the shaping of a "golden generation" (*altın nesil*) of people imbued with Islamic morals and scientific knowledge that in his view could guide Turkey toward a bright future (Agai 2003; see Gülen 1990; Gülen 1997). Before its demise after the coup attempt of July 2016, the community represented the most extensively accomplished evolution of Said Nursi's project for forging new generations of Muslims capable of living their faith in modern times. Making it particularly successful and distinct from *Suffa* was its capacity of bringing a large array of people under the same umbrella, from motivated young activists to generous economic supporters moved by an entrepreneurial spirit.

Begun in the late 1970s from a circle of students gathered around the Islamic preacher Fethullah Gülen, the community expanded soon and was able to

---

8 For a comment on this concluding sentence by the second brother and the idea of *hizmet* it incorporates, see below.

attract hundreds of thousands of adherents and sympathizers.[9] Not simply a popular preacher of the kind of Shaykh Yusuf al-Qadarawi in Egypt (see Gräf and Skovgaard-Petersen 2009), Gülen drew his force from the capacity to mobilize his followers to achieve the community's goals. Rather than asking devout Muslims to finance the construction of new mosques, as conventionally done by religious charities, he invited them to invest their gains in the opening of dormitories and secular schools (see Chapter 4). At the same time, he encouraged people to expand in the "cultural industry" by venturing into the newly emerging market for Muslim publications and entertainment activities. Since its inception, indeed, the community aimed to spread its pacifying Islamic message by relying on modern media such as magazines, journals, books, radio, and TV channels.

In 1979, the community had started publishing *Sızıntı*, a monthly magazine— later also published in English as *The Fountain*—that debated issues of science, history, and society from a Nur perspective. While the journal focused on the problems that urbanization, individualism, and social disunity had brought to Turkish society, it propounded a solution to these challenges that was certified with both religiously-grounded and science-based explanations. Gülen regularly wrote for *Sızıntı* under a pseudonym from its very first issues. The magazine remained one of the main voices of the community until 2016. *Yeni Ümit*, a journal with a more explicit theological orientation, and *Aksiyon*, a weekly magazine that dealt with more current sociopolitical issues, were added to this publication in 1988 and 1994, respectively. In the following years, thanks to the strong motivation and entrepreneurship of its adherents, the community was able to gain control of an editorial micro-empire which occupied an important slice of the Turkish cultural market for more than three decades. Apart from Gülen's turned-into-books speeches, the community's editorial group, the *Kaynak Kültür Yayın Grubu*, published anthologies of writings by classic scholars of Islam such as the Sufis Ibn Arabi and Ahmad Sirhindi (known in Turkey as *İmam Rabbani*), books of Turkish nationalist intellectuals like Mustafa Asım Köksal, Mehmet Akif Ersoy (the author of the national anthem), and the Muslim intellectual Nurettin Topçu. It also addressed the younger public by releasing a variety of books on sundry religious issues, children books, and novels.

---

9 While according to informal estimates circulated by community members, the number of adherents of the community in Turkey before 2016 was around 8 million, a research in 2011 estimated around 3 million members in Turkey (Çaha et al. 2011). However, any estimation is deemed to remain an approximation due to the high level of secrecy that wraps this and similar communities. Further, since there is no formal membership in these kinds of organizations, it is difficult to distinguish between active members and those who are only sympathizers.

These comprised of romanticized biographies of relevant historical figures of Islam, including the Prophet himself and his favorite wife *Aişe*, or characters from Ottoman-Turkish history such as Sultan Fatih Mehmet, the conqueror of Istanbul, or Adnan Menderes, the first democratically elected prime minister of Turkey.

These were more than simply "Islamic books" intended as "attractively printed mass-market texts that address such practical questions as how to live as a Muslim in the modern world" that have recently propagated widely in Muslim-majority countries (Eickelman and Salvatore 2006, 14–15; see also Eickelman and Anderson 2003). Operating at a more implicit level, these publications presented an alternative historical narrative that reinterpreted the role of important figures of the Turkish past by "Islamizing" them at the same time. A similar attitude was also reserved for important Western philosophers, such as Rousseau, Kant, and Bergson, whose publications were selected among those most quoted by Gülen. In each of the community's *NT* stores, one could find these classics of Western philosophy, which were published with the implicit intent of marking the affinity of Gülen's thought—and therefore of the community itself—with Western modernity.[10]

The flagship of the community's involvement in broader society, however, was *Zaman* (Time), the newspaper that it controlled between 1986 and 2016. Although it largely depended on compulsory conscriptions of its members and sympathizers, *Zaman* became one of the main national newspapers by reaching a circulation of 800,000 copies in the late 2000s—an unprecedented number for Turkey's editorial industry. Here, not only Muslim intellectuals such as Ali Bulaç and Ali Ünal, but also more liberal voices such as Atilla Yayla and Mustafa Erdoğan regularly wrote columns. For thirty years, *Zaman* expressed the opinion of the community's highest echelons on several public issues. It represented the platform from which the community launched its campaigns, not least the one aimed at discrediting the AKP administration in December 2013. A similar yet minor role was played by *Samanyolu TV*, the national TV broadcasting network that aired Turkish-made TV series—a very successful genre in the country—like *Tek Türkiye*, *Beşinci Boyut*, and many others, which reproduced the community's Islamically-grounded and patriotic set of values. The community also owned radio stations such as *Dünya* and *Burç FM*, which

---

10 Gülen has publicly declared that he likes European authors like Rousseau, Balzac, Dostoevsky, Pushkin, Tolstoy and the existentialists, and that he admires in particular Kant (Ünal and Williams 2000, 28–29). However, it is not clear to what degree he has read these authors, whom he probably knows from the writings of Turkish nationalist intellectuals like Nurettin Topçu and Necip Fazıl Kısakürek who lived and studied in France in the 1920s and 1930s (Guida 2014).

were followed by the conservative segments of Turkish society. More recently it had also invested in the production of theatre shows and cinematographic productions (Vicini 2015). Two examples are movies such as *The Butterfly Effect* (*Kelebek Etkisi*), which put a stress on the community's missionary and peace-building activities around the world, and Said Nursi's biographic movie *Hür Adam: Said Nursi*.[11]

Another important soft power instrument of the community was the Journalists and Writers Foundation (*Gazeteciler ve Yazarlar Vakfı*), which worked hand in hand with *Zaman* to promote the community's agenda, especially in the field of interreligious dialogue. A separate branch of the organization, the Abant Platform (*Abant Platformu*), was responsible for organizing conferences, seminars, and international meetings devoted to interreligious and "inter-civilizational" dialogue, but also to discuss current social and political issues with journalist, activists, and intellectuals who were invited from different ideological segments. These public activities reflected the community's policy of "seizure of liberal ideals of multiculturalism, tolerance, and religious freedom" (Walton 2017, 35), that it started to pursue after Gülen migrated to the United States in 1999.

Operating as a religious-cultural agglomerate, the community also established a set of economic associations and companies with the goal of implementing commercial relations among local, national and foreign businessmen. As highlighted by the scholarly literature, indeed, the Gülen community has long thrived thanks to the support of an expanding cohort of conservative businessmen, who emerged in the context of the neoliberal transformation inaugurated by Turgut Özal in the 1980s (Yavuz 2003a; Hendrick 2013). Business associations such as *İşhad, Asya Finans,* and TUSKON were founded as alternatives to both the state and the traditionally secularist TÜSIAD, as well as to the other conservative organization, MÜSIAD. They constituted an autonomous hub of social capital through which religious conservative entrepreneurs could take advantage of the community's economic and political networks—developed both at home and abroad and through a scrupulous work of lobbying (Hendrick 2013)—in return of the financial support given. In parallel, the community had invested in the bank sector by founding interest-free financial institutions such as *Bank Asya*, and a big insurance company like *Işık Sigortası*. Smaller foundations and associations included the charity *Kimse Yok Mu?*,

---

11   This movie has raised some controversy among members of the broader Nur network, because some accused the producers, and hence indirectly the Gülen community, of giving an excessively nationalist representation of Nursi turning him into a sort of hero of the Turkish Republic—while in fact he was an ethnic Kurd.

which was particularly active in those countries where the community operated abroad, especially in Africa and Indonesia.

However, all these activities were residual to the community's huge investment in the education sector. The hundreds of private schools that the community has opened in the four corners of the world were—and still are abroad—the emblem of its activism and also the main way through which it has constructed its successful image (Balci 2003; Yavuz 2003c; Agai 2003, 2007; Zengin Arslan 2009; Ebaugh 2010; Hendrick 2013; Tittensor 2014; Tee 2016). Their preparatory schools (*dershane*) were key to the recruiting strategies of the community and provided the latter with vital revenues (see Chapter 4). Hence, it is not a coincidence that the revelation of a government plan to close the *dershane* sector turned out to be the trigger of the conflict between the community and the AKP administration. Abroad, the Gülen community had begun its adventure in education in the former lands of the Ottoman Empire such as the Balkans and the Central Asian Republics—Kazakhstan, Uzbekistan, Kyrgyzstan, and Turkmenistan (Balci 2003; Turam 2007). Since the late 1990s, the community has expanded to European countries such as Germany, France, and the UK, plus non-Western countries like India, Pakistan, and Nigeria. More recently, beginning in the 2000s, it has concentrated its investments in the African continent (Dohrn 2014; Angey 2018) and South America (Dumovich 2018). As of March 2012, the community manages approximately 130 charter schools across the USA, more than anywhere else—Turkey included, following the shutdown of all its activities in 2016.[12] Here, special legislation granting freedom of school choice has created an environment where the community could expand in this as well as other fields such as in intercultural activities, commerce, construction, IT solutions, political lobbying, and education (Hendrick 2013, 7–8).

Because of the relocation of the center of the community to the United States in the late 1990s, a change of emphasis and policy has taken place in its public discourse. The community's agenda has switched from a battle with radical secularism in Turkey into a worldwide project focused on the promotion of Islam as a religion of peace and dialogue in a global world (Yavuz 2013; Tittensor 2014). In the last fifteen years, Gülen has shifted some of its positions, in particular with regard to other monotheist religions and the West in general. This has been reflected in a series of efforts to promote inter-faith dialogue, which have been brought forth by the community under the flag of organizations such as the Journalist and Writers Foundation and many other dialogue

---

12   For a journalistic account of the community's schools in Pakistan, see Tavernise (2008). With regard to the United States, see Woodall and Gatti (2011) and Saul (2011).

centers abroad. Yet the main agenda of the community, especially at home until 2016, remained to expand its networks throughout society and institutions.

3 From *Hizmet* to Individual Duty

Like people at *Suffa*, members of the Gülen community participated in weekly readings taking place in one of the thousands of private houses and dormitories located in city. Here, the books of Gülen were read in addition to the *Risale*, and tape-recordings of his weekly speeches from his residence in Pennsylvania watched in small groups of ten to thirty people.[13] Due to the higher number of affiliates and their heterogeneity compared to people at *Suffa*, a very structured and differentiated network of meetings existed, each aimed at targeting a specific group based on the level of education or occupation. Also, the social composition of the attendees was different. In line with its more elitist character, the Gülen community targeted middle and high class clerks, lawyers, doctors, state bureaucrats, and businessmen, though limited groups of laborers also existed. The more exclusive atmosphere of this community was also reflected in the identification that people here felt with the urban setting compared to their counterpart at *Suffa*.

While reading still occupied an important place during the meetings, more time was left for socializing. Elder members often paid visits and told stories about some brothers' service as teachers or managers of a school in some far-off place abroad. There was a marked emphasis on the missionary and preaching activities of the brothers within this community. This is in line with the input given by Gülen since his first years as a preacher. In his speeches, he has always encouraged people to be active in society by reminding them that in the afterlife they might be judged for the work they have not done in this life (Agai 2003). In the community, the emphasis was placed on doing more than explaining, and the matter of awareness was not thought of as simply referring to raising personal religious consciousness, but stretched to also include a concern for world's problems at large.

As exemplified by the words of the two businessmen above, the community has appropriated the idea of *hizmet* to define all activities conducted under its umbrella, to the extent that the term has become synonymous with the community itself. By extension, the word has even been used within the academic literature to name the activities of this specific group (e.g. Balci and Miller

---

13   Every Sunday, Gülen releases a sermon called *Bamteli* which is videotaped and then uploaded to the website www.herkul.org.

2012; Pandya and Gallagher 2012; Tittensor 2014; Çelik, Leman and Steenbrink 2015; Valkenberg 2015; Marty 2015; Walton 2017). Far from being specific to this community, however, the word has a long genealogy and it has been absorbed within manifold narratives in modern times. For this reason, *hizmet* has been defined by some as a "root-paradigm" (see Mardin 1989, 3–7), a word so rooted in people's language, thinking, and practice that it covers a broad field in the cultural map of Turkish-Muslim society (Bilici 2006). For example, the concept was assimilated by nationalist discourses of the mid-1950s and integrated into Turkish schoolbooks, where it was employed to extol the contribution of the Turks to world civilization and "showing them in a good light in history" (Copeaux 1996, 97). The term has been especially used within conservative circles to define any activity that Muslims brought forth, moved by the desire to achieve some higher and religious goal, regardless of their own personal interest. For example, during the Islamic revival of the 1980s, it has designated the manifold set of religious activities and initiatives that have been promoted in the public space at the time (see below).[14] Since the early 2000s, the idea of *hizmet* has also been constantly evoked by the AKP administration to highlight its way of "serving the people" (*hizmetkar olmak*) by developing infrastructures, rather than by implementing top-down paternalistic policies, as the conservative rhetoric accuses secular politicians to have done for decades following the foundation of the Republic.[15]

Originally, the word *hizmet* comes from the Arabic *khidma*. It is used in the Qur'an to refer to people's (e.g. prophets and saints) or entities' (e.g. the angels) act of total submission to God's will. The sense of submissiveness *hizmet* enshrines was maintained in successive uses of the term within the Sufi tradition, as well as outside of the religious sphere.[16] Since medieval times, the term has been employed within the Sufi orders to define the condition of the novices who accepted serving the *shaykh* (*khidmat al-shaykh*) as part of their initiation process (Uludağ 1997; Karamustafa 2007). Serving the master was the preliminary stage that the apprentice had to pass through along his path to become a Sufi disciple. Apparently, this phase could last many years, during which the

---

14 See Silverstein (2008) on how the term *hizmet* is today used within the Gümüşhanevi Sufi order, a branch of the Khalidi sub-order of the Naqshbandi brotherhood. On the use of the term by the ensemble of Islamic associations, foundations, and civic organizations that were behind the success of the Welfare Party in the 1990s, see White (2002, 178–211).

15 "We did not come to be the master of the people, we came to be of service to the people" (*Bizler millete efendi olmak için değil, hizmetkar olmak için geldik*) has been repeatedly used as a motto in political rallies across the country by today's president Recep Tayyip Erdoğan and AKP members alike (e.g. *T24* 2010).

16 For instance, in pre-Mongol Iran the word denoted the binding subordination of a slave or freeborn noble to a lord, master, or patron (Paul 2014).

apprentice was required to demonstrate his total dedication to the master (Trimingham 1971, 182ff.). Such dedication was never meant to extinguish. *Khidma* was indeed the first step of a long path of knowledge and spiritual maturation that was founded on the cultivation by the disciple of a feeling of total love for the *shaykh*. This sentiment is what the Sufi manuals call *suhba*: a form of complete attachment to a master modelled on the primary affective relationship that tied the Prophet Muhammad and his companions together (Chih 2007, 28; Werbner 2017).[17] As such, it should come as no surprise if the concept of *khidma* has also been often associated with the idea of sincerity and purity of heart (*ikhlas*) in the Sufi tradition.[18] Only by serving his master with total and sincere dedication could the disciple hope to accomplish his service properly.[19]

As an heir of the Naqshbandi Sufi tradition (Mardin 1989, 1991b; Bruinessen 2009),[20] when Nursi started to write the *Risale-i Nur* clandestinely in the 1920s, with *hizmet* he referred to his students' collective action of copying, correcting, and spreading his writings and epistles despite the risk of being arrested and persecuted by the police under the secularist regime of the early Republican era. Particularly important in Nursi's use of the term was that, rather than relying on it to reinforce the dependency of his students on his figure, he preferred to de-emphasize his own authority as a master to exalt the collective work of his followers and brothers in religion in their "service" to the Qur'an and

---

17   On the use of the concept in the Khalwati order in contemporary Egypt, see Chih (2007), while for the Muridi order in late nineteenth and early twentieth-century Senegal, see Babou (2007).

18   For an exploration of the key role played by the virtue of *ikhlas* (*ihlas* in Turkish) in the Nur tradition see especially Chapter 2.

19   Contemporary definitions of *hizmet*, such as the one offered by a Turkish dictionary of Sufi terminology, points to how the concept is immediately related to the idea of *himmet*, another central category in the Islamic pietistic path meaning "devoting oneself with all one's heart's will and purity to God" (Cebecioğlu 1997). As indicated by the entry, if the apprentice is not able to render his service with a purity of heart, this might drive him astray from the right path.

20   The Naqshbandi order is one of the major and most important Sufi brotherhoods in Islam. The Qadiri order was one of its main branches. It took its name from Abd al-Qadir al-Jilani (1077/8–1166), a Hanbali scholar active in Baghdad in the twelfth century. The Qadiri order had a great influence in the consolidation of Islamic tradition in Ottoman and Turkish history, particularly in the Eastern regions of the country where Nursi was educated (Mardin 1989, 1991b). However, at the time of Nursi, this and other older branches of the Naqshbandi order had reoriented themselves toward a new dynamic branch that came to be named Khalidi after its founder, the Kurdish *shaikh* Mawlana Khalid al-Shahrazuri (d. 1827) (Bruinessen 2009, 131). Nevertheless, quite interestingly, in his biography, Nursi reveals that throughout his whole life he has been inspired by the figure of Abd al-Qadir al-Jilani and not by that of Mawlana Khalid al-Shahrazuri (Vahide 2005, 3–5, 163–167).

Islam.[21] In this way, Nursi extended the meaning of *hizmet* to include every effort made by his followers to spread the revivalist message of the *Risale*.

However, Nursi continued to use the idea of *hizmet* to refer to activities whose main and immediate goal was oriented to the promotion of the Qur'anic message *via* the *Risale*. This is in countertrend to how the idea of *hizmet* has been lately reinterpreted within the Gülen community. For the two businessmen quoted above, engaging in *hizmet* extends far beyond direct involvement in preaching activities and includes other more mundane actions such as providing financial backing to the mission of the community. This is an important switch, especially when contextualized within the period of economic liberalization of the 1980s during which religious conservative businessmen were given unprecedented opportunity to expand their presence in the market (see below). At the time, Gülen was canny enough to understand that a traditionally religious motive such as *hizmet* could be turned into a motor for promoting Muslim engagement in society. Indeed, Gülen has been able to involve an increasing number of people into his project by turning secular occupations into a possible way of accomplishing religious service in the form of support for the community's educational mission. Under these circumstances, even the least pious Muslim could pretend to be doing "good action" when contributing to the community's mission, either by donating money or by working within one of its schools or any other of its assets. Several statements by Gülen collimate with such a view of Muslim activism, as he tells his followers to become people of action (*aksiyon insanı*) who devote as little time as possible to sleeping and other daily activities and dedicate the rest of their time to *hizmet* (Agai 2003).

From a theological perspective, one may wonder how a category that was originally circumscribed to define a dyadic pedagogical relationship between master and pupil could be widened to include such a diverse set of activities without losing its transcendent focus. How has in-worldly activism been turned into a way of sanctifying daily life in this community? A key linchpin allowing for the extension of the religious aura provided by the idea of *hizmet*

---

21 Take, as an example, these words of Nursi: "In one respect—beyond my due—you are my students, and in one respect you are my fellow students, and in one respect you are my assistants and consultants. My dear brothers! Your Master is not infallible, it is an error to suppose him to be free of error. [...] Understand this, my brothers and fellow students! I shall be happy if you tell me freely when you see a fault in me. If you hit me over the head with it even, I shall say, 'May God be pleased with you!'" (*Risale-i Nur, Barla Lahikası*, quoted from Vahide 2005, 201–202).

is found in the idea of purity and sincerity that was already central in previous formulations of *khidma/hizmet*, but that took a new strategic relevance in Gülen's discourse. According to my interlocutors, any action that brings an acquisition for the community in terms of social or economic capital can be justified, and even considered meritorious (*sevap*). The important aspect is that the real motive behind one's efforts is not to gain money or to increase one's social status, but that the accumulation of money or power is pursued with the necessary degree of detachment from any material interest, exclusively out of the sincere desire to satisfy God.

In the case of the two businessmen above, this purity and sincerity of commitment was marked by how they interpreted giving money to the community as a way to earn "God's approval" by being generous "without expecting something back." Their words can be juxtaposed to those of another elder brother whom I met at the beginning of my research. Cenep was an active member of the community who had been put in charge of an association dedicated to promoting international cooperation in relation to the community's activities abroad. He smiled when I asked what *hizmet* meant to him, because, he said, this reminded him of himself posing the same question to some brothers twenty years earlier when he first encountered the community. Trying to simplify the issue as much as possible for somebody whose understanding of *hizmet* he considered very basic, he answered: *hizmet* means "to give without expectations, thus preparing oneself for the next world."

While at the moment I could not fully understand the implications of Cenep's concise answer, it later became easier for me to interpret the emphasis he placed on the disinterested dimension of *hizmet* as an index of the constant search for sincerity and purity of intentions that ideally motivated my interlocutors' efforts. Cenep's expression, "without asking for anything in return," demarcates something more than the ideal of behaving according to the disinterested secular philanthropic motive that is highlighted by contemporary humanitarian discourse. Stemming from his words was the idea that what makes an action religiously worthwhile and meritorious for them does not stay in the nature of the action itself, but in the intentions that underlie it. Only when moved by the pure desire of pleasing God, rather than by the personal search for material or symbolic reward, does their forms of commitment become religiously meritorious. In this and other cases, the border between interested and disinterested action may appear very thin, quite specious, and anyway impossible to define properly. Yet it is central in defining the contours of religious service and motivation that lie behind people's will to support this community.

4 Modernity and the Displacement of Islamic Ethics

It is now time to take a step back and look at the challenges that Islam had to face following the set of sociopolitical transformations initiated during the late Ottoman era, concluding with the foundation of the Turkish Republic in 1923. Islam, intended as a legal, ethical, and pedagogical tradition, allowed for the administration of state-society relations through the articulation of the power-knowledge equation in the Ottoman Empire. As made clear by Sami at the beginning of this chapter, only from such a perspective can we fully appreciate Nursi's place in Islamic venture. At the time, Islam was bent to the imperatives of newly emerging forms of political authority and related techniques of power (Eickelman and Piscatori 1996; Salvatore 2001a). While Nursi agreed with the secular reformers that the country had to be modernized and the legal and education system transformed accordingly, he rebuffed their view that this could and should be realized by excluding Islam. Nursi was the proponent of a "social theology" wihch addressed the issue of Islamic civilization and its ills (Alatas 2017, 206) by calling upon fellow Muslims to look at their tradition as a source for imagining a new socio-political order. Contrary to the positivist assumptions of his time, he believed that science can effectively foster progress and prosperity only when governed by faith. His intervention in the public debate was based on the conviction that faith was a necessary precondition to heal humanity from the pathologies of unhappiness, despair, and individualism that modernity had generated.

In late Ottoman times, the intellectual and political elites had long debated how to create a path toward the modernization of state and society that was compatible with the role that Islam had played in the Empire for a long time. Since the sixteenth century, the principle at the core of the Ottoman political system was the pairing of *din u devlet* (Islamic religion and state); a link that was sealed by the figure of the *şeyhülislam* as both the supreme spiritual leader and the administrator of the religious establishment (*ilmiye*) within the Empire. This should not be confused with the common view that religion and state have always been one and the same in Islam. A separation existed, as has always existed in the history of Muslim societies, between the regulations and laws concerning the state and those having to do with religious matters (Lapidus 1975, 1996; Eickelman and Piscatori 1996, 46–47, 55–57). Rather, *din u devlet* defined both an ideology and a principle of state governance that implied a mutually-supportive relationship of state and Islamic authority in a shared sociopolitical body.

The Ottoman state culture had been largely shaped by traditions having their roots in the pre-Islamic past, such as that of the Romans and, especially, the Sassanids, as well as by Turkic/Mongol ideals of quasi-divine monarchy.

The principle of sovereignty undergirding the idea of the Ottoman Sultanate was substantially at odds with the Islamic ideal according to which the Caliph had to embody both political and religious authority (Findley 1980). This is proved, for example, by the fact that the imperial fiat of the Sultan exceeded what Islamic laws allowed (Mardin 1991a, 115). Although in this framework the *ulema*s were subordinated to the state, they operated as the depository of judiciary and educational functions, by so providing the Sultan with a seal of legitimacy and the people with mechanisms for regulating their life in society (Berkes 1998 [1964], 29–31; Toprak 1981). The legitimacy of the Sultan was not shielded by a political theory based on the idea of a contract between the rulers and the ruled, as it was in the modern liberal political model first elaborated by Thomas Hobbes (1588–1679) (Mardin 1969). Instead, it depended on the religious aura he was invested with thanks to his connection with the *ulema* class (Mardin 1971, 202–207). Since the late fifteenth century, the *medrese*s and the body of the *ulema*s had been regularized and ranked in a strict hierarchy under the control of the state (Hefner 2007, 13–14) as they began to take on an important role in the administration of justice within the Empire. In this regard, the role of Islam as a total system granting connectivity between the center of the Empire and its farthest reaches was pivotal for its survival, especially if one considers the inherent tension existing between the court culture of the elites speaking Ottoman language and reading poetry (*Divan*) on the one hand, and the large masses of Turkish-speaking Anatolian peasants living in the periphery, on the other.[22]

Beginning in the nineteenth century, this system began to creak as Ottoman reformers decided to introduce some innovations in the Empire, feeling pressured by the military and scientific supremacy of their European rivals. Before the *Tanzimat* reform period (1839–1876), changes in the legal and educational institutions were sometimes introduced with the favor and cooperation of the highest *ulema*s, some of whom believed they could strengthen their position within the state apparatus (Heyd 1961). However, the reforms led to the opposite; the progressive erosion of the old system. Within the legal field, the codification and enforcement of the *shari'a* in a European-style civil code (*mecelle*) during the last quarter of the nineteenth century resulted in the limitation of the *ulema*s' jurisdiction to the domains of the family, marriage, and personal law.[23] A parallel process took place in the education system. New civilian

---

22   At the time, the term "Turk" was synonymous with uneducated and uncivilized peasant, and an Ottoman gentleman would have considered it an insult if somebody had addressed him with this title (Lewis 1968 [1961], 1–2; Toprak 1981, 61; Ahmad 1993, 78).

23   On the deployment of a similar process in late nineteenth-century Egypt, see Asad (2003).

schools modelled on the European example (*rüşdiye*) were opened with the goal of raising civil servants. Similarly, medical, technical, and military schools inspired by those found in other Imperial capitals of the time were established. It followed that traditional *medrese*s began occupying a secondary role in the system and the *ulema*s lost the hegemony they had exercised for centuries over the domain of knowledge.[24]

Although these transformations did not imply the complete fading away of the *ulema*s—who maintained an important role in shaping public debate on issues of morality even after the emergence of nation-states in the region (Zaman 2002; Bein 2011)—the transmission of the legislative authority to the state and the spread of secular education made them lose the central role they had once played within the *din u devlet* system. As highlighted by Şerif Mardin, when operating as judges (*kadı*), the *ulema*s did not just apply a pre-codified set of rules as occurs in secular law, but were careful to implement a distributive kind of justice based on "measuring various parties' contribution to total solidarity and to working for the equipoise of society" (Mardin 2006, 263).[25] When accomplishing their duties, the *ulema*s relied on those ethically-grounded hermeneutic abilities that were necessary to interpret the complex body of Islamic jurisprudence and that they had learned in the *medrese*s. While secular law is mainly based on the formal application of legal codes, in Islamic jurisprudence the law was interpreted according to the specificities of each particular case.[26] The administration of justice in the Ottoman Empire passed through a delicate operation of interpretation of Islamic jurisprudence in order to fit the local circumstances within which the infraction of a particular norm had occurred (Hallaq 2009, 2013). With the introduction of European-like codes during the *Tanzimat*, now-secular judges applied the law with little, if any, consideration for context and interpretation. Whereas before a judge's authority was based on his transpersonal character as a broker in the

---

24 For a deep and insightful analysis of how the *Tanzimat* reforms were enacted in colonial Egypt, see Mitchell (1988).
25 Among the different concepts that Mardin has used to explain the role of Islam in the Ottoman Empire, the one I like most is "distributive justice." I am less satisfied with "cultural idiom," a terminology Mardin has often used in his works (e.g. Mardin 1997, 71), not least in his seminal study on Said Nursi and socio-religious change in Turkey (Mardin 1989). While I do not intend to neglect the idiomatic aspects related to Islam's sway over Ottoman-Turkish culture, I think an emphasis on cognitive aspects must be integrated with a consideration of the role played by social authority and power.
26 For a contemporary illustration of how judges learn to accomplish such complex tasks by embodying specific reasoning dispositions, see Nakissa (2014).

construction of the social bond at the local level (Salvatore 2007, 169), now his authority was diluted into the state-machine with its impersonal codes of law.[27]

The reform in the field of law was accompanied by the unfolding of a parallel process within the public sphere, by which Islam no longer provided the values and the hierarchy of goods that guided public debate but was instead reduced to be referred to as a symbol of national unity within debates concerned with the emerging idea of "national interest." Since the nineteenth century, this transformation was related to the gradual development of a new "modern" kind of public sphere, with its own specific rules of public persuasion. This notion is not intended here in its positive modern meaning, which sees the public sphere as a natural space where public confrontation amongst rational subjects takes place. Rather, it is approached as "a modern field of power" whose emergence involved "the institutionalization of the practice of discussing questions of common interest for society" (Salvatore 2001b, 127). The fact that public debates focused on how to achieve the national interest contributed to what I call a process of "objectification" or "ideologization" of the Islamic tradition. The institutionalization and successive consolidation of a modern kind of public sphere in the late Ottoman Empire has indeed been part, together with the reforms in the legal domain, of a process of gradual dispossession of Islam from its old regulative function. In the process, Islam has been confined within the limits allowed by modern intellectual public confrontation on the fate of the nation.

As it has been proven by a broad body of scholarship, a public sphere intended as a space for debate around the common good has always been present in the Ottoman Empire (Salvatore and Eickelman 2002, 2006; Gerber 2002; Özbek 2005). Yet it was only with the emergence of a modern kind of public sphere that Islam started to become an object of intellectual speculation and debate beyond the restricted space of the mosque and the *medrese*s. This was a debate upon which the *ulema*s could no longer retain an intellectual monopoly. Rather, they had to enter a confrontation with secular-educated public intellectuals. Trained in the new European-like schools and often devoid of knowledge in Islamic jurisprudence, the latter were the bearers of modern, technocratic knowledge. More relevantly, they possessed those skills that were now required to debate in public, namely being able to argue against others around topics of national interest. It follows that the *ulema*s not only lost their

---

27 The process has also been observed by Brinkley Messick (1993) with regard to the codification of Islamic law for application in Western-style court systems in late nineteenth-century Yemen. As he argues, this process resulted in the reification of Islamic jurisprudence.

position in the system, but also the rhetorical skills and competencies they had to possess in order to be regarded as authoritative by the public. A system had collapsed and a new one had emerged, generating a process of fragmentation of traditional religious and political authority; a transformation that was later accelerated by the emergence of mass higher education (Eickelman 1992) and the diffusion of new media (Eickelman and Anderson 2003) in the twentieth century.

Borrowing his terminology from Kara (1998 [1990]), Mardin (2006, 268–269) has described this process in terms of an increasing "intellectualization" of the sphere of knowledge, whose origins can be traced back to the Young Ottomans (1865–1876), and particularly to Namık Kemal (1844–1888). Like other Young Ottomans, Kemal envisioned a political order that had to remain sealed by the figure of the Sultan and sanctioned by the *shari'a*. In Kemal's writings, however, Mardin sees a process of transformation of the *shari'a* into a mere symbolic and formal referent only serving to promote collective solidarity within the framework of a proto-national Ottoman state. According to Mardin, Kemal had already internalized a view of Islam as sundered from the legal and ethical roles it had historically played in the Empire, thus inaugurating what later became a common pattern of modern political argumentation. This view found its mature version in the writings of Republican nationalist intellectuals such as Ziya Gökalp. Largely indebted to Emile Durkheim's idea of religion and morality as functional to granting social cohesion, Gökalp was a proponent of a view of Islam as an instrument for consolidating the nation's moral health. He thought that Islam was a rational and moral religion that could function as the glue of a new national identity based on the combination of Western technical civilization with a Muslim ethos. In his view—which had a strong impact on the constitutive process of the Turkish nation in the 1920s and would influence Turkish political thought for decades to come—the newly established national education system should have a central role in instilling this sense of identity in the Turkish citizens (Gökalp 1959; Akşit 1991).

The process of ideologization of Islam saw its completion with the foundation of the Republic, when a set of programmatic reforms also known as Kemalism—from the name of the national hero and general Mustafa Kemal Atatürk (1881–1938) from whom they were inspired—were enacted. The secular revolution had already sanctioned the abolition of the Sultanate (1922) and now enforced a set of other radical institutional transformations. These included the forced closure of all the *medrese*s, the Sufi lodges (*tekke*), and their sanctuaries (*türbe*). All the pious endowments (*vakıf*) that presided over the provision of educational, economic, and social services to the population were also closed down. European-like codes of law were introduced and the definitive secularization of the education system took place (Ahmad 1993, 78 ff.). Conscious of the importance Islam had for the masses, however, the Kemalist elites decided to maintain the *ulema* class within the structure of the Republican machine. In line with the Ottoman tradition of interpenetration of state and Islam delineated above (see also Mardin 2005; Vicini 2016), the Turkish version of state secularism (*laiklik*) was conceived as an extension of the state's control over religion instead of as implying a clear separation of state and religion, as it is in French *laïcisme* (Davison 2003). In this regard, the Directorate of Religious Affairs was established in 1923 to supervise all religious activities, from the administration of the thousands of mosques scattered around the country to the education of religious functionaries (now called *imam*s in place of *ulema*s). The *imam*s had to be educated in newly established schools called *İmam Hatip Mektepleri*, whose teachers, textbooks, and curricula were overseen by the Directorate. By these means, in the early years of the Republic, *imam*s were charged with the precise mission of addressing those coming to Friday-sermons as "citizens" and of orienting their moral choices and fidelity toward the nation-state. One can see the assimilation of the *imam*s into the state machine as being in a line of continuity with the role the *ulema*s had played within the Ottoman Empire. However, there is quite a significant difference in that Islam had now been expropriated from the ethical and juridical function it had in the past. The acquisition of the Islamic legitimizing aura by the nascent nation-state was indeed the other side of a process of ideologization by which Islam was reduced to an empty referent.

Not exclusive to the Turkish case alone, Gregory Starrett (1998) has illustrated how a similar process has taken place in modern Egypt. There too, with the emergence of the modern nation-state, Islam was deprived of its old centrality in the administrative system to be "functionalized" into a moral system that had to be inculcated in the citizens of the new nation through modern schooling. There is an inseparable link between the processes of intellectualization of Islam and the emergence of a modern order based on the nation-state. It is the same link that can be established between these processes and secularization intended neither as religious waning nor as social differentiation. It consists of the redefinition of the way religion has come to be practiced and thought of in modern times, that is, something to remain confined within the private domain of personal belief (see Asad 2003; cf. Casanova 1994).

It is against this modern secular backdrop that Said Nursi elaborated his "social theology" (Alatas 2017). An eclectic intellectual who had initially been educated within informal Sufi circles of the Naqshbandi-Khalidi order in Eastern Anatolia, he later undertook a self-taught itinerant path that led him to live at the court of local governors. While there, he became passionate about reading European scientific treaties and manuals. Later, he became a politically active figure and public intellectual supporting constitutional reform and the pan-Islamic ideas of the Young Ottomans. Apparently, he had initially thought that a compromise was possible between the old and the new order, but the virulence of the Kemalist reform program made him change his mind and threw him into a deep personal crisis. Coming out of this crisis, he rejected his previous life as an emerging public intellectual and was convinced of the need to go back to Islamic core teachings. It is this "New Said" that emerged after 1923 to initiate the Nur movement with the goal of revitalizing Islamic intellectual repertoires, rebuilding under new forms what had become disjoined forms of Muslim connectivity.[28] The movement he established survived his death and developed into new organizational forms as it resettled in major urban centers in the 1960s.

5   The Islamic Revival, Urban Life and Community

The capillary control that the Republic attempted to exercise over Islam did not correspond to a real capacity of conveying the charismatic and connective force of the tradition to society during the first decades of the Republic. After all, it was not the intention of the Kemalists to make Islam an explicit component of the official ideology. The Republic was devoted to the principles of laicism, scientific positivism, and European-style modernization. Only later, following the end of the one-party era in 1948, but particularly during the 1980s, a significant shift in national ideology combined with macro urban and economic transformations allowed for an until-recently-unexpected flourishing in terms of Islamic books, pamphlets, dresses, symbols, and forms of devotion. More than a mark of discontinuity in religious zeal regarding the past decades, however, the Islamic revival is better described as Muslims' return to the public space as soon as it was allowed by new sociopolitical conditions. In particular, the revival was the result of two strictly interconnected phenomena: the progressive integration of the countryside into the national system and the gradual reconfiguration of the state's official ideology in a direction more open to Islamic instances after the 1980 military coup.

During the one-party regime (1923–1946), Atatürk's Republican People's Party (*Cumhuriyet Halk Partisi*, CHP) made a special effort to spread the republican values across the whole country, including the rural areas, although most of

---

28   Nursi himself divided his life into three periods; the "old Said" (from his birth to 1923), the "New Said" (1923–1950), during which he produced the *Risale*, and the "Third Said" (1950–1960), living during the Democratic Party era.

the measures were ineffective. While Kemalist ideals were assimilated by the urbanized elites living in the major urban centers, they only affected the people living in Anatolian small towns and villages to a limited extent (Ahmad 1993, 82–84). This is in line with the contrast between the "culture of the periphery" and the "culture of the elite" that I have described above in relation to Ottoman times, and that was replicated in similar ways within the Republic. As argued by Mardin (1973), just as the people living in the countryside under the Ottomans perceived the state as a distant, alien, and oppressive institution, the attempts that were made by the CHP to implement the Kemalist reforms were likely perceived as an imposition by the religious conservative people living in rural areas. In this regard, the secularist reforms contributed to maintaining, and sometimes even widening, the gap that had historically separated these masses from the elites in previous centuries. In the countryside, even if dispossessed of its old institutional power, Islam continued to survive as a fragmentary set of practices, ideals, and values that were transmitted through popular culture within the conservative religious families, or within those religious networks that continued to survive underground. Many people from rural areas had indeed remained attached to a culture made of daily Islamic practices, saint veneration, shrines visitations, the Qur'an, *Mevlud* poems recalling and celebrating the birth of the prophet Muhammad, and reverence to men of religious knowledge; a legacy that Kemalism was never really able to tarnish (Mardin 1989).[29]

Following the democratic opening of the 1950s, new and old Islamic networks resettled in the main Turkish cities. Between 1950 and the end of the 1970s, the Democratic Party (*Demokrat Parti*) and its successor, the Justice Party (*Adalet Partisi*), had shifted the economic policy of the country from agriculture to industrialization, causing the failure of the majority of small-size farms (Danielson and Keleş 1985; Atasoy 1997). This caused the migration of many peasants from the countryside to the main urban centers in search for occupation in the manufacturing and construction sectors. Here, they amassed at the outskirts of major cities, where they settled in small houses erected overnight (*gecekondu*). Either by finding occupation in these sectors or surviving by other means, newcomers were often disoriented by the city lifestyle, its customs and rhythms. One way of recreating regional patterns of sociality and solidarity was the institution of associations of migrants coming from the same regional capital or town (*hemşehri dernekleri*), which offered both a first-time support and forms of aggregation based on common customs to the new migrants, thus

---

29 See Hart (2013) on how this culture still structures a great part of rural life in contemporary Turkey.

allowing them to familiarize themselves with the urban environment (Erder 1996). Besides these associations, religious networks also had a fundamental role in allowing for the construction of transversal bonds of solidarity and trust among people of different provenance in the big, anonymous cities of Istanbul, Izmir, and Ankara.

In an urban context, Islamic networks reorganized themselves into organically structured organizational forms based on the idea of community (*cemaat*). These networks were immunized from outside society and possessed their inner rules and codes of comportment. Apart from offering help on several practical matters, they provided migrants with a message of social justice and moral integrity that they felt had been lost in the hostile urban environment (Yavuz 2003a, 83–86; see also Bulaç 2007). More significantly, the *cemaat*s offered the sons of these immigrants educational facilities and small scholarships that allowed these new generations of religious conservative people the opportunity to get a higher education and acquire the sociocultural capital they needed to achieve better jobs and climb the social ladder. Also, the Justice Party introduced some educational policies in favor of the migrants with the double goal of dealing with the swelling number of people settling at the outskirts of the Turkish cities and gaining their votes in the elections. The party supported the opening of vocational schools (*imam hatip lisesi*) and their better integration into the national education system. Operating under the supervision of the *Diyanet*, these schools had been instituted with the goal of training mosque preachers. They were generally preferred by religiously conservative families because they were the only education institution with a religious curriculum. Since the 1950s, the number of *imam hatip* schools has been growing exponentially, and it almost quintupled from 1970 to 1980, jumping from 72 to 374 (Bilici 1993).

When an increasing number of students from Anatolia were willing to enroll in these schools in the major Turkish cities, the *cemaat*s offered them low-cost accommodation and other facilities, without which they would not have been able to sustain their studies. The investments of the *cemaat*s in education were facilitated by a lenient 1967 legislation on *vakıf*s that *de facto* gave religious communities the opportunity to re-open foundations after more than forty years of prohibition. This allowed them to operate in a more effective way than was possible in the recent past.[30] Although foundations had a secularized

---

30 Despite new rules prohibiting foundations from having political goals or links with a particular group, the *cemaat*s took advantage of the vagueness of the law to bypass it (Bilici 1993)

appearance, religious groups used their legal façade to redirect the money they collected through informal networks toward the construction of mosques, health centers, charitable associations, and, particularly, the subsidization of students. Apart from the Nur movement, other groups, such as those affiliated with the Naqshbandi Sufi order, could also rely on a tradition of activism boosted by inner puritanism and a moral sense of commitment, making them particularly suitable to take advantage of the new circumstances (Mardin 1991b, 2006; Weismann 2007). Not only focused on civic activism, these groups gathered around the figure of Mehmet Zahid Kotku in the 1960s, who encouraged the active participation of his followers in formal politics. Prominent political figures like Necmettin Erbakan, the leader of numerous Islamist parties in the 1970s, came from such a political tradition. Korkut Özal, the brother of the future prime minister and then president Turgut Özal between 1984 and 1991, also emerged from these networks. It is reported that leading members of the AKP, including Recep Tayyip Erdoğan, also come from these circles (Mardin 1991b, 2006; Yavuz 2003a). In contrast, the Nur movement generally remained outside of party politics.[31] Although Nursi's followers have, at times, supported one political party or another, they have very rarely become deputies. Rather, they preferred to focus on a bottom-up project of social reform based on the promotion of the *Risale*.

This process of progressive integration of the religious conservative strata within the urban fabric and their gradual adaptation to modern lifestyles prepared the ground for the Islamic revival of the 1980s. In those years, an unprecedented variety of forms of Islamic expression started to appear in the public space, such as Islamic-style dresses and beards, but also an entirely new market of publications in Islamic theology, history, and philosophy (see Göle 1997, 2002; Navaro-Yashin 2002b; Saktanber 2002b). The revival was favored by the convergence of diverse social, economic, and political factors. The 1970s were characterized by a deep crisis in the state-led model of industrialization, with the country having risked bankruptcy. Meanwhile, profound political tensions traversed the nation, leading to violent confrontations between extremist

---

31 Said Nursi had constantly discouraged his students from entering politics by suggesting that they should devote all their efforts to religious service. However, in the 1950s he did not hide his sympathy for the Democratic Party. Then, in later years, some Nur branches, more or less openly, supported political parties, as was the case for the *Nesil* group's support for the aforementioned Justice Party in the late 1970s. In the 1980s the Gülen group supported Özal's center-right Motherland party (*Anavatan Partisi, ANAP*) and the AKP until their clash in 2013.

groups of the right and the left. The coup of 12 September 1980, was intended to put an end to this turbulent situation by presenting the nation with a new ideological outlook that could pacify the state's relationship with religious conservative groups and ground the social pact on new fresh foundations. After almost sixty years, during which it had remained excluded from official discourse and erased from the curricula, Islam was now reaccepted in public discourse as a topic that could be debated in the media. It also reappeared in schoolbooks and other publications recommended by the Ministry of National Education and the *Diyanet*, which aimed to foster a renewed sense of national unity.[32]

These were the years of Turgut Özal's program for economic liberalization, which further favored Islamic communities' extension into the editorial and media sectors.[33] This was the period when a new generation of Muslim intellectuals began playing a more visible role in society as they found a new listening public in the masses of well-educated and urbanized Muslims who were being raised within the religious communities. More critical than their predecessors of the West and of its democratic liberal values, public figures such as Ali Bulaç, Rasim Özdenören, İsmet Özel, and Hayreddin Karaman began advocating the need for reconsidering the modernist intellectual premises of the previous years and reevaluating Ottoman-Islamic sociopolitical models (Meeker 1991; Mardin 2006; Guida 2010).[34] At the same time, an emerging network of devout businessmen dubbed the "Anatolian tigers" provided a new economic underpinning for Islamic communities and their educational services, as well as for the expansion of these communities in other areas of the cultural industry, such as the publishing sector (Yavuz 2003a, 88–91).

It is at this juncture that the *Suffa* and the Gülen communities were established in large urban centers like Istanbul. As illustrated, the Gülen community occupies a special place among all others in terms of capillarity and capacity of extending its activities to many financial, economic, and cultural sectors. The expansion of this community was initially looked at with sympathy by Özal

---

32   On publications issued or recommended by the *Diyanet* in the 1980s that stressed the relevance of Islam in education and in young people's assimilation of "Islamic morality," see Akşit (1991, 160–163) and, particularly, Saktanber (1991).

33   For an analysis of some of the religious communities' publications of the 1980s, see Güneş-Ayata (1991) and Acar (1991).

34   Unlike nationalist intellectuals of the 1920s and 1930s, new Muslim intellectuals did not completely "objectify" Islam. When they highlight that Islam, as an ethical system, must be put again at the center of Muslim patterns of sociopolitical organization, they seem to escape the limits of intellectualization. However, when they exceed in their historicization of Islamic social forms, they risk falling back in this tendency. As we will see in Chapter 4 and 5, a partial process of objectification of Islam is not extraneous to the Gülen community itself.

and some segments of the state who thought that Gülen could represent the kind of moderate Islamic preacher they needed to pacify Turkey under the shield of a peaceful and Western-oriented Islamic message. In this period, Gülen was allowed to release speeches in the main national mosques, a liberty that had no precedent in Republican history, and to appear in main newspapers and TV channels to offer his opinion on several public issues. In turn, he did not hesitate to publicize an image of himself as the representative of an enlightened and docile version of Islam, fitting the needs of the new Turkey that had emerged in those years under Özal. The weaving together of Islamic and national narratives emerged clearly in his speeches and publications of the 1980s and 1990s (e.g. Gülen 1998c). In these, he argued that a positive and allegedly unique Turkish version of Islam exists and should be taken as a model for other Muslims as well (Özdalga 2006; Koyuncu-Lorasdağı 2010).

The symbiosis between Gülen and the state became even more pronounced in the 1990s, when the community started opening Turkish schools in Central Asia and the Balkans where national values were promoted (Balci 2003; Turam 2007). Yet this situation was short-lived. On February 28, 1997, a military-driven campaign against Islamic groups forced the cabinet, led by Erbakan, the first prime minister backed by an Islamist party to be elected in Turkish history (in charge between 1997 and 1998), to resign. At first, Gülen maintained a low profile and even justified the coup. Soon, however, some fragments of old videotaped speeches where he advised his adherents to infiltrate state institutions were broadcasted on national TV. Afterwards, he received an arrest warrant on charges of planning to overthrow the state. Gülen rejected the accusation but decided to take refuge in the United States in 1999, officially to undergo medical treatment. After relocating to the United States, Gülen has taken advantage of the antinomy between "good" and "bad" Muslims to appear as an important, emerging, and moderate voice of global Islam (Mamdani 2002; Hendrick 2018; Tee 2018). He has claimed to be the spiritual leader of a global movement of volunteers motivated by peaceful goals and spurred by the will of promoting universal values of brotherhood, love, and tolerance. Meanwhile, in Turkey, the community continued to expand its networks in a coordinated way by both embracing important spheres of Muslim civil society and increasing its presence in the institutions. Although its epicenter had moved abroad, the community continued to operate in the motherland where it drew most of its financial support until the failed coup attempt of July 15, 2016.

•••

Memories of the anti-Islamic campaign of 28 February 1997, and of the measures and imprisonments that followed are still vivid in the mind of many religious conservative people in Turkey. These memories also explain, in part, the large political success that the AKP continues to achieve today. Religious conservative strata supporting the AKP administration are indeed afraid that if the secularists come in power they will take revenge against them by applying measures similar to those they took in those days. However, the events of February 1997 are just a memory today. With the rise to power of the AKP in 2002, Islamic discourse has publicly reemerged in an unprecedented way. Today's Turkey appears completely different compared to how it might have appeared to a visitor in the early Republican period, or even in the 1960s and the 1970s. The influence of religious groups has increased exponentially in the last two decades, thereby harming secularists' sensibilities and definitively rattling their certitude that Turkey would continue along the path outlined by Atatürk more than nine decades before.[35]

The following chapters are dedicated to an exploration of how two contemporary Islamic groups have operated during this new era with the goal of educating new generations of Muslims with specific worldviews and ideas about how to contribute to the progress of their country. As illustrated in this chapter, both the *Suffa* and the Gülen communities have contributed to reigniting a process of solidarity reconstruction from below, which has influenced the course of Turkish history more than their effective public visibility might suggest. As it will be shown, by establishing a deep and tangled link between modern life and faith, both communities have indeed offered new generations of religiously conservative people attractive ways of living a Muslim life prompted by Islamic ideas of responsibility and activism in society. To explore how this has been possible, it is necessary to begin by illustrating how longstanding, yet renewed, Islamic ideals are reflected upon and actualized in concrete life within these two communities.

---

35   For an analysis of the revival of secularism as a response to the Islamic revival in Turkey, see Özyürek (2006) and (Navaro-Yashin 2002a, b).

CHAPTER 2

Living the Brotherhood

Located within one of the thousands of apartment blocks neighboring each other along the ups and downs of Istanbul's hilly urban landscape, the houses managed by the *Suffa* and the Gülen communities worked both as residences for university students and as weekly meeting points for the community. They were usually large flats equipped with sizeable living rooms and numerous bedrooms that had the capacity to host between five and ten students. Today, these houses have all the comforts of modern life including dishwashers, water-boilers, refrigerators, washing machines, and vacuum cleaners. Yet this had not been the case in the past. Elder community brothers often liked to remind their younger companions that when they were students they did not even have a heating system, this being a serious problem for houses located in isolated central Anatolian towns where winter temperatures could easily drop below zero. At times, even food could be scarce. Yet—they conjectured nostalgically—perhaps those hard conditions allowed them to forge stronger links of comradeship and brotherhood than they do today.

First established in the early 1930s as places where Said Nursi's followers read, copied, and disseminated the *Risale-i Nur*, houses affiliated with the Nur movement have traditionally been referred to as *dershane*s within the Nur circles—literally "lesson (*ders*) space (*hane*)"—because they acted as a venue for collective readings of Nursi's writings. This is how they are still addressed within the *Suffa* community in Turkey today, whereas they were preferably called "houses of service" (*hizmet evleri*) by the Gülen people before their closure after 15 July 2016. The difference in pedagogical paths between the *Suffa* and the Gülen communities will be illustrated in detail in Chapter 3 and 4 respectively. Instead, in this chapter, I offer an overview of the practices that structured and defined communal living among fellow brothers within both the *Suffa* and the Gülen houses, without marking a clear distinction between the two. In this regard, indeed, the commonalities between them abundantly outnumber the differences.

In both communities, the houses circumscribed an enclosed environment where a process of Muslim socialization took place separate from the one taking place in the public space. In the eyes of the elder community members, the houses provided students with a safe and welcoming environment that was conducive to the embodiment of key Islamic virtues. Community life here unfolded along the flexible inter-subjective bond of religious brotherhood (*uhuvvet* or *kardeşlik*). This represented a key organizational principle of daily interactions that was an alternative to that of "community" (*gemeinschaft*) intended as a pre-modern form of organization distinct from society, as traditional sociological literature has generally depicted it. Indeed, the idea of brotherhood within the *Suffa* and the Gülen communities worked as an acephalous matrix fostering Muslim connectedness among their members. But absent the traditional role played by the master in the Sufi path, the idea also functioned as a pedagogical path that was enlivened in all community practices, including the most ordinary ones, shaping the process by which students embodied the cardinal virtue of sincerity and purity of faith (*ihlas*).

The idea of brotherhood is also useful from a theoretical point of view to soften the rigid link between discipline and subjectivity construction that is too often established within the anthropological scholarship on Islam. As I will show, rather than simply marking the model of an idealized Muslim "conduct," the *sunna* of the prophet Muhammad was part of a broader pattern for intersubjective engagement which was strongly embedded into the matrix of the brotherhood. Muslim life in the houses of the *Suffa* and the Gülen communities was punctuated by the intervals between prayers and infused by a spiritual atmosphere (*maneviyat*). All these moments were framed within a brotherhood-based framework of Muslim sociability and peer dynamics that diluted the place of individual self-scrutiny and self-interrogation in the pedagogical path. Toward the end of the chapter, I will follow Milbank's (2006 [1990]) critique of MacIntyre's account of religious virtue to shed light on these moments and explain how the brotherhood represents a horizon of imagination and practice of Muslim virtues—and particularly of the cardinal virtue of *ihlas*—that is actualized in daily life in the houses.

1   Daily Life in the Houses

The house of the Gülen community where I spent part of my fieldwork was a two-floor flat located in the district of Şişli. Positioned north of the European side of Istanbul, only a few metro stations from its symbolic center of *Taksim* square, this is one of the most important business centers in city. The house was occupied by students attending some of the best national universities such as Istanbul Technical University (*İTÜ*) and Bosporus University (*Boğaziçi Üniversitesi*), and regularly visited by younger students going to similarly prestigious high-schools like the *Galatasaray lisesi* and the Robert College. The first floor consisted of a big living room, kitchen, one bathroom, and two double bedrooms. A wooden staircase led to the upper floor, where there were two other double bedrooms, one bathroom, one storage room, and one big carpet-covered room with four bed-sofas and wardrobes where visiting high-school students stayed during weekends. The flat of the *Suffa* community was located in the notoriously pious neighborhood of Fatih, on the ancient side of the town. Not far from the Theodosian walls, the area is well-known for hosting the major Islamist organizations and some of the most important Naqshbandi confraternities. It is always here that the most important Islamic fashion companies open their shops. In the imagination of secularist people in Turkey, the neighborhood is generally perceived as the cradle of the city's cultural and religious backwardness (Navaro-Yashin 2002a).

While *Suffa*'s flat was a little smaller than the one in Şişli, it had a very similar composition. Indeed, all the houses of the two communities that I visited were arranged to allow for a precise separation between private and public spaces, between moments of individual study and moments of collective sociality and rituals. While the sitting room was the main place of social interaction, students used their bedrooms to focus on their individual studies and readings, and take a pause from collective life. In line with a precise code of conduct that intended to prevent students from seeing others naked or in other improper situations, flat-mates were expected to knock and wait for permission before entering. Instead, when students wanted to socialize, they went to the sitting room. Here they could find other brothers intently reading religious texts, or simply passing the time chatting and drinking tea. This was indeed the main place where conversation with other residents was made. The sitting room was also where the two main meals (breakfast and dinner) and the evening collective tea (*çay*) that followed dinner were consumed. A bookcase full of the community's "red books" was always present here. Red is the color of the cover with which the 14-volume set of the *Risale* is usually printed. Bookshelves in more conventional Nur houses such as those of *Suffa* were stocked with multiple copies of the collection in order to allow several brothers to read the same text simultaneously. Instead, bookshelves within the Gülen community houses were generally replete with Fethullah Gülen's books and only one copy of the *Risale* was present. This copy was from a new edition bound in the less garish, brown binding adopted by their publishing house.

As these first notes already illustrate, the houses were meant to create a specific kind of space separate from outside society, where secular sociability forms and hedonistic values were perceived as prevalent. Despite the increasing presence of Islamic symbols in public since the Islamic revival of the 1980s, life in contemporary Turkey follows the modern rhythms of work and consumption.

For this reason, those willing to conform to a more conventional kind of Muslim life are left alone in their attempts. Within this context, the hermetic character of community spaces met a precise need that the *Suffa* and the Gülen communities had: to provide well-suited places for the actualization of Muslim ways of life and sociality to their members. The separation between inside and outside was physically marked by the house's threshold, whose passage was symbolically accompanied by students' habit of taking off their shoes. A widely diffused Turkish custom, in this specific case taking off one's shoes responded to Islamic prescriptions concerning the purity of the soil, which is a prerequisite for performing the daily prayer (see Henkel 2007). Similarly, the curtains were always kept closely drawn by the students to prevent indiscreet gazes from outsiders curious about their activities. This habit was also a precaution (*tedbir*) they took to hide their affiliation with the community and served to prevent them from encountering tempting feminine gazes on the street.

In order to preserve the spiritual atmosphere of the house, the interiors had sober and religiously-attuned tones. Posters or pictures were absent from the walls and no music was played that could remind members of outer areligious, hedonistic life. Writings in Arabic, generally Qur'anic passages, sayings from the prophets, or words of Said Nursi and Fethullah Gülen decorated the walls instead. All these traits served to remind those present of the link between the houses and Islamic civilization, as well as to immunize these spaces from unwanted external influences. Similarly, no television or internet connection was present—though the former could be exceptionally found in some Gülen houses.[1] Such exclusion may certainly be read as an attempt by both communities to prevent students from viewing sinful images or being influenced by negative behaviors. However, quite interestingly, my interlocutors also explained that watching the television and surfing the internet were "useless occupations" (*malayaniyet*) that would have wasted their time and energy, diminishing their capacity to adhere to the house program and actively contribute to communal life. The lack of television and internet responded to the need of limiting students' laziness and relaxation, favoring the fruitful occupation of their time for studying, reading, and spending time in community with other students.[2]

---

1 This is explained by the added importance that the Gülen community gives to socializing activities as a way for attracting younger middle-school students, as well as less disciplined, but successful, university students (see Chapter 4). However, even in these cases, the use of television was limited in time and regulated by the *abis*.
2 Notice that while my interlocutors had mobile phones, in 2010 mobile internet connections were still quite slow and expensive and hence not widely spread.

The separation between life inside and outside of the houses was also clearly marked by authoritative discourses through which elder brothers warned younger students of the perils of outside society. One of the first issues to be addressed with males in their early twenties, indeed, was that concerning how to keep their sexual drives under control. Similarly, students were discouraged from exploring life in a modern metropolis like Istanbul; something young people coming from the countryside would likely be curious of.

The care and control of the self is a longstanding concern within Islamic pedagogy, which takes a new dimension in modern urban contexts. In this regard, take as an example the words of Fatih *abi*, a brother from the Gülen community in his mid-twenties, to a group of around 20 university students. Though not much older than his audience, Fatih was responsible for 12 houses of the community in the Şişli district.[3] As the *abi* in charge of the students, once every month or two he organized a one-day reading camp (*kamp*) in one of the community's dormitories.[4] For the collective reading (*sohbet*) of that day, Fatih had brought a book significantly entitled *How Do We Protect Our Gaze From Forbidden Things?* (Güven 2010). After pulling the book out of his bag, he turned it a bit in his hands and then began his speech by saying: "Summer is coming, and with it the hot weather ... that is why, together with other elder brothers, we decided to talk about this issue." Without being any clearer, it was obvious to everybody what the brother meant with these words: with the end of winter and the warming of the weather, women were going to leave some forbidden (*haram*) parts of their bodies uncovered and students needed to be ready to keep their gazes away from those *haram* things.

Then Fatih read the book's extract from the back cover, in which the author compared God's prescriptions for humankind—including those about prohibited things—to those of a doctor for people's health. Following a metaphor that is widely used by Nursi that parallels medicine to religion and the solutions provided by the *Risale* to the prescriptions of a doctor, the meaning of the extract can be summarized as follows: if a doctor prescribes us a medicine, do

---

3 To understand how a limited age difference between elder brothers and students is played within pedagogical practices in the Gülen community, see Vicini (2013) and Chapter 4 of this work.

4 *Kamp*s were sort of collective out-of-town holiday-trips organized a couple of times per year aimed at gathering a group of students in one place to make intensive readings, worshiping, and Qur'anic memorization. One-day meetings where students followed similar programs like the one I am discussing here were also called *kamp*s, specifically mini-camps (*mini-kamp*). While camps are a common trait of many Islamic communities in Turkey including both those considered here, they retain a particular historical importance for the Gülen community (see Chapter 4).

we not take it? Hence, since God has prescribed the avoidance of some things, should we not then avoid them? Then Fatih opened the book at a page he had previously bookmarked and started to read the text by commenting on some passages. In one of his comments, he explained: "In man, there are three things that have no limits (*sınırsız*): intellect (*akıl*), wrath (*öfke*), lust (*şehvet*).[5] [...] Without people's self-control, the second and the third characteristics get the upper hand over the first." To avoid letting our sensual feelings overshadow our mind, Fatih adds, "We have to maintain self-control." As he explained, "When we see some pictures from newspapers, movie scenes or advertising boards with forbidden content, we have to skip past them." After having laid out the theoretical basis for his argument, Fatih then concluded his 15-minute speech with a precise warning to the students:

> If you get bored by staying within the houses the solution is not to go outside and start to walk around ... to stay outside and go to the market ... [...] Rather let's stay in the house. Let's read the Qur'an and the *Risale*. [...] These are the right things to do ... Because it is clear where we will end up after death. [...] But if we go outside, we know that we might easily meet the Devil.

This short ethnographic excerpt is a good example of the primary concerns of the elder brothers for their younger companions. Admonitions of this kind reflected their general view of outside society as a space dominated by ignorance and lack of awareness of the Islamic message (*cahillik*). Since young students had to attend those environments daily while going to school, they could be dangerously attracted by their values and thus be deceived. Similar warnings often appear in the *Risale* as well.[6] In the text, young people are those who are more easily pulled in by devilish temptations, both because of their inexperience and because of the strength of their sexual appetites. It is exactly because the devil can exercise a major attractive power in those places where Islamic regulations are not followed that students were warmly invited to stay in the

---

5 After the reading meeting, Nizam explained to me that, for them, whether one feels *şehvet* or not is a distinctive element in discerning a sinful action from a sinless one. If a man looks at a woman who is dressed according to Islamic standards with *şehvet*, he is sinning anyway. In reverse, if he sees something *haram* accidentally, he is not committing a sin. He does only when he willingly looks at that thing a second time. In line with ideals of purity and sincerity that were extolled in both the communities, intention (*niyet*) is an important dimension in their economy of proper religious action.

6 In the houses, it was common to find a pamphlet called *Gençlik Rehberi* (A Guide for Youth) which is a collection of fragments of the *Risale* dealing with this particular topic.

houses of the community as much as possible. In the view of the elder brothers, the sincere and spiritual atmosphere stemming from community life would safeguard them from devilish whispers and help them keep control over their carnal impulses.

2 Discipline and Prayer

The daily prayer (*namaz*; in Arabic, *salat*), a common requirement for all observant Muslims, was the most important duty the students had to accomplish. In their words, this was the first indication of their act of submitting to God.[7] Influential anthropological discussions of this main Islamic obligation have tended to drive attention away from its normative aspects and redirect it to the performative efficacy of this practice. In her *Politics of Piety*, Saba Mahmood offered one of the most sophisticated explanations of the Islamic prayer, representing it as a key disciplinary practice by means of which the Muslim women of the mosque movement in Egypt embodied key Islamic virtues such as humility and related feelings of fear and awe (Mahmood 2005). In her dense ethnographic account, Mahmood followed the lead of Talal Asad (1993) in advancing a compelling critique of those studies in the anthropology of religion that, since Durkheim, have tended to see collective rituals as means for the public expression of what were more profound, inner feelings or emotions. Mahmood's study has been particularly effective in turning these conventional sociological views upside down and showing how ritualized bodily practice has a central role in shaping a specific cultural and historical set of emotions—rather than simply being the expression of an allegedly natural set of universal feelings. In this way, she also persuasively questioned the distinction between social and individual experience that surreptitiously plagued these approaches.

For my interlocutors, the prayer represented a way of experiencing and embodying certain Muslim emotions and their related virtues, such as humility. Some stressed how one of the most difficult things for them to accept was that they had to lower their head to the ground five times per day. No matter how humiliating this practice might be at the beginning, however, it was necessary to continuously remind themselves that their lower self (*nefs*; in Arabic, *nafs*) had to be tamed in order to better themselves as faithful Muslims. The daily

---

7 Submitting to God is the key prerequisite of Islamic faith as indicated by the fact that this is exactly the Arabic meaning of the word "Islam," while the word "Muslim" can be translated as "submitter," and is a participle from the same verb (Hodgson 1974, 72).

prayer was indeed part of a broader set of techniques and exercises, both bodily and intellective, through which my interlocutors aimed at disciplining their *nefs*. This is in line with a longstanding Islamic pedagogical tradition, which maintains one of its main goals of taming the lower self by keeping its impulses at bay—this being the precondition for the achievement of any successive development of the person in terms of ethical conduct and spiritual maturation. In this regard, discussions of the nature of the self in Islam have generally grappled with the difficult task of differentiating between the two overlapping concepts of *nafs* and *ruh* (also in Arabic, the human soul) (Calverley 1943). The distinction acquired some greater clarity when Ibn Arabi (1165–1240) described the path to human sainthood and higher spiritual perfection (*al-insan al-kamil*) as one based on the discipline of the *nafs* in accordance with the high ethical dispositions indicated by the *ruh*. In this pedagogical configuration, only the *ruh* is receptive to God's will and, accordingly, the *nafs* has to be tuned with it (Ibid.; see also Sviri 2002).

Analogously, my interlocutors thought of their self as the articulation of a similar duality of a "lower part," or *nefs*, dominated by human-animal instincts, and another more "spiritual" part, the soul or *ruh*, which should guide the former along a process of progressive spiritual growth. Only by surrendering their carnal desires could my interlocutors aspire to achieve the kind of awareness they wished to cultivate. The distinction should not be understood as Manichean, however. Neither for Ibn Arabi nor for my interlocutors should the *nefs* be thought of only as the place of irrational desire and instinct, or something to be tamed through one's intellectual faculties. This is how post-Enlightenment secular liberal conceptions of the self which are centered on the dichotomy of body and mind would suggest to conceive it (Asad 2003; Salvatore 2007). As also illustrated by the entry of the Persian/Ottoman-Turkish dictionary (*Lügat*) widely used within the student houses (Yeğin 2005), the *nefs* is "the devilish strength of the low instincts of lust and wrath (*şehvet ve gadabın [öfke] mebdei olan kuvve-i nefsaniye*)." Alternatively, it is defined as the desires that stem from the individual's natural inclinations (*fıtri meyil*) and sensual drives (*bedenin hissi istekleri*). Yet the *nefs* is also interestingly designated as the human "push," energy and inclination (*gayret*) toward persevering human life. As such, it is seen as an indispensable element of human nature (*fıtrat*) that one can never be completely rid of—a definition that echoes the Western philosophical notion of *conatus*.[8]

---

8 This was also confirmed to me by Ali Ünal, a high-level member of the Gülen community, author of many books and editor of an important new Turkish edition of the Qur'an. As part of human *fıtrat*, human beings need the *nefs* to defend themselves from both internal (e.g.

In sum, taming the lower self to drive oneself away from sin and toward meritorious and proper actions occupies a central place in Islamic pedagogy in general, and particularly in the view of my interlocutors. And since the daily prayer was for them a way of continuously remembering God and their subordinate status with regard to Him, it occupied an important position in their pedagogical path. However, contrary to what is implied by Mahmood's analysis, my interlocutors' strict abidance to the *namaz* went beyond the goal of disciplining the self and embodying key virtues. For them, the prayer was, first of all, a duty they had to accomplish for God's sake as a sign of their submission to His will. In this regard, the act of submission implicit in the prayer had a strong relation to principles of sincerity and purity of commitment to faith that I have introduced above. Even when they acknowledged that the prayer could be a way of increasing their spiritual status, students of the *Suffa* and the Gülen communities immediately clarified that if such intent had been put in the foreground, this would have undermined the key principle according to which they perform the prayer—as well as every other Islamic duty or activity. In their view, any religious performance or conduct has to first emerge out of purity and sincerity of commitment, namely without having any other ulterior motive in mind, not even that of cultivating Islamic virtues.

As with any reference to sincerity and purity of intentions, these claims may appear as pointless, slippery, or deceptive. However, they raise one important theme that will return at several junctures in this work. The emphasis put on sincerity reflected my interlocutors' view of the prayer as one of the most powerful means to establish, reinforce, and constantly maintain a personal connection with God. From this perspective, rather than simply responding to a disciplinary intention, performing the *namaz* was a way of constantly renewing their relation (*irtibat*) with transcendence, that is, with a cosmic order in which to frame their own existence. As will be explored in detail in Chapter 3, it is only by projecting their life onto a transcendent framework that my interlocutors could achieve the kind of spiritual awareness they wished to cultivate. An important moment of everyday life, the prayer was a way of regularly reminding themselves of their spiritual (*manevi*) inner life (*içtenlik*) and of the link that the soul has to establish with God and His commandments. As such, it was one of the most effective ways of detaching themselves from ephemeral

---

microbes and sickness) and external attacks. As such, the *nefs* is intrinsically neither good nor bad. As exemplified by Ünal through the example of sexual desire (*şehvet*), if this desire is correctly channeled toward marriage (e.i. family and reproduction) it is good, but if it is not, instead, it may drive people toward committing adultery (*zina*).

worldly preoccupations, commitments, and passions to establish such a connection.

3 Time and Prayer

In her ethnography of rural life in two villages of Western Turkey, Kimberly Hart has vividly described how life in the countryside unfolded in accordance with a "cosmological construction of Islamic time" (Hart 2013, 44). This is reflected in the recurrence of daily activities and in the succession of major life-course events. The daily prayer occupied a central position among these activities, as it allowed her interlocutors to attune their existence to the flow of natural life dictated by the sun's rise and fall, and the changing of the seasons. In line with such an Anatolian rural culture made of Muslim rituals and cosmologies, community life within the student houses of the *Suffa* and the Gülen communities also followed a specific kind of Muslim temporality. The cadence of the five obligatory daily prayers dictated the rhythms of the day and defined its schedule strictly by imbuing life in the houses with an intense spiritual atmosphere.

University students woke up at dawn about 30 minutes before the sunrise in order to awaken sleepier brothers in time to make the ablution (*abdest*) and perform the morning prayer (*sabah*). According to a consolidated path within the Nur movement, after the *sabah* it was considered a good thing to stay awake and read some pages from the *Risale-i Nur* for about an hour until breakfast. However, in both the *Suffa* and the Gülen houses I only saw the elder and more disciplined brothers do this occasionally. Students often went back to bed to sleep for another one or two hours, or even longer if they had no lessons to attend in the morning. After breakfast, students went to school. Therefore, they often had to perform the noon prayer (*öğle*) and the afternoon prayer (*ikindi*) outside, either in a mosque or in one of the small prayer places (*mescit*) scattered throughout the city. The evening prayer (*akşam*), however, was usually performed together with the other students in the house before or after dinner. Late in the evening, before going to bed (around 11 p.m.), students performed the night prayer (*yatsı*). Although this was meant to mark the end of the day, students sometimes liked to stay up chatting, drinking tea, and eating biscuits, chips, or dried fruits. On such occasions, they could even decide to postpone the *yatsı* to a later hour.[9]

---

9 Sometimes, especially during weekends when chatting lasted until late at night, students could opt to wait until before the dawn to perform the *yatsı* and then wait for the next

The daily schedule was regulated by the obligation of performing the prayer within the prescribed time slots. The *muezzin*'s call to prayer (*ezan*) marked a hiatus in daily life that could not be ignored by the students. I remember one day during the holiday break from school, at the end of a slow and relaxed brunch in the Gülen house of Şişli, Kamil decided to show me and three other students some videos on his laptop. After playing a video on the Day of Judgment, he then opted to show us something less disturbing: a fragment of an American cartoon series he had recently downloaded. Suddenly, the *muezzin*'s first two cadenced utterances "God is magnificent, God is magnificent" (*Allahü Ekber*) were heard in the background. With a slow but resolute move, Kamil stopped the video, lowered the computer screen, and said, "Let's take a small break ... It has been called for." Kamil and the students turned completely silent staring into the air with a grave look. Only when the *muezzin* had finished uttering the *ezan* did we continue to watch the video.

The prayer also marked the most important moment of the day, when all the students gathered in the big saloon after dinner to perform the last prayer of the day (*yatsı*) together as a community (*cemaat olarak*). In these moments, the *namaz* was led by the most authoritative brother in the house, normally an older or more experienced student. Grouped in short lines behind him, the students followed his recitations and movements, falling synchronically on the floor at each genuflection. After performing the compulsory prayer-cycles (*rekat*), the students started reciting the ritualized repetition of God's names (*tesbihat*) in unison, beginning with the utterance of the three main ones (*Sübhanallah, Elhamdülillah, Allahu Ekber*) 33 times each.[10] The ritual was concluded with one or more additional silent prayers (*dua*) that the students performed individually. These were followed by the recitation of one chapter of the Qur'an (*surah*) by the brother who had led the prayer. Once finished, the leader generally gave instructions for the following day and invited all those present to join the compulsory hour of evening reading of community texts in the living room.

---

time-slot to also perform the morning prayer before going to bed. This allowed them to sleep until before the *ikindi* the following day.

10 Every evening, in the Gülen community, the students also recited nearly the totality of the remaining 96 names, on a total of 99 that human beings know of the infinite number of God's attributes. They did this by following a melody that was specific to the community. The sequence of the names as well as the whole ritual for each of the five prayers was contained in a small pamphlet called *Namaz Tesbihatı* that less experienced brothers could follow during the performance.

4 Living by Example

The ritual prayer was just one of the many daily practices through which students and community brothers imitated the exemplary conduct of the Prophet Muhammad. The *sunna* is a set of reports on the way Muhammad resolved certain disputes, spoke, or behaved in a specific circumstance during his lifetime. These reports have historically retained a high practical importance for Muslims, as they provide guidance on many aspects of Islamic conduct that are not explained in the Qur'an, such as how to pray or perform ritual bodily purification. Today, living in line with the *sunna* is often associated with Salafism, a reformist branch within Sunni Islam which is famous for following Muhammad's conduct in detail, including his way of dressing and appearing. Emphasis on the *sunna* is indeed a trait of this and other reformist movements that emerged in the late nineteenth century in response to Western colonization and from a felt dissatisfaction with the state of decadence of their societies. Muslim reformers explained such decadence as the result of corruption and deviation from the original teachings of Muhammad and found the example provided by the life of the Prophet to be a natural source of inspiration for revitalizing the Islamic faith (Rahman 1979 [1966], 210).

Nevertheless, the boundaries between contemporary Islamic reformist and Sufi-inspired movements are quite porous, as references to the *sunna* can be found on both sides of the spectrum (Malik 2018). As new historical works point out, since the origins of Sufism, the *sunna* has often been invoked with the Qur'an to sustain the centrality of a personal commitment to faith and active membership in organized brotherhoods, in opposition to more formalist interpretations of the tradition (Salvatore and Rahimi 2018). Analogously, even in contemporary communities originating from the Nur movement—which, as noted, is a reformed branch of the Naqshbandi-Khalidi Sufi order—like the *Suffa* and the Gülen's, the *sunna* occupied an important place in community life. Distinct from the Salafists, wearing traditional Islamic clothes and growing a beard were highly discouraged in these communities. However, in the houses students and elder brothers alike strove to conform to the exemplary conduct of the Prophet Muhammad down to the minutest detail.

A first example is the prayer, which was performed together as a community (*cemaat olarak*) under the guidance of a leader wearing a special robe (*cübbe*) and hat (*takke*), and by adding a number of supplementary prayer-cycles, as the Prophet and his community used to do. Another case is the way the students accomplished religiously meritorious extra practices, including weekly fasts (*oruç*) on Mondays and Thursdays, or additional prayers at night (*teheccüd*). But beyond the prayer, the *sunna* shaped the entire set of behaviors, etiquettes, and inter-subjective paths that distinguished communal life in the houses, including daily activities such as eating, drinking and sleeping. For instance, apart from the customary Muslim hygienic rule of eating with the right hand, meals were generally consumed on the floor by sitting with one of the two knees leaning on the ground and the other bent on itself. This foot was steadily planted on the carpet-covered floor and the upper part of the thigh pushed against the lower part of the intestine. The habit allegedly corresponds to the way the Prophet used to eat, and it was indicated as good for human health. Students believed that by keeping one of their legs pushed against their intestine they could better understand when they were satiated and thus avoid overeating, which would be not only unhealthy but also not in compliance with community rules of self-restraint (see below). Similarly, students also used to drink by kneeling and by swallowing in three separate sips.

In line with the combination of scientism and faith that distinguishes the Nur movement in general, and the Gülen community in particular (Zengin Arslan 2009; Tee 2016), the *sunna* was believed by my interlocutors to be the reflection of God's commandments, and hence as shielding a hidden scientific knowledge which scientists must discover. The thesis of the scientific reliability of the *sunna* (but also of the whole Qur'anic message) has been taken to its extremes in the Gülen community, which has promoted it through some of its most important publications, particularly *Sızıntı*. Consider the case of sleeping habits. Students of the Gülen community used to sleep lying on their right side, keeping their legs slightly bent and their hands under the head. While they first justified this practice by saying that they were following the *sunna*, they also argued that the habit was good for their health. Their stance was supported by seemingly scientific articles that I found in both old and new issues of *Sızıntı*, aimed at demonstrating that sleeping on the right side was better for the heart, blood circulation, and other bodily functions, whereas sleeping on the opposite side was harmful (Coşkun 2006). Rather than medicalizing the *sunna* to justify the need of keeping up with it, however, these cases should be seen as the opposite. The Prophet's model of conduct was seen by them as above any scientific discovery because it is suggested and favored by God. As such, the *sunna* does not contain a model of perfect conduct because it is healthy, but it is healthy because it is in line with a God-given order.

While all the examples I have mentioned so far refer to individual behavioral norms, the *sunna* had a far-reaching implication on community life. The idea of "Islamic conduct" that is generally used to indicate the set of behaviors that pious Muslims are expected to comply with rests on a view of Muslim life as mainly concerned with the formal respect of outer rules. Instead, for my interlocutors living by the *sunna* also meant to inhabit Muslim life in a specific way that included forms of solidarity and sociality. As I have illustrated elsewhere, the exemplary conduct of the Prophet in community life was externalized into a dynamic path of civic behavior that traversed inter-subjective relations among my interlocutors and was an integral part of the practices through which they cultivated their Muslim selves (Vicini 2014a). The *sunna* shaped all sociability forms within the community, from more informal and relaxed moments like drinking tea, eating chips, or chatting, to more formal ones such as collective meetings. Sociability forms are here intended as "people's capability of inhabiting a particular social space by interacting with other people according to certain standards of behavior and etiquette, but which cannot be reduced to the outward performance of a habit" as they also include people's own ideas of the self and how this is thought of in relation to other selves (Ibid., 96).

This is where, in the view of my interlocutors, the *sunna* is conflated with the other two interrelated notions of *adab* (norms of virtuous behavior) and *ahlak* (ethics). In pre-Islamic times, the term *adab* was often used as a synonym of *sunna*. The original Arabic meaning of the term can be rendered as "tradition" intended as "habit, hereditary norm of conduct, custom derived from ancestors and other persons who are looked up to as models" (Gabrieli 2011). In the course of history, different layers of meaning have been added to the word, from more ethical and social connotations implying ideas of good upbringing, urbanity, and courtesy, to more intellectual ones referring to the sum of knowledge that made a man apt to court life. It is in this regard that, during the Middle Periods of Islamic history (945–1503), *adab* developed into an original element of Islamicate civility indicating a "knowledge tradition" inherited from Persianate court culture that "embraced the ensemble of the ethical and practical norms of virtuous and beautiful life ideally cultivated by a class of literati" (Salvatore 2016, 123).

As noted by others, since *adab* is a malleable word that has taken different connotations in different places and moments, it "is [better] defined by the multiplicity of its uses" than by a specific set of practices (Farag 2001, 94). In the *Suffa* and the Gülen communities, the word overlapped with the concepts of *ahlak* and *sunna*, indicating the set of rules of etiquette and correct manners through which my interlocutors addressed each other. Therefore, students were said to be following the Prophet's *adap* and *ahlak* when they addressed their fellow brothers in polite and gentle tones, using the respect form "*siz*" (you plural), calling them elder brother (*abi*) rather than using their first names, avoiding slang, or greeting new people by standing up and replying to the proverbial form of salutation *selamün aleyküm* with *aleyküm selam*.

These and other relational forms became particularly manifest during visits (*ziyaret*) by members of the community students were not familiar with and whom had to be addressed more formally. During these events, after salutation, the guests approached the students who were standing in a circle. Following a counterclockwise order, they shook the students' hands and hugged them twice, first on the left and then on the right side. Then, they would sit within the circle with the older guests sitting in better places at the right side of the most authoritative brother present. Finally, all participants briefly introduced themselves, and only after the ritual presentation had ended would mutual conversation begin, inspired by love for their fellow brothers (*muhabbet*). During these *ziyaret*s, the attendees displayed a certain ability to find topics of conversation, even if they did not know each other well. The important aspect was to avoid moments of silence that could bring about embarrassment or improper arguments that could cause disputes or disagreement. The brothers were careful not to raise their voice and to speak gently. Normal conversations were usually full of jokes, which often served to break the ice. However, joking was done by behaving respectfully toward others. It was important to arouse collective amusement and laughter rather than having jokes that would exclude some people. Brothers always behaved toward each other with extreme gentleness and smiles.

This model of interaction was inspired by the way the Prophet Muhammad and his companions allegedly behaved when they gathered to discuss religion, economics, or pressing political issues. It defined a path of inter-subjective interaction that wrapped up all community meetings, from more decisional ones (*istişare*) to normal *ziyaret*s. Compliance with the *sunna* absorbed time and space into a way of life in which good manners, moral conduct, individual and collective behavior, and the Islamic past and present converged. In this sense, for my interlocutors, the Prophet's tradition did not merely represent the utmost example for moral individual conduct, but the all-encompassing model of organization of community life in which most daily activities, ritualized performances, and meditative practices could not be separated from each other. As such, these inter-individual patterns draw attention to the inter-subjective substratum that underlies Muslim life, as other studies have done (Tapper and Tapper 1987; Bowen 1993; Lambek 1993; Marsden 2005; Rasanayagam 2010), and invite us to think of Muslim life beyond the contours of Islamic discipline.

Given how the Prophet's exemplary conduct shapes community life, it would be tempting to rely on the Wittgensteinian notion of form of life. Important anthropological studies of Islam have indeed resorted to this notion to stress how the cultivation of key virtues in Muslim life cannot be separated from the commitment to a set of external behaviors through which these same virtues are embodied. In particular, the concept of form of life has often been used by Talal Asad (1993, 2003) to indicate the process through which people embody a tradition, intended as a complete set of emotional, practical, and intellectual dispositions that a man cannot learn in the conventional sense of the term, but can only inherit, by learning it through practice from some ancestors. Like in Wittgenstein, the emphasis is "on the fact that *what is learnt is not a doctrine (rules) but a mode of being*, not a thread one can pick up or drop whenever one feels like it but a *capacity* for experiencing another in a way that can't be renounced" (first emphasis added) (Asad 2015, 167). However, I will resist the temptation to use this notion for three reasons. First, I do not espouse the way Asad seems to see forms of life and related embodiment practices as a distinctive element of religious practice in opposition to modern secular forms of life. In my view, "secular" emotions and feelings are as much embodied as religious dispositions are, though the feelings and emotions involved—and probably also the ways through which they are embodied—are certainly different from those prescribed within the religious domain (e.g. Fadil 2011). Secondly, as already discussed in the introduction, I believe that an excessive emphasis on embodiment processes tends to squeeze tradition into the still important, yet limited, space of disciplinary practice, thus overtly highlighting the prescriptive dimension of Islamic tradition on the one hand and disempowering the place of reflection in the way Muslims cultivate their faith on the other.

Lastly, the rehabilitation of the notion of form of life in the scholarship was not accidentally inspired by the exploration of the monastic rule in Christianity (Foucault 1982; Asad 1993; Agamben 2013). According to one of the possible definitions of the notion provided by Giorgio Agamben in his study of monastic life, a form of life designs "a way of life that, insofar as it strictly adheres to a form or model from which it cannot be separated, is thus constituted as an example" (Agamben 2013, 95). The same juxtaposition of model and life that is highlighted by Asad is found also in Agamben who explains how his definition of form of life is derived from his analysis of monastic life as opposed to post-Westphalian conceptions of the Rule of law. In his view, contrarily to codified, disembodied, and abstract norms contained in modern law, monastic rule consisted in a way of life that did not separate the form (that is the rule, the law) from its realization in concrete life.

However, while this opposition may be useful to define what happened in the Christian tradition, Islam never witnessed such a clearly defined distinction between form and life, between a set of external rules and human life.

As it is now largely recognized by the literature on the topic, the crystallization of the *shariʿa* into a corpus of codified and abstract laws has largely been the result of colonialism or, as in the Ottoman-Turkish case, of a movement of inner reform inspired by foreign models. As described in Chapter 1, before the *Tanzimat* the *shariʿa* was a flexible body of law that was contextually applied in court as well as an ethical code guiding Muslim life. As such, it was neither abstracted from concrete life nor ever sacralized into a set of codified "natural laws"—this being a process whose genealogy can be traced back to historical developments within Christianity and that was consolidated by modern liberal political thought (Salvatore 2011, 2016, 97–99). For this reason, rather than through the notion of form of life, I suggest that the figuration of community life in the *Suffa* and the Gülen houses is better grasped when seen as taking place following the recent reshaping of latent civility patterns from within Islamic tradition such as brotherhood.

5 Brotherhood between Pedagogy and Authority

If living in compliance with the *sunna* can be seen as a dimension of my interlocutors' commitment to a Muslim life, the path that allowed for the articulation of community life in the houses is the flexible inter-individual bond provided by the ideal of brotherhood in religion. As illustrated by Armando Salvatore (2011, 2016, 73–102), brotherhood is a longstanding pattern of civility and collective action that largely predates modern forms of social cohesion based on national or ethnic identity. Within Islamic history, it has represented a key "matrix of civility" that has developed in opposition to modern liberal state-centered and corporative solidarity models. This was especially prominent within Sufi networks beginning in the Middle Period following the Mongol conquests (see Hodgson 1977; Salvatore 2016). Brotherhood defines a pattern through which solidarity is reproduced among Muslims in a diverse ensemble of settings (in the *tarika*s in particular, but also in communities such as *Suffa*) and, as such, it is quite diverse from other forms of solidarity that have emerged in Europe since modern times. Autonomous offices based on abstract forms of legislation like the guilds, which gradually emancipated themselves from feudal structures in late-medieval Europe, were the antecedent to modern forms of impersonal Law in the West. On the contrary, the pattern of civility offered by the brotherhood in Islamicate societies has historically "stood out for warranting a quite strong (and conscious) immunization against consecrating any institution in the form of a corporation" (Salvatore 2016, 32).

Rather than defining a corporate kind of personality based on formal membership tied to a defined territory, the idea of brotherhood has historically provided Muslims with a flexible pattern for organizing interpersonal relations along delocalized transregional networks. The idea is still useful today for thinking of themselves as members of a global community of brothers in religion, the *ummah*, based on a relation of mutual partnership under God's aegis. In the case of the *Suffa* and the Gülen communities, however, brotherhood was primarily used by my interlocutors as a model for organizing community life within the houses. It worked as a flexible pattern of interaction among peers which allowed for the simultaneous articulation of the two apparently opposing principles of authority and amity in brother-to-brother relations. Authority was indeed much less present than it may be thought in the two communities, as it was mitigated through knowledge and brotherhood in the form of a specific articulation of what Salvatore (2016) has called the "power-knowledge equation." In this regard, brotherhood functioned as a dyadic pattern of intersubjective relations that served to dilute and regulate Muslim forms of knowledge and authority.

New university students residing in the houses could already be accustomed to life in religious communities, either because they had occasionally frequented the Nur houses with relatives or friends before, or because—especially in the Gülen community—they had visited these places during their middle or high-school years (see Chapter 4). Yet this was generally the first time they had to adhere in such a scrupulous way to the program, rules, and behaviors that were upheld by the community. Elder brothers knew that the more experienced peers had an important role in facilitating the adaptation process of the new students. For this reason, they tried to establish an appropriate mix of more and less experienced students (generally half and half) in each house. This maintained the equilibrium of community life and, at the same, a certain degree of pedagogical efficacy. There was only one role that was clearly defined: the one that distinguished the house's leader (*imam abi*) from the other students. The *imam abi* had some administrative responsibilities (he was usually the one who collected students' rent and paid the domestic bills), but his most important role was to ensure that life within the houses unfolded in consonance with community patterns. The first function gave him access to decision-making meetings of the next echelon of the community. Indeed, the *imam abi* regularly reported back to brothers occupying higher positions about the successes, shortcomings, or problems that may have occurred among the students. However, this was the only real power he had on his co-residents. If a student was not disciplined enough, he could report this to elder brothers who might admonish the defiant boy privately or in collective meetings, or even decide to expel him from the house. This certainly had an inhibiting effect, especially on the poorest students, for whom departure from the house would have implied the loss of their scholarship and/or favorable rent payments.[11] However, this was the very last resort. Authoritative brothers only rarely intervened and the *imam abi* did his best to manage situations by other means, never reminding students of his authority and preferring jokes and explanations to reprimands.

In this regard, it is important to highlight how authority was always diluted along brotherly lines and articulated through the principle of mastery of knowledge. The *imam abi* was usually the oldest student in the house. He was chosen by the elder brothers according to his degree of command of community life and his demonstrated sense of commitment to the community's ideal of service. Rather than deriving from bestowal, authority depended on the *imam abi*'s degree of knowledge of the community's books, exemplary conduct and embodiment of community ideals. It stemmed from the expertise he had acquired while being socialized within the houses for a sufficiently long period of time and depended on the acknowledgment by the others of him as an exemplary model.[12]

In order to better understand this point, it might be useful to reconsider MacIntyre's aforementioned application of the Aristotelian "craft metaphor" to the domain of apprenticeship. This is analogous to the other metaphor of chess playing that MacIntyre (1984 [1981], 188–191)—probably inspired by Wittgenstein's (1986 [1958]) use of the same analogy—relies on to explain his understanding of virtuous practice. In his account of the virtues, MacIntyre distinguishes between external goods that consist of the rewards attached to a specific practice "by the accidents of social circumstance" on the one hand, and the internal goods of a practice, which are instead exclusively related to the practice itself, on the other. Internal goods are those that are constitutive of a tradition intended as a set of discourses and related practices that practitioners can absorb only through participation in the social world in which this tradition is lived. In the case of chess, internal goods are the rules and aims of the game that the player learns to like and practice without attachment to any external goal other than the virtue of becoming a good and honorable chess player. Instead, external goods are those collateral ends that one may achieve

---

11 Although my research has not dealt with economic issues, they must be considered if we want to understand the sense of constriction that poor students might feel on some occasions.

12 On exemplariness in religious education within the Gülen houses, see Vicini (2013) and Chapter 4.

as a result of his success in pursuing the internal goods, such as the fame and honor a chess-player champion may reach.

Although below I will follow Milbank in going beyond MacIntyre, the latter's description of how people learn to inhabit a tradition by mastering its internal goods through constant practice is still useful to approach an understanding of how students of the *Suffa* and the Gülen communities learned to live the brotherhood and developed a related sense of the self in the houses. Like the chess-player improves his expertise in the game by knowing and appreciating its intrinsic goods day by day, what ideally makes a particular student more authoritative than others is not his attachment to a set of external rewards or the bestowing upon him of such a power by more authoritative brothers. Rather, it is the embodiment of those virtuous behaviors that are required to function as a guide for others. While the power dimension is certainly present, it does not explain everything.

Attributing excessive importance to authority and power would prevent us from appreciating the mechanisms through which these factors are softened through charisma. Charisma is understood here as the reflex of the embodiment of exemplary virtues and behaviors, not as a sort of fascinating effect that authoritative figures exert on the subjects of power (Salvatore 2016, 24). Not only was the *imam abi*'s authority never made explicit, it was also dissimulated by him. Rather than the submission to a magical sort of charismatic aura, the respect that students felt for the *imam abi* was based on the shared acknowledgment that he exemplified a model for them. The way the pattern of brotherhood organized horizontal inter-individual relations was central in the process of dissimulation of power/authority. In the houses, students lived together in equality, respectfully calling each other *abi* and sharing communal deeds like buying food, cooking, and cleaning. This was the norm, and when conflicts arose, students who could not get on well with others in the house were normally transferred to another place. Although differences in expertise were sometimes evident, these were never flaunted by students as a mark of their distinction and authority. Quite to the contrary, the *imam abi*s often happened to carry out some of the humblest occupations within the houses, which was also seen as one of the best ways of embodying the key virtue of sincerity (see below). By dissimulating his higher position and foregrounding his humility, the *imam abi* also gained in respect, as he once more manifested his embodiment of community values.

Further, the authority of the *imam abi* was mitigated by the level of expertise of the other students and the responsibilities they were charged with. Apart from the novices, a good number of the residents had already spent one or more years within the houses, and even if they had not yet been designated as *imams*, they were in the process of progressively ascending the invisible hierarchy of the community as they increased their expertise. Though they did not exert direct authority over less experienced students, they were still recognized as authoritative by the latter for their higher mastery of community virtues. Moreover, according to a path of progressive adaptation to community life—that was parallel to that of responsibilization (see especially Chapter 4 and 5)—after the first year of residence in one house each student was expected to become responsible for a particular aspect of community life, such as taking care of some high-school students or overseeing the cleaning of the house. This responded to an ascending model of authority and responsibility which further softened the weight of hierarchy within the houses.

It is useful to acknowledge that a certain ambivalence in the nature of the distribution of authority along brotherly lines is not a novelty of the two communities under study, or of the Nur movement in general. Michael Gilsenan had already noticed a similar mechanism at work in a conventional Sufi brotherhood like the *Hamidiya Shadhiliya* of Egypt back in the 1960s (Gilsenan 1973, 112). Apart from the vertical relationship of subordination to a master, a gradual and not necessarily explicit hierarchy of relations of brotherliness occupied an important pedagogical function in this context as well. However, if in Sufism this path has generally been thought of as only complementary to the key one based on the companionship and love for the *shaykh*, it has become the rule in the Nur movement. In this case it is the horizontal relationship of brotherhood and the ideal of communal life that prevails over the centralization of the knowledge-power equation in the hands of the master.

Finally, one should also consider the plain fact that my interlocutors were young students attending modern secular schools and mingling in outside society. Consequently, the general sense of equality that was present among the students also stemmed from their shared status and condition. The fact that they experienced similar problems and difficulties at school, but also maintained expectations related to university life and work in the future, was an additional factor that lessened the weight of authority within the houses. On the other hand, the prevalent view of outside society as the reign of ignorance and unbelief had an important role in leading the students to emphasize cohesiveness and parity, and to shun hierarchical differences among themselves. The atmosphere of sincerity and purity that permeated from community life made students feel as though they could trust their brothers in ways that were not possible outside. Yet, at this point, an additional element has to be added to the analysis: the way the principles of brotherhood were used within the houses to think of the community's organizational form as opposed to secular associative forms that have become prevalent in modern times.

6   Brotherhood between Civility and Corporate Personality

It was one rainy day in November when Ferhat, the brother at *Suffa* who was held responsible for the group of university students I lived with, came to pay a visit. A couple of new young students had recently joined the house and Ferhat had decided to make a lesson to introduce them to some of the key principles that regulate life in the community. He read the 21st *Lema*, a chapter of the *Risale*'s volume "The Flashes" (*Lemalar*) (Nursi 1995b), which is considered particularly important, and to which Ferhat referred as the "constitution of *hizmet*."[13] Said Nursi had indeed suggested reading this section every 15 days, as this is the passage where he focused on the key community virtue of sincerity and purity of intentions (*ihlas*). While the place of *ihlas* as a virtue *sui generis* that regulates community life will be discussed in the next section, here I focus on *ihlas* as a key principle in granting unity along brotherly lines within the community.

Ferhat *abi* began his lesson by explaining the common root of the term *ihlas* with that of other Islamic words, and then translating it into *içtenlik* or *samimiyet*, two quasi-synonymous terms that may be rendered as "sincerity and purity of heart."[14] To highlight the importance of the concept for Muslims, he added, "an action made with *ihlas* is greater than thousands done without it." In an effort to explain how such a principle should be understood as inseparable from the experience of brotherhood that is recreated in the houses of the community, he added that "It is not clear at all where *ihlas* is," and by referring to a deed that Ismail, one of the two students attending the lesson, had accomplished the same day, he concluded, "It may also be in putting a bookcase in order." As an ending to this prefatory explication, Ferhat specified that the important point for an action to be considered sincere is that it is accomplished "without hypocrisy" (*riyasız*), "without showing off" (*göstersiz*), "without searching for appreciation" (*beğensiler yok*), and excluding "admiration" (*takdir*) or "acclamation" (*alkış*). Such an action has to be so sincere, he added,

---

13   The passage is also called *İhlas Risalesi* (the epistle of sincerity). Although *ihlas* appears in different parts of the *Risale*, this is the section where Nursi explicitly theorizes upon the concept and suggests four principles that brothers have to follow in order to attain this virtue. Due to its centrality, the passage will be further discussed in other sections of Chapter 3 and 5. The other main section where Nursi explicitly discusses *ihlas*, though less systematically, is the 20th *Lema*.

14   In the community's Arabic/Persian-Turkish dictionary (Yeğin 2005), *samimiyet* is translated as "love and connectedness coming from the interior/heart" (*içten ve kalpten olan sevgi ve bağlılık*). *İhlas* instead comes from *hulus* (pure) and is translated as "to make the heart pure," "sincere love coming from inside," and "rightness and connectedness imbued of sincere love."

that it must be performed, "God willing, just for the sake of God" (*Sadece Allah razı olsun, inşallah*), without any other goal in mind.

Then, Ferhat started to read the introductory section of the 21st *Lema*:

> O my brothers of the Hereafter! And O my companions in the service of the Qur'an! You should know—and you do know—that in this world sincerity is the most important principle in works pertaining to the Hereafter in particular; it is the greatest strength, and the most acceptable intercessor, and the firmest point of support, and the shortest way to reality [truth (*hakikat*)], and the most acceptable prayer, and the most wondrous means of achieving one's goal, and the highest quality, and the purest worship [subservience to God (*ubudiyet*)]. Since in sincerity lies much strength and many lights like those mentioned above; and since at this dreadful time, despite our few number and weak, impoverished, and powerless state and our being confronted by terrible enemies and suffering severe oppression in the midst of aggressive innovations and misguidance, an extremely heavy, important, general and sacred duty [*umumi ve kudsi bir vazife-i imaniye*] of serving belief and the Qur'an has been placed on our shoulders by Divine grace, we are certainly compelled more than anyone to work with all our strength to gain sincerity [*bütün kuvvetimizle ihlası kazanmaya mecbur ve mükellefiz*]. [...] My brothers! There are many obstacles before great works of good. Satan put up a powerful struggle against those who assist those works. One has to rely on the strength of sincerity in the face of these obstacles and satans. You should avoid things which harm sincerity the same as you avoid snakes and scorpions. [...] Do not let egotism and the soul [lowest self (*nefs*)] deceive you.[15]

Exclamations and calls to brotherhood like the one that opens this passage are found in almost every chapter of the *Risale*. Nevertheless, during their meetings, the brothers often commented upon them to keep reminding their audiences of the importance of brotherhood for the achievement of sincerity. In this case, the appeal to a sense of unity among brothers functioned as an incipit of a broader discourse by Ferhat on the centrality of sincerity for the achievement of their collective mission for revitalizing Islam. In the passage, Nursi makes a not-too-veiled reference to the threats that Kemalist policies and other forces such as hedonistic individualism and the market were to the survival of Islam and the maintenance of the integrity of the Muslim

---

15   Nursi 1995b, 212–213.

community during his time. For Nursi, these challenges could be faced only by means of a unity of intents. And only sincerity and purity of brotherhood could allow them to succeed in strengthening such a renewed solidarity pact and fight together against these new enemies.

In relation to this point, Ferhat *abi* further explained to the two novices why Said Nursi had put so much stress on the idea of brotherhood:

> Look, those straying from the right path (*ehl-i dalalet*), those who are unaware of Islamic truths (*ehl-i gaflet*) ... What did they do? They became a collective personality (*şahs-ı manevi*). How did they become a collective personality? They appeared as a collective personality, a committee. They started to behave with the spirit of a committee. [...] How do they attack? They attack through television, through the internet ... They openly show immodest things ... In this or the other way they [form] an alliance [...] And what shall we do? We also have to become a collective personality against them ... We have to ally with one another...

According to Ferhat, the main problem with outside society is not just that its principles contradict those defended by the community, but also that the forces of unbelief in this modern era have organized themselves into "collective personalities" that cooperate to undermine the status of religion. Literally meaning "spiritual (*manevi*) personality (*şahıs*)," the expression *şahsı manevi* is a neologism that was introduced in Ottoman lands during the nineteenth century, probably through the writings of the Young Ottoman Namık Kemal, who may have assimilated it from Rousseau's moral and collective body (*corps moral et collectif*) (Vahide 2005, 368, n. 21; see also Mardin 2000 [1962], 333–334, 399–400). In Rousseau's theory of the social contract, the idea of collective personality delineates a rational-legal kind of pact that an ideal ensemble of individuals subscribes to in order to render their sovereignty to the ruler (Merriam 1999 [1900], 85–89). On his part, Nursi confers a religious and spiritual connotation to the idea, which is a way for him to highlight that, beyond circumscribing a rational kind of agreement, these modern configurations of power also involve a commonality of interests. Not just to be found in the state, this unity is also present in other modern legal formations such as the corporation, the commune, and the Church, which are all based on contractual forms of solidarity. By offering an updated reading of the concept of *şahsı manevi*, in his lesson, Ferhat highlights how today these corporate personalities can penetrate and undermine community life by means of television, advertising, and the internet. However, following Nursi, he also sees in them a possible source of inspiration for their organizational form. If today anti-religious actors are organized in powerful "committees," Ferhat argues, they also have to aim at such a firm unity and resolution in bringing forth their religious mission.

If, as suggested by Ferhat, modern organizational forms must provide inspiration for rethinking brotherhood in a more intra-communitarian way, what does this imply for the organizational form and the purposes of the two communities under study?[16] What happens when a flexible dyadic model of inter-individual relations is reconceived along the lines of a corporative kind of personality? Most certainly, in these passages of the *Risale* Nursi is using a simile to emphasize that they must reinforce their brotherly relations to establish a strong alliance against their enemies. Yet these words also seem to suggest the possible future transition of the Nur movement toward new organizational forms, as happened when the network split in separate and shielded communities as it relocated into the urban fabric. As illustrated above, the Nur movement's settlement to major urban centers since the 1960s corresponded to a parallel process of re-organization of what were previously the poles of a flexible network of reading centers of the *Risale* into self-enclosed communities (*cemaat*) with their own restricted agendas and goals. As it will be noted in Chapter 5, this transformation is particularly evident in the case of the Gülen community, within which the idea of brotherhood served to uphold a corporate-kind of collective enterprise mainly aimed at the mobilization of people in society. As it will be noted, this attitude resulted in the reduced capacity of this community to rely on the ideal of brotherhood as a civilizational tool for promoting solidarity beyond community walls.

7   Virtues of Mutuality

The indissoluble link that the Nur brothers established between brotherhood and the key virtue of *ihlas* is not accidental but reflects the need of linking Muslim processes of ethical formation with new forms of organization in a modern context. Within the *Suffa* and the Gülen communities there is indeed a circular relationship between the basic goals of taming the *nefs*, the process of embodiment of the key virtue of *ihlas*, and the cultivation of a sense of the self that was diluted into the ideal of religious brotherhood. An interesting mark of this circular relationship is, for example, the highly ignominious character that was attributed to the sin of gossiping and talking behind one's back

---

16   For a discussion of how brotherhood was, instead, conceived in universalistic terms within salvation religions emerging from the axial breakthrough, see the discussion of Bellah (1999) and Weber (1978) in Chapter 5.

(*gıybet*) within these communities. The topic was constantly discussed in the houses when students jokingly warned those who complained about some small flaw in other students' character or attitude not to commit *gıybet*. But it was also the subject of specific reading sections, such as the one Yasin, a young doctor and former student residing in the houses of the *Suffa* community, conducted in front of a group of university students one evening.[17] His lesson was based on the concluding section (*hatime*) of the 22nd chapter of "The Letters" (*Mektubat*) (Nursi 1997), a writing that Nursi had entirely dedicated to this particular sin. In it, Nursi examines the *Surah Al-Hujurat*'s sentence "Would any of you like to eat the flesh of his dead brother?" (Qur'an 49:12).

Yasin introduced the passage by referring to a *hadith* in which, after admonishing one of his companions for backbiting another, the Prophet Muhammad reportedly ordered her to spit out the piece of meat she had in her mouth, which was indeed immediately expelled.[18] Yasin emphasized how committing such a sin should be hated like perpetrating cannibalistic or inhuman acts. Then he started reading the text at a point where Said Nursi interrogates an imaginary interlocutor about what had happened to his sense of civility that pushed him to commit such a vile and wild act. Of particular interest is the 5th passage of the chapter, in which Nursi compares the sin of *gıybet* to "mercilessly (*insafsızca*) biting the corporate personality (*şahsı manevi*)," of which the imaginary sinner does not realize he is himself part of, so that he is inadvertently "biting his own limbs." As also mentioned by Yasin, backbiting is a sort of poison (*zehir*) that can spread easily and fast through the community if somebody starts committing it. Luckily, he added, it does not seem to be a concern for their community today, but he warned the students to always keep their guard up because it is easy to start gossiping about other brothers. Interestingly, Yasin concluded by observing that this would compromise not only the capacity of the single individual to achieve sincerity of faith, but also that of the whole community, which would risk crumbling.

This example is further proof of how the *Suffa* and the Gülen communities are, *via* Nursi, part of a long-standing trend within Sufism, in which sincerity and purity of intentions occupy a central place. The origin of the word *ihlas* stems from a semantic root indicating purity, cleanliness, and freedom from admixture. As such, it appears in both the Qur'an (e.g. 4:146) and the *hadith*

---

17 The topic was also discussed in writing. Gülen has dedicated at least two of his weekly editorials to the subject (Gülen 2010b, a).
18 According to the sources, the interlocutor and reporter of the *hadith* was Prophet Muhammad's third and youngest wife Aisha herself, who had just observed how the skirt of a woman who had passed by was too long (es-Suyuti 1994, 200–202).

literature, where it indicates the act of pure and sincere submission to God as expressed by the declaration of belief in the Oneness of God and the Prophecy of Muhammad (*shahada*). Not accidentally, one of the main goals of the *shahada* is to turn the heart and mind away from everything other than God (Chittick 2000, 11). Because it originates from the Prophet Muhammad's intimate religious experience, *ihlas* has taken an important place in the development of pietistic Sufism since late ninth/early tenth century. An early example is "the Path of Blame" of the Malamati way, in which the concept was associated with practices aimed at narrowing the sense of the lower self by blaming it. Developed in the region of Khorasan, this path consisted of a constant and unrelenting suspicion against the *nefs*, which was oriented to self-restraint to such an extent that it refused to indulge in any kind of visible praiseworthy act or of public display of piety (Karamustafa 2007, 48). Later in history, the principle of *ihlas* has been discussed largely by Muslim scholars, among which are the great Hanbali mystic Khwajah Abdullah al-Ansari (1006–1088) and the theologian and Sufi scholar Abu Hamid al-Ghazali (1058–1111), to whom we probably owe the most extensive treatment of the term (Gardet 2011b). Today, the virtue of *ihlas* is associated with practices aimed at controlling the egotist desires of the lower self in total submission to God, which are still particularly distinctive of Sufism. For example, in Turkey the virtue of sincerity pervades key moments of disciplinary practice in contemporary Sufi Naqshbandi brotherhoods (Silverstein 2011, 147).

What is more original in Nursi is the way he circularly linked the cultivation of this principle to unity within the brotherhood. According to the first of the four key principles of *ihlas* listed by Nursi in the above-mentioned 21st *Lema*, such virtue has to be searched for individually, only for the sake of achieving it. Yet in the following three axioms Nursi explicitly highlights how *ihlas* has to be sought as a way of strengthening the brotherhood. It is through purity and sincerity, which implies not criticizing other brothers (second principle) and instead praising them (fourth principle), that Muslims may stay united and be strengthened by each other's purity/sincerity (third principle) in order to counter worldly temptations (Nursi 1995b).

To understand the intra-social character that the virtue of *ihlas* had for Nursi and for my interlocutors, it is useful to follow John Milbank (2006 [1990]) in his search for a conception of the embodiment of virtues that goes beyond models centered on individual self-fashioning. Although Milbank moves within Christianity rather than Islam, he offers important insights for our analysis of the virtue of *ihlas* as related to a search for connectedness in brotherhood. As a Christian theologian, he criticizes the entire Western philosophical tradition from Late Antiquity to modernity—including Hegel, Marx, and postmodernists like Nietzsche, Foucault, and Deleuze—for maintaining a perspective that remains within what he defines as "a secular horizon." In his opinion, this horizon rests on a fundamental "ontology of violence," upon which the entire edifice of modern Western philosophy is built. Such ontology assumes that "the priority of force" prevails over any other essential human principle and takes "how this force is best managed and confined by counter-force" as its main subject of inquiry (Ibid., 4). Milbank dedicates several pages to illustrate the long genesis of this tradition and indicates Hobbes as one of its most eminent representatives. More decisively than others, the Scottish political philosopher introduced the idea that human behavior is essentially driven by the primordial will of each individual of prevailing over others. As notoriously exemplified by his maxim, "man is a wolf to man." If human beings were not bound by the social contract they ideally signed among themselves under the aegis of the Leviathan, they would tear each other apart in a lawless war for power. Although not all the above-mentioned modern philosophers would openly agree with Hobbes, according to Milbank they remain oriented by an essentially immanent horizon of meaning in which individual interests and desires occupy a central position, and human beings are understood to make moral decisions with the goal of satisfying such interests and desires. In his view, modern Western philosophers are the multivocal expression of an established and well rooted secular ontological perspective which assumes that the individual's desiring and willing self *is* the universal subject of ethical deliberation.[19]

In opposition to this tradition, Milbank places himself in the classical and medieval inheritance of Platonic-Aristotelian-Augustinian-Thomist genealogy along with Macintyre, with whom he agrees on his emphasis on virtue, narrative, and tradition in opposition to the "nihilistic" voice of modern philosophy. In search for a conception of the virtues that transcends individual contingent experience, however, Milbank also criticizes MacIntyre, particularly for being "too Aristotelian"—and probably "not enough Christian"—in his account of the virtues. According to Milbank, MacIntyre is too much indebted to the Aristotelian ideal of the "magnanimous man," that is, of a man who gets his honor from the heroic and uncompromising way he sticks to his social role, no matter what it may cost him. Think of anyone of the heroes of the Greek tragedy. All sought honors and rewards that, to use the MacIntyrian vocabulary I have

---

19   For a more detailed discussion of modern secular conceptions of the self that emerged within the Philosophers of the Scottish Enlightenment and how these are distinct from Muslim formulations, see my discussions of Macintyre (1988), Asad (2003) and Salvatore (2007) in Chapter 5.

illustrated above, are "internal" to the goods of a tradition. As highlighted by Milbank, all the characters of the tragedies of Ancient Greece behaved in a partly heroic, and decidedly aristocratic, framework and were "still primarily motivated by this seeking for public acclaim" (Ibid., 354). No matter how honorable the aristocratic act of the magnanimous man might be, it had as its main goal the public display of honor and not the pure cultivation of a virtuous behavior. This implies that the virtues that sustained his heroism in the tragedy remained tied to the contingent world, oriented toward a horizon of immanence rather than toward one of transcendence. While MacIntyre has developed his model of the virtues over time by integrating Aristotelian ethics with a Thomistic framework (cf. MacIntyre 1984 [1981], 1988), according to Milbank he was never able to get rid of this heroic inflection. In other words, whereas as clarified in the introduction to this book, Laidlaw (2014) criticizes MacIntyre for not being Aristotelian enough, Milbank accuses him of being excessively so.

To this view, Milbank opposes a Christian understanding of the virtues that, in his opinion, genuinely surpasses magnanimity because it transcends the search for mundane honors. By foregrounding Thomas Aquinas's exploration of the cardinal virtue of charity (*caritas*), Milbank proposes a post-heroic understanding of what a virtue is and makes it such. Differently from the civic ideal of the "magnanimous man," the person of charity is a person whose very mode of existence is a constant and disinterested act of giving; an act that can be exercised even in negative situations of poverty and weakness, and without occupying powerful positions. As such, *caritas* epitomizes the least honorable of the virtues, that is, a kind of virtue that is intrinsically contrary to public acclaim. In order to be so, it cannot simply stem from the human disposition. Rather, it can be enacted only as the expression of the higher transcendent principle represented by God's charity toward humanity. In this light, human charity is and can only be manifested as the reflex of divine grace (Milbank 2006 [1990], 363). Inasmuch as charity transcends the contingency of any other sort of worldly-grounded virtuous behavior, it represents *the* virtue par excellence, the cardinal virtue that surrounds all other virtues within a genuine ethical life. In Milbank's words, *caritas* "is not merely the highest ethical ideal: it is also what makes virtue virtuous, the very 'form of the virtues' according to Aquinas" (Ibid., 364).

There are two additional points that are worth highlighting. First, for Aquinas *caritas* is a virtue whose achievement is ontologically grounded in the practice of mutuality in friendship and as such cannot be sought individually. While Milbank observes that Aristotle has made a similar point about friendship, he also remarks that neither Aristotle nor MacIntyre have ever put the mutual dimension of the virtues at the apex of their conceptions. Par opposition, in Milbank's proposition, the virtues are first sought for the sake of the neighbor and for the achievement of God's grace itself rather than being conceived as a "self-contained, internal matter" (Ibid., 363). This view of the virtues is essentially based on mutuality and connectedness. As such, it is defiant toward any form of authority or any search for honor. Second, as mentioned, *caritas* is not a simple virtue. Rather, it is a cardinal virtue that provides orientation to all other virtues. Inasmuch as it expresses the most immediate manifestation of the transcendent order of God, it is the superior and regulating principle of ethical conduct that circumscribes all the other virtues. For this reason, Milbank elevates it to the rank of the highest virtue, of "what makes virtue virtuous."

It follows that there is a double parallel that can be traced between Milbank's understanding of the virtues and that of my interlocutors. Like charity can only be thought of and achieved within an ontological framework grounded in friendship, also *ihlas* must be sought for within and through brotherly ties. Second, similarly to how *caritas* is the foundation of all virtues in Aquinas, *ihals* is what makes all other Islamic principles virtuous in the perspective of the *Risale*—a perspective which, as it will be shown in Chapter 3, is oriented toward a transcendent principle exceeding "secular reason." In this vein, even when drawn from the Christian tradition, Milbank's theologically-grounded account of the virtues opens a venue for rethinking virtuous behavior, in Islamic tradition too, as the worldly expression of cardinal virtues having a strong transcendent anchor. In place of *caritas*, it is mutual recognition in concrete life forms through the exercise of *ihlas* that regulates community life in the Nur houses. As an overarching and comprehensive virtue, *ihlas* takes into account a wider set of ethical dispositions that include patience, humility, love, self-restraint, and self-sacrifice for the other brothers. As I further remark in the following section, all these attitudes were daily enlivened in the houses and were a way of achieving sincerity and purity of commitment to faith.

8   Living Sincerity

In a circular way, we have come back to where we had started. Within the student houses of the *Suffa* and the Gülen communities, taming the self is the underlying goal of a broader pedagogy oriented toward practicing self-control and self-restraint, which is in turn aimed at fostering brotherhood on the basis of unity and pureness of intentions. To shed light on the final link between the cultivation of the key virtue of sincerity and brotherhood within the houses, it is useful to quote from the rest of Ferhat's lesson introduced above. After having attentively read the first paragraph of the 21st *Lema*, Ferhat added: "Purity and sincerity are the highest moral (*en yüksek ahlaktır*)" and, conversely, "the highest level of morals are purity and sincerity (*ahlak'ın en yüksek seviyesi ihlastır*)." Then, Ferhat articulated a discourse in which he established an interesting nexus between a set of humble works related to community life and the process of cultivating sincerity. Commenting upon the second part of the same passage of the *Risale* quoted above, he highlighted some qualities such as patience and, by implication, humility as ways for people to attain sincerity and move closer to God. Even more interesting is the way Ferhat linked the achievement of these qualities, and indirectly of *ihlas*, to the daily practices and duties of communal living, rather than to practices of devotion such as performing the daily prayer or reading Islamic texts.

Ferhat first stressed the importance of exercising patience toward others and of not making trouble. He introduced the argument this way: "Let's say, for example, that we have some trouble here in the house [...] I have to be patient (*sabır*). Why? For God's sake. This gets you closer to purity/sincerity (*ihlas'a yaklaştır*)." To elucidate this point, he used a concrete example related to living together that students might have to face in the course of their residence in the houses. By taking the tea-glass that he had just emptied in his right hand, Ferhat said:

> For example, let's say that this glass hasn't been washed. If I start saying [*simulating a shouting voice*] 'Why hasn't it been washed? Why this and that...?' This way, I have worn myself down. Instead, what should I do? My brother has not washed it. For God's sake, I wash it. God knows what I have done and if I have done it with sincerity. In this way, I haven't worsened the situation. If our actions are based on *ihlas* we aren't weakening *hizmet*.

From Ferhat's words emerges the idea that remaining calm and showing patience toward a companion who has left his duty undone is a mark of sincerity in one's commitment. The issue is not framed only as a matter of personal discipline and control but as part of a broader dynamic that also contemplates the need for maintaining a good atmosphere in the house in order to foster a sense of communion and brotherhood. As he claims at the end, showing patience and calmness is conducive to preserving human relationships that are the foundation of *hizmet*. If one is sincerely committed to the duty of service, he is not disturbed by somebody else's shortcomings and does not complain about them. Rather, he puts all his efforts to fix the problem, behaving patiently, moved by the will of self-sacrificing and dedicating himself to his fellow brothers.

This leads us to the second example presented by Ferhat, in which he relates the virtue of humility (*tevazu*) to the communal work of cleaning the lavatories:

> The most valued thing is the cleaning of the bathrooms. Why? Because there is no self-pride (*onur*) in doing it. We don't pretend to be special while doing it. The highest services to salvation (*en selametli hizmet*), the most distinct means to spiritual advancement are the services that go unseen; the services whose plaudits are not received. For example, I, Ferhat, could be proud of myself ... Let's imagine that I say 'I've done a really good job at giving this lesson today,' 'I've expressed myself very well' and so on ... These things can make my vanity (*enaniyet*) increase, right? But whoever cleans the bathrooms doesn't have vanity. He does it as such, for the sake of God.

As in the case of the glass above, Ferhat associates the accomplishment of an action related to community life to the virtue of humility. While he does not mention this virtue explicitly, he does it indirectly by referring to the corresponding vices of "vanity" and "self-pride" that may arise if one does not perform his deeds out of sincerity. Particularly significant in this quotation is the association that Ferhat establishes between humble work, the capacity of controlling one's lower impulses, and the achievement of *ihlas*. He could have given the example of the prayer or of any other individual or collective practice of devotion. Why did he not do this? Why was the cleaning of bathrooms or washing of dishes more meritorious to him than the act of piety and surrendering to God embodied by the prayer? The answer lies where Milbank's (2006 [1990]) understanding of religious virtue leads us: because there is no possible pride that can come from cleaning the bathrooms. Whereas one may still feel proud of, for example, how scrupulous he has been in performing the prayer, no such a feeling can accompany these other activities. Ferhat is stressing this point when he says that the "highest services to salvation" and the "most distinct means to spiritual advancement" are those services "that go unseen," those "whose plaudits are not received."

This is something he had also mentioned at the beginning of his speech when he defined sincere actions as those that are done "without hypocrisy," "without showing off." In this regard, Ferhat's words illustrate an economy of religious action that can be brought back to the first goal students have to aim for if they want to live a pious life. The engagement in humble acts, like cleaning or serving other brothers, is the expression of a view of virtuous behavior as rooted in a constant preoccupation and concern for the traps of the lower self and for how taming it. As stressed by Ferhat, in other practices that may reflect a higher degree of authority or knowledge on behalf of the practitioner, there is always the risk of awakening one's lower self and increasing one's vanity, hence of breaking the principle of *ihlas*. Instead, these risks are reduced to the lowest level when doing humble deeds. The circle of brotherhood, purity of action, and control of the lower self is here closed. Each element of the circle cannot be strengthened without the other, and community life is where this triad comes together and is put into practice day by day within the houses.

∴

In the eyes of my interlocutors, the houses provided an uncontaminated and safe environment where they could enliven patterns of Muslim life and sociality that are no longer allowed in outside society. Communal life was marked by the cadence of the five daily prayers and by an exemplary conduct made of Muslim sociability, Islamic deeds, good manners, and morals that were exemplified by the *sunna*. Here, the pedagogical pattern worked in absentia of a master, though it did not completely break with longstanding Islamic patterns of authority and knowledge. The brotherhood functioned as an acephalous matrix of power-knowledge that both structured pedagogical relations and was generative of Muslim connectedness. Within the houses, newcomers could experience firsthand brotherhood as a horizon of imagination and practice of key Muslim virtues through a constant practice of self-restraint and self-denial. Living in the houses was a way for them of "unbuilding" the self, rather than simply taming the *nefs*, by constantly deconstructing it through brother-to-brother interactions. Only in this way was it then possible to rejoice of a new sense of unity and cohesion in the brotherhood. As concluded by Ferhat when commenting upon another passage of the 21st *Lema*:

> 'As one of man's hands cannot compete with the other, neither can one of his eyes criticize the other, nor his tongue object to his ear' (Nursi 1995b, 214) … We also have to be like this. Like a tongue and an ear, not like quarrelers. We have to do this way: working for understanding, meeting half way, finding the middle way, always being accommodating, being the solution to the problems and being peacemakers. For example, by saying 'If you like, let's do this way, my brother,' […] 'Let's start from here,' 'Look, there is a point from which we can start,' 'If you want let's do this way.' I mean, we always have to work toward meeting half way.

Like the organs of the body do not compete with each other, so the brothers have to learn to cooperate and be united by a sincere feeling of brotherhood. Not just a place to cultivate Islamic virtuous behavior, the houses are also where students and brothers reinforced their unity and supported each other against the external world. As mentioned, such an emphasis on cohesion also contains the seeds of a new corporativist element taken from the modern experience which is at work in the way the pattern of brotherhood has been reinterpreted within the *Suffa* and the Gülen communities. However, in the idea of brotherhood there is also the potential for thinking of religious action beyond secular reason, that is, as a form of engagement in the world that is still oriented toward the search for universal unity; no matter how uncertain and precarious this search may be. I will come back to consider such tension in Chapter 5. An important step to accomplish before, however, is to explore how specific intellective practices underlie the patterns of civility that were upheld within the houses. It is only by framing their lives into a broader Islamic cosmological order, indeed, that my interlocutors could justify their renunciation for the satisfaction of their immediate and contingent desires in the name of universal brotherhood and the search of God.

CHAPTER 3

Reading, Reflection and the Search for Transcendence

During my stay in the houses of the *Suffa* and the Gülen communities, the most important moments of community life were accompanied by readings of key religious texts: the *Risale-i Nur* in the *Suffa*, and this work or one of Gülen's books in the Gülen community. After morning and evening prayers, fellow brothers met in the central hall to read one of these texts individually or collectively. When they read collectively, the more authoritative brother read aloud and commented on the paragraphs, lingering on the most important passages. Those present listened silently, nodding and whispering words of approval in response. Whether conducted individually or collectively, reading is a central and constitutive practice of these two communities.

Reading had also been a survival strategy of the Nur movement during its formative period. In the time Nursi spent in prison and exile between 1923 and 1950, his ideas were diffused by way of letters smuggled and copied by his students which were read in clandestine meetings (Mardin 1989; Vahide 2005). It is through the multiplication of these reading circles across the country that the movement expanded initially. Motivated by the need of escaping persecution by the state, the view that the *Risale* could be read independently of the presence of their master by the growing number of Nursi's followers gradually gained ground in the community and became one of its distinctive traits. This was a rather unconventional practice compared to traditional patterns of transmission of Islamic knowledge in which the presence of the master was recommended, if not essential. However, it also reflected the mutated epistemological conditions of the time, which emerged in parallel with the encroachment of modern forms of political authority and related techniques of power in the late Ottoman Empire. New understandings of knowledge prescribed that Muslims should have direct access to the sources and be able to scrutinize them autonomously. Apparently aware of these shifting conditions, Nursi became the promoter of an approach that winked at these new views and conceived the *Risale* accordingly, as such inclination responded to his desire to produce a text that could revitalize the faith of the ordinary believer.

Shifts in the practice of reading are part of a long-standing trend that has been explored by scholars with particular regard to the West. Studies on the social history of reading in Europe have generally noted how the passage from classical and medieval forms of reading to modern ones has involved a rupture in terms of the public nature of the practice and of the involvement of one's senses in it (Saenger 1997; Johnson 2000; Stroumsa 2015). As it is well-established in the literature, by the fourth century St. Augustine was bewildered by seeing St. Ambrose practicing silent reading as this habit was not very common in Europe until the thirteenth century.[1] This is not to say that the habit of reading texts aloud disappeared entirely after that time. However, it became less prominent than in the past, when reading was generally conducted in a spoken manner by an orator addressing a listening public. In philosophical and religious circles especially, the readings consisted of performative acts that involved the entire body of the listener, his senses and feelings, as they were aimed to generate a transformation of his inner states and dispositions. This image contrasts sharply with that of the silent reader of national newspapers of the nineteenth century, for whom reading has mainly turned into a means of accessing information and imagining the nation (Anderson 1991 [1983]).

The transition from one way of reading to the other was gradual and dictated by broader social transformations. The introduction of new printing technologies, along with the rise of literacy rates and the major use of vernacular languages, all significantly impacted the consumption of books in Europe. Radical shifts within the religious field also played an important role. The Protestant Reformation made direct access to religious sources the main banner of its proposal for lessening the weight of ecclesiastic authority and emancipating religious practice from its yoke. Facilitated by the emergence of printing, the Reformation introduced the idea that individual believers could autonomously read religious texts without the need for intercession by the class of religious scholars. In this light, the Reformation is commonly acknowledged as the motor of a radical transformation in the approach to the texts which paralleled and contributed to the process of individualization and internalization of reading processes both within and outside the religious field.

Said Nursi's efforts to convey the Qur'anic message in a vernacular language accessible to the ordinary Muslim resonates widely with these shifts and could be seen as an attempt at refashioning Islamic exegetical forms in a "Protestant fashion." In line with this narrative, some authors have suggested that the movement initiated by Nursi in the 1930s might be better defined as a "textual

---

1   The first to bring to scholarly attention the famous passage by Augustine was Norden (1923 [1989]). Yet the interpretation of the passage is controversial. Moreover, as it has been widely demonstrated by the literature, it is mistaken to think that silent reading was totally absent in the past. What changed was the prominence that silent reading took over public reading in time. For a reconstruction of the debate, see Johnson (2000).

community," namely a community in which the greater accessibility to the sources has brought about a process of democratization of religious knowledge similar to the one initiated centuries before in Europe (Yavuz 2003a, b). It is undeniable that the simplification and transliteration of Nursi's work into the modern Turkish alphabet have contributed positively to the circulation of his ideas among a newly emerging public of Muslims educated in the new national schools.[2] However, the question remains of whether this narrative may occlude some more complex mechanisms of transformation and renewal of the Islamic tradition in relation to the changes brought about by the advent of new technologies and media. To what extent has the introduction of printing and modern forms of communication impacted on Islamic intellective practice and what are the eventual hybrid outcomes of these transformations?

These considerations sit within a broad anthropological debate concerning the impact of literacy, modern education, and new communication technologies in Muslim-majority countries. This scholarship has generally questioned grand narratives such as those delineated above by studies on European social history. In general, it has suggested that although the diffusion of schooling and the impact of modern media across the region have contributed to the transformation of the mechanisms of authorization and justification of Islamic knowledge, they have not determined a total turn toward individualized forms of authority and media consumption (Eickelman 1978; Messick 1993; Eickelman and Anderson 2003; Hirschkind 2006; Silverstein 2011; Spadola 2014). These studies have widely agree that more research is needed to explore how old and new technologies have intertwined with the religious tradition in each specific context. However, anthropologists have dissented about the impact of these transformations. While some have emphasized the role of new media in favoring a "democratization" of religious authority (Eickelman and Anderson 2003), their critics have observed that highlighting the way new media have made religious contents more accessible than in the past reflects a common tendency within liberal thought to conceal the role of authority in shaping the public reception of both religious and secular discourse (Hirschkind 2006).

---

2 Please notice that, however, the people *Reading Islam* describes are members of two enclosed religious communities who, as such, do not represent a transversal public of "cultured" Muslims like the one explored in some recent ethnographies of Islamic public culture (e.g. Aishima 2016). The discourse would be different if this work was about those who read the *Risale* alone without being members of any specific community.

Both approaches are relevant for understanding reading practices of the *Risale* in relation to issues of continuity and change in the Islamic tradition. While religious texts were often read individually in both the *Suffa* and the Gülen communities, the reading of the *Risale* continued to be conducted by more experienced brothers during collective meetings. However, in this chapter I am concerned less with changes in forms of authority and more with exploring to what extent the broad epistemological and hermeneutical shifts that distinguish the modern era have impacted the Islamic tradition. In this vein, I point to how longstanding Islamic modalities of intellectual engagement have survived underneath apparently more "modern" ways of approaching the tradition such as the reading of religious texts in vernacular language.

The exploration of the reading practices of the *Risale* within the *Suffa* community shows that the transition to new unmediated ways of approaching a text within the Nur movement has *not* undermined the founding ontological and heuristic assumptions about how proper knowledge should be attained in the Islamic tradition.[3] Longstanding forms of Islamic intellectual engagement grounded in the heart and relying on human imaginative faculties remain central in reading practices of the *Risale*. In opposition to what a modernist view of the history of reading would imply, the reading of this text maintains a specific religiously grounded heuristic dimension even when conducted alone and in silence. Whereas the use of the intellect was highlighted by my interlocutors as a mark of the "modern" character of their way of living Islam vis-à-vis that of other Muslims, I will show that their exercises of meditative reflection (*tefekkür*) were based on a specific conceptualization of the relationship between an inner sensitivity of the heart and intellectual capacities, which has its genealogy in Islamic—particularly Sufi—tradition. Accordingly, I will argue that a new anthropology of reading in Islam and beyond should be more

---

3 Although reading the *Risale* is a central practice in both the Gülen and the *Suffa* communities, all the ethnographic materials that I rely on in this chapter are drawn from my research into the latter. In the *Suffa* community, reading the *Risale* was more frequent and scrupulously conducted than in the Gülen community. This does not mean that what I say in this chapter is not valid for the Gülen case as well, where reading still maintains a central place. However, as it will be illustrated in the next chapter, another pedagogy based mainly on exemplariness has become more prominent in the Gülen case. Further, it is not by accident that in this chapter I will talk of those reading modalities that are specifically associated with the *Risale-i Nur*, and not, for example, with Fethullah Gülen's books. Indeed, it is in relation to his own work that Said Nursi elaborated the idea of meditative reflection on nature and existence that I explore below.

attentive toward the historically-specific intellectual exercises that are attached to reading practices in each context.

1 Appealing to the Imagination

> Sixty years ago, I was searching for a way to reach reality that was appropriate for the present age. [...] First I had recourse to the way of the philosophers; I wanted to reach the truth with just the reason. But I reached it only twice [and] with extreme difficulty. Then I looked and saw that even the greatest geniuses of mankind had gone only half the way, and that only one or two had been able to reach the truth by means of the reason alone. So I told myself that a way that even they had been unable to take could not be made general, and I gave it up ... Then I had recourse to the way of Sufism and studied it. I saw that it was truly luminous and effulgent, but that it needed the greatest caution. Only the highest of the elite could take that way. So, saying that this cannot be the way for everyone at this time, either, I sought help from the Qur'an. And thanks be to God, the *Risale-i Nur* was bestowed on me, which is a safe, short way inspired by the Qur'an for the believers of the present time.[4]

Contrary to what Nursi implies in this passage, historical scholarship has abundantly proven that Sufism has never been just an elitist tradition as it has been often associated with practices aimed at making the divine message accessible to the non-lettered masses (Hodgson 1977; Salvatore and Rahimi 2018; Malik 2018). According to Nursi, however, Sufism was no longer able to provide an efficient way of cultivating a Muslim life in an epoch dominated by the Western worldview. Under the newly established Turkish Republic, Muslims were being educated in modern secular schools and lived in a society that was dominated by modern rhythms and lifestyle. They would not be capable of engaging in pedagogical paths like those undertaken by students of the *medrese*s or by members of the Sufi lodges in Ottoman times even if they wished. This is the main reason why Nursi wrote the *Risale*: to offer ordinary Muslims a way to embrace and strengthen their faith in a "modern" world in which old Muslim pedagogical paths and forms of commitment were unable to survive or no longer represented a practicable path.

---

[4] Reported by Said Nursi's former student and now authoritative brother of the Nur communities, Mustafa Sungur (Şahiner 1979, 399; quoted in Vahide 2005, 167).

Written in an elevated language using many Arabic and Persian terms from the Ottoman lexicon, the *Risale* is a work of approximately 6,000 pages containing concepts that are not easily comprehensible for the ordinary reader. The vocabulary, rhetoric, and language employed were eradicated from common use following the lexical purification of the Turkish language initiated by Mustafa Kemal Atatürk after 1923—which also introduced the Latin script to replace the Arabic one (Lewis 1968 [1961]; Zürcher 1993; see also Lewis 1999). For this reason, a new reader of the *Risale* must gain a certain degree of acquaintance with the text in order to fully grasp the contents, something only achievable with time and repeated readings. Yet, however difficult the *Risale* may be to understand—and especially some of its volumes, like "The Rays" (*Şualar*)—the fact that it was written in a vernacular language instead of Arabic was something new in the panorama of Islamic texts in Turkey. Initially dictated by Nursi and transcribed in Ottoman script by his students in the 1930s and 1940s, the text was partly simplified and transliterated in Latin script under the supervision of Said Nursi himself in the 1950s. Nursi considered making the *Risale* accessible to a growing public of graduates of modern secular schools to be an integral part of the Nur movement's mission of saving the Islamic faith. In his pioneering study on Nursi and social change in Turkey, Şerif Mardin (1989) compared the use of vernacular language in the *Risale* with coeval attempts at making literary culture more accessible to citizens of the emerging modern European nations. This choice responded to Nursi's attempt at offering a new kind of literary work which was imbued with Islamicate culture to new generations of Muslims who felt culturally dispossessed under the secular Republic.

As shown by Mardin, one of the main reasons for the *Risale*'s success was the use of a particular *idiom* made up of "clusters" and "reservoirs" of meaning taken from the Muslim culture of the Anatolian countryside. Nursi used an "allusive, superficially obscure" literary style full of cognitive clusters, symbols, and metaphors, which had a particular hold over a readership raised in those peripheral lands of the country where such cultural repertoires still retained a constitutive social role (Mardin 1989, 34–39, 176–177). The use of an often cryptic language was also evocative of the style of the Qur'an, which is full of allegories and metaphors with ambiguous meanings. As noted by Mardin, the intellectually elaborate vocabulary, poetic images, references to mythical figures, and consistent degree of obscurity of several passages conferred a quasi-magical aura on the *Risale* that struck a chord with people who had been raised in the Muslim culture of the Anatolian periphery. Mardin suggests that Nursi's appeal derived from an intuitive understanding of what the Italian philosopher Giambattista Vico (1668–1744) has called "poetic imagination." By this term, the Neapolitan philosopher referred to the capacity of poetry to affect human behavior—especially the behavior of an ethical nature—more effectively and easily than speculative philosophical discourse (Mardin 1989, 176–178).[5]

Poetry was a central trait of Muhammadan prophetic discourse and had a primary importance in the subsequent development of Muslim societies. As has been lucidly expressed by the historian of Islamic civilization Marshall Hodgson, poetical language has historically survived in Islamicate societies as "that art which every class could indulge in"—unlike other forms of art that were condemned for requiring a certain "aristocratic taste" (Hodgson 1974, 369). In the Anatolian region, this sphere of intellectual production blended easily with mythology and Islamic religion. Accordingly, Nursi's interest in the more obscure and cryptic Qur'anic verses may conceal his hidden awareness that these passages could have a more direct impact upon ordinary people and could be more effective than speculative discourses in communicating ethical principles. In this sense, one might also think of Nursi as an unconscious heir to the Islamic philosopher Ibn Sina, who first formulated a theory of religion as a sort of philosophy for the masses—a theory which found new interpreters among leading modern European thinkers, such as Spinoza, Vico, and even Gramsci (Salvatore 2007, 146).

Nursi was educated within the Sufi Naqshbandi circles that dominated Turkey's Eastern regions at the time (Mardin 1989, 1991b; Bruinessen 2009; see also Hourani 1981). Reference to the ambiguous verses of the Qur'an (*mutashabihat*) is a common practice in Sufi currents. It is also possible to find such references among the most reformist-oriented Sufis, such as the sixteenth-century Indian scholar Ahmad Sirhindi (1546–1624) whom Nursi quoted often (Friedmann 2008; Weismann 2011). Sufi scholars have generally preferred to emphasize the inner aspects (*batin*) of the Qur'anic message, rather than the outward and more explicit ones (*zahir*). Although Nursi refused to define himself as a Sufi, his focus on those sections of the Qur'an that lack an immediate meaning can be read as the natural outcome of his education. As we will see in detail below, Nursi retained much more from Sufism than he was ready to admit. Indeed, the *Risale* can be seen as a work of synthesis through which he aimed at simplifying the complex meanings of the Qur'an and the Sufi cosmology for the ordinary Muslim (see also Vicini 2017).

---

5 See Salvatore (2007) for a discussion of Vico's idea of *poiesis* and its role in the elaboration of a conception of the common good and the social bond which is alternative to that purported by the modern liberal idea of the social contract. My interpretation of the *Risale*'s discourse as one providing a broad public of ordinary Muslims with an accessible "philosophy of life"—namely with clear ontological and cosmological views—is highly indebted to Salvatore's analysis of this Vichian framework. See LeVine and Salvatore (2009) for a Gramscian analysis of the counter-hegemonic potential of poetic language in Muslim cultures.

Yet, in order to be successful in this endeavor, Nursi needed to simplify complex theological concepts in a way that would be understandable by people who had not taken a course of studies in classical Islamic knowledge. With this goal in mind, Nursi accompanied all 33 sections of the first volume of the *Risale*, the *Sözler* ("The Words"), as well as other parts of the text, with one or more "representative" allegorical stories (*hikaye-i temsiliye*). Narrated in a parabolic form, these stories usually tell of a man who is faced with a dilemma where one solution leads to the certainties of Islam and the other to perdition. Another common plot is that of two men, one of whom is a true believer and the other an atheist. Through their actions, they reveal two opposite attitudes—respectively, faithful and materialistic—toward existence, life, and God, thereby showing the aptness of the former with respect to Islamic truths, wisdom, and knowledge compared to the latter. This is not a novelty as the narration of parabolic stories (*hikaya*) has had important didactic, etiological, or mythic functions in both folk and scholarly Muslim literature.[6] Nursi's reliance on parables and short stories to explain the meaning of key Qur'anic verses is not new: it was employed before by Mevlana Jalaluddin Rumi as well as by other Sufis to simplify complex concepts (Cooper 1999 [1993]). Likewise, Nursi relied on stories to crystallize abstract theological concepts for his readers, such as the concept of God's unity, magnificence, and bounty, without resorting to a refined verbiage.

Another important narrative device present in the *Risale* is the epistolary nature of most of its pieces. This was a longstanding genre in Sufism, especially within Naqshbandi circles in the wake of Ahmad Sirhindi's letters (*Maktubat*). Nursi underwent periods of great hardship during the first thirty years of the newly-founded Republic. He spent many of these years in forced retreat or prison, and attempts were made on his life. For this reason, the *Risale* collection includes a significant number of letters written to his students from the different places in which he was in captivity. Apart from the volume entitled "The Letters" (*Mektubat*)—which is one of the four main books of the *Risale*, along with "The Words" (*Sözler*), "The Flashes" (*Lemalar*), and "The Rays" (*Şualar*)—Nursi's work also includes collections (*lahika*) of letters like *Barla lahikası* and *Kastamonu lahikası*. Epistles are a commonly used genre among the scholars of Islam. What makes Nursi's usage more specific is the affected and emotional tones used in his letters. As Nursi was reporting on the adversity he and his fellow brothers were facing at the time, he never forgot to reassure

---

6 A thin but not always clear distinction of genre can be traced between the *hikaya* and fictional stories (*qissa* in Arabic) according to which the latter were generally more preoccupied with literary effect than with telling truths (Moosa 2005, 71).

and comfort his students about the strength he felt by thinking of them. When my interlocutors read these epistles together, I noticed how the direct style of the letter format conferred a high degree of immediacy and actuality upon Nursi's words. It was as though they entered an imaginary co-presence with the former Nur community, from which they gained strength and conviction in their actions.

The form, syntaxes, and language of the *Risale* cannot be separated from Nursi's main purpose of providing new generations of Muslims with an engaging text that could appeal to their imagination and convey key Islamic messages in a simple and attractive form. As I will show below, the *Risale*'s reliance on a metaphorically dense language that appeals to the human imagination played a role in arousing intellectual engagement in the reader. Before investigating this point further, however, it is important to linger for a moment on the way my interlocutors understood their continuous and repeated engagement with their main text.

2   Iterative Reading

According to common contemporary formulations of reading, once a text is read and its contents assimilated, it is time to move to another piece of writing in order to advance to a successive step along the path of knowledge. On the contrary, my interlocutors cyclically re-read the *Risale* and almost completely ignored other religious texts. While this might be considered one of the results of the glorification of Nursi as a *müceddit*, it is also the outcome of the more basic fact that reading that specific text was pivotal in my interlocutors' path toward the cultivation, achievement, and maintenance of their state of awareness as Muslims. When asked why they cyclically re-read the *Risale*, the first reason my interlocutors generally invoked was the semantic depth of the text. To use their own words, the *Risale* is "a work whose meanings have been hidden within" so that every new reading can open new "windows" and "doors" to the reader's understanding. Interpretations like this one are in line with conventional Qur'anic hermeneutics highlighting how the founding text of Islam hides a multiplicity of meanings which are progressively disclosed at each new reading. The hermeneutical depth of the Qur'an has always been foregrounded by Muslims across time and has been of particular concern within Sufism. The Qur'an calls its own verses and any divine revelation a "sign" (*ayat*), a term that is also non-accidentally employed in the text to refer to the phenomena of the universe (Chittick 2007, 17). The Sufis have been more inclined than Muslim philosophers and theologians to point to this hermeneutical dimension of revelation, as it allowed them to uphold their claim that a more fundamental esoteric level of knowledge existed than the one sought after by the rationalists.

Later I will illustrate in detail that, as suggested by some Qur'anic verses such as 41:53 and 3:190–191, such hermeneutics upholds the practices of meditative reflection of my interlocutors. It suffices to say for the moment that the reality of God, of which the cosmos is but a manifestation, cannot be easily and immediately disclosed to the Muslim practitioner according to a general Sufi epistemology. Disclosure can only take place gradually and progressively, as the disciple advances along the spiritual path, and develops an "openness" to receiving the message of revelation. Similarly, in the view of my interlocutors, the truths of the Qur'an can only be accessed gradually, as they advance in their comprehension of the *Risale*. The *Risale* points to the entirety of concealed truths of revelation through its dense metaphors, but a full comprehension of certain passages—if ever possible—requires the repeated reading of the text over time. According to a story commonly told within the Nur circles, even Said Nursi himself had to re-read his work over 10,000 times in order to fully grasp the meaning of what he had written![7]

This explanation is confirmed by the following statement offered by Furkan, a student who had been residing in the *Suffa* foundation's house in Fatih for the last three years but who also had attended the community's meetings since his adolescence in his village in the Eastern province of Bitlis:

> The truths of faith do not take hold in the spirit (*ruha yerleşmiyor*) by reading the *Risale* just once. The heart cannot fully grasp and absorb them on the first go. It might not even make sense to you the first time you read it. [...] Now, it's impossible to understand the *Kader Risalesi* by reading it just one time. Two times, three times, four, five, maybe by reading it ten times you might finally get it. Because [...] there are solemn meanings of God's names that have been hidden from you behind windows. There are meanings laid out for you behind doors. That is, when you enter within the [deep meanings of the] *Kader Risalesi*, this reveals God's meanings [hidden in His names].

---

7 Although Nursi was certainly considered a new kind of Muslim scholar, part of his biography is still surrounded by a charismatic aura that attributes to him some of the qualities of the saints and the prophets. Accordingly, the Nur brothers believe, as confirmed by Nursi himself in the *Risale*, that when dictating the text to his students he was directly inspired by God and might not have been fully aware of some of the things he stated. That would explain why Nursi had to re-read the text himself over time. Clearly, these sorts of statements are also part of a strategy of sanctification and promotion of the Nur message.

To explain to me how deep the meaning of the *Risale* is, Furkan took the *Risale*'s 26th Word as an example. Also known as the "Treatise on Divine Predestination" (*Kader Risalesi*), this is a particularly complex section where Nursi deals with the problem of theodicy and human will. For the Nur brothers, the whole universe, including the existent world with all its living beings, is but the reflection of God and His 99 names, which are the subject of constant remembrance by Muslims all over the world. In order to provide access to this complex reality, the *Risale* must contain a deliberate degree of complexity, at least in certain passages like the 26th Word. Inasmuch as God's truths are not immediately visible, so the text conceals from its readers some hidden Qur'anic meanings. While this complexity is reduced to a certain point by the use of metaphors and the exemplifying stories mentioned above, further reading is required to fully grasp the meaning of many passages.

All this brings us to the other main reason for the cyclical re-reading of the *Risale*: the semantic complexity of the text should be seen as reflecting the corresponding deep complexity of the esoteric reality it explores. Within Sufism, reality can only be accessed through an all-involving, endless, and disciplined process. Similarly, for members of the *Suffa* and the Gülen communities, reading was part of a gradual pedagogical pattern. As clarified again by Furkan during the same conversation:

> ... But this cannot be reached in one journey [reading] (*sefer*). It only happens when you are continuously engaged in such an effort—that is, in accordance with what you are occupied with in the world. Once this happens, whatever your intention (*niyet*) is, your actions too come into accordance with it. It is really like this.

To Furkan, reading the *Risale* is a formative practice through which they progressively penetrated the secret meanings of revelation. For this to happen, they had to maintain permanent engagement with the text. It was by continuously attuning their thoughts and demeanors to the truths of faith contained in the *Risale* that they could harmonize their view with that of Islamic revelation. In this sense, as further stressed by Furkan, reading the *Risale* was associated with a long and never-ending process of progressive spiritual maturation:

> In order not to commit sins we must continuously renew our faith, we must continuously travel within the world of the *Risale-i Nur*. Because the *Risale* is a work consisting of the Truths of faith, which ripens our faith, and which perfects it.

Furkan's use of the image of an individual who is traveling in a new kind of world where truths are disclosed by means of reading the *Risale* is taken from the seventh Ray (*Şua*) (Nursi 1993a, 123 ff.), an important passage of the collection which is also known as the "Supreme Sign." The section also circulates in the Nur communities as a pamphlet and was often mentioned by my interlocutors in our conversations. In this treatise, Nursi compares the condition of a human being to that of a traveler—a *topos* in Sufi literature—undertaking a journey of the mind through the universe to learn about its creator. Throughout this imaginary trip, the traveler ponders the universe's different realms (first the heavens, then the atmosphere, the winds, the clouds, and the rain, and, finally, the Earth) which testify to the necessary existence and unity of their maker, God. At the same time, the traveler goes through 33 different and progressively higher degrees of faith, thereby passing from the status of "imitative" faith (*taklidi*) to that of "true," certain, and verified faith (*hakiki*)[8] (on this, see also Vahide 2005, 233–237). A brief quotation from this chapter of the *Risale* is useful here:

> Then [the traveler] looks at the rain and sees that within it are contained benefits as numerous as the raindrops, and manifestations of the Most Merciful One as multiple as the particles of rain, and instances of wisdom as plentiful as its atoms. Those sweet, delicate, and blessed drops are, moreover, created in so beautiful and ordered a fashion, that particularly the rain sent in the summertime is dispatched and caused to fall with such balance and regularity that not even stormy winds that cause large objects to collide can destroy its equilibrium and order; the drops do not collide with each other or merge in such fashion as to become harmful masses of water. Water, composed of two simple elements like hydrogen and oxygen, is employed in hundreds of thousands of otherwise, purposeful tasks and arts, particularly in animate beings, although it is itself

---

8 More precisely, Nursi states that these steps would allow "… our belief to advance [*iblağ etmek*] from imitation to realization [*taklitten tahkike*], from realization to knowledge of certainty [*tahkikten ilmelyakin*], from knowledge of certainty to vision of certainty [*ilmelyakinden aynelyakine*], and from vision of certainty to absolute certainty [*aynelyakinden hakkalyakine*]." Such a statement shows once again how, despite the fact that Nursi distinguished his path from that of the Sufis, he still largely drew upon Sufi vocabulary, in this case to explain the degree of knowledge-ascendancy related to the practice of *tefekkür* (see below). *Ilmelyakin* and *aynelyakin* define the two successive levels of religious awareness that can be achieved along the Sufi path and that precede the most elevated and final degree of certitude and final knowledge of God (*hakkalyakin*) which only saints are believed to be able to achieve (Chittick 1989, 166; Schimmel 1994, 141–142).

inanimate and unconscious. Rain, which is then the very embodiment of divine mercy, can only be manufactured in the unseen treasury of mercy of One Most Compassionate and Merciful, and on its descent expounds in physical form the verse: 'And He it is Who sends down rain after men have despaired, and thus spreads out His mercy.'[9]

In this passage, the regularity of rainfall during the summer and its simple chemical composition are both signs that point to the divine origin of its existence. The person reflecting on this is here allegorically represented through the Sufi *topos* of the traveler in search of knowledge. He travels through the world and the universe, and ascends the ladder of knowledge, progressively increasing his awareness as he acknowledges the necessary existence of God behind this world. The *Risale* is "the door" to this sort of hidden esoteric knowledge, and meditative reflection is the way to enter it. In line with this metaphorical account, it is through constantly renewed engagement with the *Risale* that its readers aim to achieve and maintain their Muslim awareness. In this sense, the repeated reading of this religious text is a practice implying a total reconfiguration of one's way of looking at and perceiving worldly reality. For my interlocutors, it was a way of constantly renovating their connection with the *Risale* and with the truths of faith that are revealed within it. Not simply consisting of a mechanical act of repentance, this habit is part of a path of cultivation of their spiritual awareness which is rooted in forms of meditative reflection on the world, nature, and the cosmos that I explore below.

3   Reading as Cultural Practice

As previously mentioned, anthropological scholarship has demonstrated that the diffusion of printing and the rise of literacy rates have had a significant impact on forms of knowledge transmission within the Islamic tradition (see Eickelman 1978, 1992; Messick 1993; Eickelman and Anderson 2003). In partial disagreement with this scholarship, I divert attention from shifting patterns of mediatization brought about by modernization to focus on lines of continuity within Islamic practice with particular emphasis on the intellectual exercises that are generated by the reading of the *Risale*. In this light, I propose an anthropology that approaches reading as a specific modality of relying on a written text which draws upon historically and locally specific forms of intellectual

---

9 This last sentence is taken from Qur'an, 42:28. The entire passage is quoted from Vahide (2005, 234).

engagement, rather than as a neutral practice with a merely technical function. My search for the cultural specificity of my interlocutors' practices of reading the *Risale* was greatly inspired by the work of Brinkley Messick. In a critical reconsideration of his own previous work, in which he presented the Islamic scholarly tradition in Yemen in terms of decisive ruptures and gradual shifts with respect to the past, Messick (1997) later advanced the idea that a more compelling comparison of discursive diversity within non-Western traditions should be undertaken. In his words, this enterprise must look for a new synthesis and hybrid forms of scholarly consumption, rather than be governed by a logic that highlights linear progressive passages from longstanding to modern forms of textual consumption.

Messick's suggestion that transformations in the domain of reading should be explored contextually and by remaining open to possible alternative outcomes came to me as particularly refreshing in terms of questioning the linearity that is implicit in social histories of reading in Europe. However, my analysis differs from the one he suggested in two important respects. The first difference is related to a matter of context. Messick was interested in the interpolation of memory-based and text-based forms of discursive authority within predominantly formal scholarly settings. But in the Nur movement the master and his voice have lost the centrality they had in the past and been replaced by textual consumption within much less institutionalized pedagogical environments. More relevantly, however, my perspective also differs in terms of approach. Messick was mainly concerned with the technical aspects of text consumption: with the different weights that text-supported knowledge and orally-transmitted knowledge had in the specific socio-historically educational settings he considered. In his analysis, he did not look at reading as a practice that could affect faculties other than those of memory or sight. He also failed to consider the possibility that texts could be engaged by means of different kinds of intellectual endeavor.

In contrast, the exploration of the reading practices of the *Risale* reveals a specific way of engaging with texts, which is connected with a distinct form of intellectual practice. My interlocutors associated the reading of the *Risale* with *tefekkür*, a specific kind of meditative exercise grounded on the perceptive capacities of the heart and the related faculty of imagination which is aimed at deciphering God from the observation of natural phenomena. For the exercise to be effective it does not matter whether the reading is conducted individually or in group. Even if the collective reading of the *Risale* is a key community practice, solitary reading was often conducted by students. Some of my interlocutors even suggested that the latter might be preferable as it allowed them to undertake a much greater reflection on the text than when reading was conducted in a group. This might appear as a rather modern understanding of reading intended as an individual practice requiring a focus on a single topic. However, rather than reintroducing this or other similar dichotomies that are generally accepted in social histories of reading—such as individual and collective, reflective and ecstatic, written and oral—I suggest to focus on the cultural and historical specificity of the practice of reading the *Risale* and of the kind of meditative exercise it is expected to engender in the reader.

The central place that *tefekkür* occupies in the reading practices of my interlocutors was well exemplified by a saying of the Prophet Muhammad that they often repeated: "One hour's reflection is better than one year's [voluntary] worship."[10] This *hadith* was often quoted by early Persian Sufis, but is also reported by al-Ghazali in his authoritative work, *The Revival of the Religious Sciences* (*Ihya Ulum al-Din*). In the chapter on meditation (*Kitab al-Tafakkur*), al-Ghazali refers to this prophetic saying to rhetorically indicate the great importance of meditation within Islam (Waley 1999 [1993], 502, see also next section). This *hadith* had particular importance for Nursi, too. He thoroughly explained its meaning in *Hizb al-Nuri*, a 45-page piece he wrote in Arabic, but also in several parts of the *Risale* such as the above-mentioned "Supreme Sign." In the 29th *Lema*, Nursi discusses the *hadith* as a key to interpreting those Qur'anic verses that legitimize reflective thought. This is the same place in which he explains that his decision to embrace *tefekkür* as a key religious technique coincided with the very moment he underwent a personal crisis that marked the passage from the "old" to the "new" Said following the foundation of the Turkish Republic in 1923 (Nursi 1995b, 380 ff.).[11]

It was again Furkan who first drew my attention to the centrality of the practice of *tefekkür*. At the time I had become quite accustomed to the *Suffa* foundation's reading meetings. Yet this sense of acquaintance was accompanied by an uncomfortable feeling. In my view, when commenting upon the *Risale*, the brothers often repeated the same arguments and examples taken from the most disparate aspects of the natural world. These examples included concepts such as a man's memory being contained in a gland (the hippocampus) as big as a nut, the thickness of the atmosphere compared to its fundamental role in protecting the Earth from the rays of the sun, or the vastness of the universe. By accurately describing these phenomena, including related biological

---

10 Voluntary (*nafile*) worship is practiced in addition to obligatory prescriptions by more devout Muslims.
11 The Qur'anic verses Nursi considers in this chapter of the *Risale* are: "That you may consider" (2:219, 2:226); "Perchance they may reflect" (7:176); "Do they not reflect in their own minds, did God create the heavens and the Earth?" (30:8); "There are signs for those who consider" (13:3). These are quoted in Nursi (1995b, 380).

and physical measurements, the brothers wanted to emphasize the slender mechanisms that regulate the natural world and highlight them as evidence marking the necessary existence of God. This was also a way for them to counter materialist philosophies by relying on arguments similar to theirs taken from scientific discourse. In their eyes, the coordinate and precise—actually perfect—functioning of the complex mechanisms of nature that is well illustrated by scientific descriptions is the most immediate proof that God exists.

Returning from a reading one evening, I confessed to Furkan that I found the arguments of the lessons quite repetitive. Furkan started by clarifying that the repetition of some examples was part of the precise rhetoric of the *Risale*, which aims to explain faith through concrete and easily observable examples:

> Generally, we abstain from using abstract expressions when explaining faith. This was *üstad*'s [Said Nursi] strategy. *Üstad* explained all things starting from the concrete. Why should we use abstract ways of explaining things when we have concrete ones? This is how we think. [...] When do you understand something best? ... When your eye can see that thing. [...] It is always from season-change, flowers, nature, etc., that examples are given in the readings. It is so because these are all things that are before the eye. I mean, you can see them. [...] The trees' leaves fall in autumn and they grow again in springtime. [...] It comes as a very normal fact. But if you think about the wisdom (*hikmet*) these changes conceal ... [you understand that God is behind them].

The alternation of the seasons and the revival of nature every spring which Furkan referred to was another of the most recurrent examples used as unshakable proof of God's power and magnificence in the reading meetings. Similar examples from nature were seen as the simplest way to represent and describe God to a public of ordinary Muslims. Such images were particularly effective for people coming from the Anatolian hinterlands, or their sons and nephews, as these people still felt nostalgia for these landscapes which they continued to associate with ideals of purity, peace, and simplicity.[12]

As I failed to understand the point of repeating these kinds of examples at every meeting, I told Furkan that I found this strategy somewhat redundant and that I would have expected that their readings would be associated with

---

12   See Hermansen (2007) on the preference for natural symbols in the narratives of the Gülen community. As the author notes, the name of the community's main magazine, *Sızıntı* (leak), is also indicative of this preference.

some other kind of speculative or theoretical consideration. In response, Furkan made the following statement:

> *Abi*, think a little. Night has come. How has night come? Wow! From the morning the sky has darkened. It is a very basic occurrence, a monotonous one. It is like this. Since it has always been like this, it seems ordinary to us. But think a little brother, reflect a little (*bir tefekkür et*) ... Have you understood now why I gave you this concrete example? [...] What do we say? We say: "*Abi* take this apple and reflect (*tefekkür*) a bit on it." Look at the apple-tree, that in springtime its apples come out, that in autumn the leaves fall, that after all this every spring they come back to life again, that there is an entity (*Zat*) bringing them back to life, that this entity is God, that the One ruling all the universe is Him, that [...] He has created us from nothingness...

As was finally clarified to me by Furkan, the repetition of analogous examples at their reading meetings was motivated by the need to instill and maintain a new disposition in the participants when reflecting on nature—a disposition that differs from that of secular readings of natural phenomena diffused in schools and through the media. My interlocutors were not engaged in an inferential exercise when they pointed to examples drawn from the natural world as evidence of God's existence. They were not expected to draw a set of logical consequences from the empirical observation of natural facts, and from the latter to reconstruct a chain of ontologically disembodied series of reasons and mechanisms that would explain their functioning, like in modern scientific thought. Rather, they engaged in an inductive exercise based on the thoughtful observance of natural phenomena from which they concluded that God must exist, given the pre-ordered and perfect functioning of existence.

The whole edifice of modernity since the Enlightenment has been based on the idea that God must be definitively separate from the worldly domain. By acquiring a full awareness of their rational faculties, humans were now able to rule their societies by relying solely on themselves, without any transcendent assistance. As observed by a tradition of inquiry in the sociology of religion going back to Max Weber, the same idea of modernization is grounded upon "disenchantment"—namely, humans' final realization that extra-worldly forces do not intervene in the world and should not be taken into consideration by modern people (Weber 2005 [1930]). Boosted by modern scientific discourse, this disenchanted view of nature as an autonomous machine has profoundly affected people's perception of the world around them. Today, people at all latitudes tend to look at natural phenomena as normal and observe them in a very detached and objectifying manner. As a result, the passing of the daytime into the darkness of the night and the descent of the sun and rising of the stars to which Furkan refers are commonly accepted by people as being routine and hence not worthy of consideration.

Subverting this perspective, my interlocutors pointed to the miraculous character of these simple and regular phenomena and practiced reflection upon nature to cultivate a view of worldly reality as a manifestation of the deeper and truer reality of God. As observed by Abdel Rahman (2003, 203), a sense of the wondrous and miraculous with respect to the most common natural facts is the basis of the kind of awareness that the Nur brothers aim to attain through the repeated reading of the *Risale*. This is exactly what my interlocutors were doing in their readings: using scientific descriptions of the mechanisms that regulate the natural world to highlight the perfection, and hence "miraculous" and supernatural character of the universe and its functioning. Rather than being the expression of a "backward" way of looking at nature, as a modernist view would suggest, this childlike kind of amazement toward natural phenomena is intended to be a complete reversal of the modern scientific view. It reflects a call for a re-enchantment of people's gaze with respect to existence.

Attention to the miraculous and wondrous aspects of nature is certainly not a novelty of these communities, or of Islam in general. From Late Antiquity to before the Enlightenment, a long-lived cohort of European theologians and philosophers have looked at wonderment as a main object of investigation. Even Christian clerics such as St. Augustine relied on the symbolic use of wonders to interpret the holy scriptures, or as repositories of moral lessons and testimonies to the omnipotence of God (Daston and Park 1998, 39–48). On the other hand, popular cosmographical works by Muslim scholars such as the *Kharidat al-Aja'ib wa Faridat al-Ghara'ib*—which was translated in Ottoman language by Mahmud al-Hatib in 1562–63—incorporated a great deal of material on the wondrous and strange aspects of existence, as well as related themes such as the perfection of the cosmic order and the wisdom and justice of God (Coşkun 2011). It is within Sufism, however, that the attention for the wondrous as a reflection of God's power and majesty acquired a systemized form and was turned into specific meditative practices. In this tradition, speculation over the wondrous is coupled with a thorough reflection on existence, the cosmos, and the place of humanity within it. The way in which the exercise of *tefekkür* is rooted in a longstanding Sufi tradition of the region, and how Nursi re-elaborated the latter in response to modern epistemology, is the subject of the following two sections.

4 Genealogies of Reflection

The term *tefekkür* (*tafakkur* in Arabic) comes from the Arabic root *f-k-r* (also referred to as *fikr*), literally meaning "to think." In Islam it generally refers to the intellectual faculty of thought or of reflecting upon an object (Gardet 2011a). Encompassing a broad field of intellectually-based speculative practices within Islamic philosophy, *tafakkur* has also traditionally been practiced within Sufism. Beginning with the inception of this tradition during the early Persian Sufi period, the term has been utilized for a specific kind of meditative practice (Waley 1999 [1993]). As I will illustrate in a moment, many scholars of Islam have been suspicious of the perils of the excessive intellectualism centered on *fikr*, and have for this reason suggested to take a cautious approach to using the intellect for heuristic purposes. However, *fikr* has never been interpreted as being entirely severed from other forms of meditative practice, including the more commonly known Sufi practice of *dhikr* (in Turkish, *zikr*) (remembrance or invocation of God) (Ibid.; cf. Netton 2000 for contemporary uses of the term). The two terms have often appeared together in some important Qur'anic passages, like the aforementioned 3:190–1 and 45:13, but also in 16:44, which suggests that both *fikr* and *dhikr* are similar and reliable methods for contemplating God by looking into the signs He has left throughout the cosmos.

One of the most detailed expositions of *tafakkur* is found in the previously mentioned "Chapter on meditation" (*Kitab al-Tafakkur*) contained in al-Ghazali's *Ihya Ulum al-Din* (Waley 1999 [1993], 542–544). In this section, al-Ghazali distinguishes *tafakkur* from ordinary thinking. Whereas the latter is a purely logical kind of exercise merely aimed at drawing cause-effect relations from the observation of natural phenomena, *tafakkur* consists of the application of reflection on human qualities and actions or on God's creation. For al-Ghazali, the way the divine attributes of God become refracted across the cosmos (from the universe to human soul) provides a particularly fertile ground for *tafakkur*. Indeed, he held meditative reflection in very high regard, to the extent that he argued that *tafakkur* could be of a potentially greater benefit than *dhikr* with regards to how Muslims could firmly root the faith in their heart. However, al-Ghazali was also troubled by the potential for deception of this technique. In particular, he strictly warned against the reliance on *tafakkur* when it comes to the innermost essence of God. Reflection on this matter had already been forbidden by the Prophet Muhammad himself, who had clarified that the capacity of the human mind is too limited to be able to grasp God's essence. For this reason, reflection on the essence of God has been considered sinful in Islam, leading to either heresy or madness (Schimmel 1994, 220).

Another Sufi scholar, Shaykh Ahmad-i Jam (d. 1141–2), praised *fikr* as one of the main Sufi techniques, while noting some limitations. He thought that reflection was only appropriate for those who were in an advanced stage of the spiritual path and had already "lived in the spiritual realm" (*alam-i batin*), whereas, for novices who were still in the "material realm" (*alam-i arkan*), invocation (*dhikr*) was considered preferable to *fikr*. In his view, *dhikr* was an essential and preliminary exercise that served to "soften" the heart and "illuminate its eye" in preparation for *fikr*. Only once the Sufi practitioner had achieved a sufficient "knowledge of the heart" would he be ready for meditative reflection (Waley 1999 [1993], 545–546). The great Sufi scholar Muhammad Ibn Arabi (1165–1240), for his part, had a more negative opinion about *fikr*, claiming that it brought the risk of a drift toward rationalism. In his opinion, this was the typical error of the Muslim peripatetic philosophers who not only attempted the impossible and intellectually deviating task of grasping the essence of God, but also thought that religious knowledge could be achieved by means of abstraction rather than through what he considered to be the key heuristic faculty of imagination. For this reason, Ibn Arabi generally looked coolly on reflection and suggested that it be used with much caution, and only applied to those Qur'anic verses that refer to it explicitly (Chittick 1989, 62; Zamboni 2005; see also Gardet 2011a).

From this brief excursus, it emerges that while medieval Muslim scholars recognized the importance of reflection in the heuristic path, they also generally agreed upon the fact that an excessive reliance on reflection could be misleading. Paradoxically, for the same reasons that *fikr* raised these concerns, centuries later Said Nursi praised *tefekkür* and distinguished it from *dhikr* in more radical terms than these same scholars would have done (Nursi 1995b, 217). In this, Nursi was almost certainly influenced by the conditions of his times, when the Sufis were under attack by both reformist scholars and modern nationalist discourse (Ewing 1997; Sirriyeh 1999; Bruinessen 2009). Said Nursi's intellectual genealogy is indeed a complex one. On the one hand, his vision of Islam was largely influenced by the Sufi ontology and worldview he had assimilated as a young boy in local Naqshbandi circles of Eastern Anatolia. On the other, by only partly reflecting the views of Muslim modernist intellectuals such as Jamal al-Din al-Afghani (1838–1897) and Rashid Rida (1865–1935) who stigmatized Sufi views as backward (Malik 2018), Nursi thought that Sufism was behind the time. In this regard, the more immediate semantic resonance of *tefekkür* with a modern epistemology highlighting reasoning over more esoteric practices such as *dhikr* made it more fit for the times. Accordingly, Nursi opted for establishing the *Risale*'s path on this kind of meditative practice.

However, Nursi's preference for a vocabulary that better matched modern epistemologies does not prevent us from looking at intellectual meditation within the Nur tradition for what it is, namely a technique aimed at the contemplation of God's all-comprehensive Wisdom (Kuşpınar 1996). Although Nursi's emphasis on the intellectual dimension of meditation was the reflection of preoccupations similar to those of modernist Muslim scholars, the practice of *tefekkür* draws abundantly upon Ibn Arabi's cosmology; much more than Nursi would admit. For precisely the reasons raised by medieval Muslim scholars, Nursi warned his followers that an excessive reliance on rational faculties would be misleading, causing them to adopt a materialist view of nature as disembodied from God's majesty. Similar to mainstream Islamic and Sufi understandings of speculative exercise, the use of intellectual rational faculties in the Nur eidetic framework always had to be mediated by the heart. The heart is the center of the soul (*ruh*) and of any human attempt to communicate with transcendence. Discourses about the heart as the locus of spiritual life and as the most effective possible link with the transcendent reality of God were an ever present and recurrent theme within both the *Suffa* and the Gülen communities. Take, as an example, the following passage from a reading delivered by Ferhat on the importance of reading the *Risale-i Nur*:

> We have to strengthen our inner world (*hususi dünyamız*), to radiate out the lights of Truth at an angelical degree. At that point, earthly things do not matter and therefore cannot harm the human heart. [...] Once Sungur *abi*[13] said the following: 'Night invocations (*evrad*) give strength and power to the heart.' On that occasion I understood [...] that to be occupied with elevated-spiritual (*nurani*) things gives strength to one's heart. Our master [Said Nursi] says: '[...] Do not drown in nothingness (*bir şeyle batma*)... Don't get caught up in small things.' That is to say, if you do not give strength and power to your heart, it will be suffocated. Your senses are overwhelmed, [they] break down... Why? Because the heart is not strong. Why? Because the necessary precautions have not been taken, because my heart has not been filled up with the truths of faith.

The importance of the heart as the center of Islamic faith, human life, intelligence, and intentions is acknowledged by the Qur'an and is supported by many *hadith*s, such as "Faith is a light that God casts into the heart of whomsoever He will" (Chittick 2007, 6). Within Sufism especially, the heart has traditionally

---

13   A renowned Nur brother and, formerly, Said Nursi's student.

been imagined as the depository of human intellectual faculties and perceptive capacity to grasp things "instinctively"—that is, even before the mind is able to articulate conscious thought. The achievement of the particular state of Sufi ascension and spiritual closeness to God, which the Sufis aimed to achieve beginning with their emergence in eighth-century Baghdad, has depended on the heart as the center of people's spiritual life and striving for self-perfection (Schimmel 2011 [1975]; Karamustafa 2007; Green 2012).

Relatedly, according to Ibn Arabi, the heart was the epicenter of the faculty of imagination (*khayal*): the most important and powerful of the human soul's faculties, together with reason and the senses. In Ibn Arabi's micro-cosmology of the human self, *khayal* lies beside reason and the senses and is capable of combining these two faculties in ways that allow human beings to perceive that the reality they see is but a veil hiding the manifestation of the Truth of God. According to him, it is by means of imagination that human beings can navigate through the only apparent contradictions between existence, death, and revelation to grasp the true meaning lying behind reality. The prominent medieval Sufi scholar had elaborated his theory in an open polemic aimed at the rationalist Muslim theologians, who tended to dismiss imagination as corrupting and misleading. He argued that *khayal* was at the core of any heuristic attempt to comprehend the micro-cosmology of the self as well as the broader macro-cosmology that is made of the different layers of existence (Chittick 1989, 115–123). Later, I will sketch out how this and the Nur cosmologies overlap in important ways. For the moment, it suffices to say that Ibn Arabi saw the heart as the locus of imagination and knowledge rather than of sentiments and feelings. Contrary to post-Enlightenment Manichean distinctions between mind and body, he endowed the heart with a tremendous heuristic capacity that sits on its direct connection with God.

Similarly, within the Nur eidetic framework, the heart is the organ that is endowed with the intuitive and immediate capacities necessary to grasp the reality of existence before any process of rational abstraction of this reality can take place. In line with the Sufi tradition, the heart is seen as the center of the manifestation of the realities of the universe (Kuşpınar 1996), the organ designated to deflect human intellectual efforts away from mundane reality and redirect them toward transcendence. If my interlocutors sought to feel God's presence through meditative reflection on existence, they would only achieve this through the intuitive capacity of this organ. It is by means of the heart's perceptive faculties that, when practicing *tefekkür*, the Nur brothers were able to exceed mere formal intellectual speculation over the constituent parts of the universe and penetrate the underlying meanings and "signs" that they stay for. Only in this way could they acquire the kind of religious awareness they aimed for.

5   Toward a Sufi Cosmology

Another way of approaching an understanding of *tefekkür* in the Nur tradition is to look at the cosmological framework that upholds this practice and the way such framework relates to transcendence. In order to introduce this aspect, look at the following excerpt taken from "The Words" (*Sözler*), the 24th Window of the 33rd Word, and at the comment made by Ferhat *abi* as he was addressing a group of university students living in the house in Fatih. This chapter of the *Risale* consists of Nursi's comment on the Qur'anic verse: "There is no God but He, everything will perish save His countenance, His is the command and to Him shall you return" [28:88] (Nursi 1993b, 708):

> [*Text:*] Both with their existences do living beings point to the existence of a Necessarily Existent One, and with their deaths do those living beings testify to the eternity and unity of an Ever-Living Eternal One. For example, the face of the Earth, which is a single living creature, points to its Maker with its order and circumstances; so too it points to Him when it dies. That is, when winter conceals the Earth's face with its white shroud, it turns the gazes of men away from itself—their gaze moves to the past behind the corpse of that departing spring—and it shows them a far wider scene.
> [*Ferhat* abi:] Now, for example, spring has come. Construction projects are beginning. Billions of plants are being made to flourish. With the seeds from which the roots rise, with things, with atoms, what happens? His Excellency the Just [God (*Cenabı Hakk*)] has set springtime. Then, the spring dies. Immediately, where does the gaze shift to? It goes 'to the past behind the corpse' [conditions or events of the past (*maziye*)]. [...] How many times has springtime come? It has been spring one thousand times! And a thousand times the spring has died... [...] Every year this domain is broken down. Then it is made anew. [*Now reading from the text*] 'Their gaze moves to the past behind the corpse of that departing spring—and it shows them a far wider scene.' What is this scene? [*Quoting from the following portion of the text*] 'That is to say, all the past springs of the Earth, which were all miracles of power, inform them that new living springtime creatures of the Earth will come...'

Ferhat's words offer a vivid account of human life and death through the image of the cyclical blossoming of nature at spring and its withering with the coming of winter, a recurrent trope in the *Suffa* meetings. During the readings, the ephemeral and transitory character of worldly life was constantly reiterated and compared to the endless existence of God. By reference to these metaphoric examples, the attendants inferred the necessary existence of God behind the universe. The reiterated character of all these natural events is what conferred force, reliability, and consistency to the argument of the Nur brothers. In their view, it was the expression of the fact that all natural processes visible to the human eye are only temporary manifestations of another greater underlying principle. Once one realizes that these manifestations are but fluctuations of the permanent existence of the only Existing One, their material consistency dissolves.

Notwithstanding the fact that Said Nursi distanced himself from Sufism, this representation of nature as the most evident and immediate expression of a cosmos in which God becomes manifest to human beings through the multiple and diversified expression of His attributes is highly indebted to a Sufi cosmology as formulated in its most exhaustive form by Ibn Arabi. One of the most intricate philosophical problems in the Islamic tradition has been reconciling the key principle and pillar of faith concerning the indivisible oneness of God (*tawhid*) with the idea that everything that exists originates *from* God. In his account of Ibn Arabi's *magnum opus The Meccan Illuminations (Al-Futuhat al-Makkiyya)*, William Chittick (1989, 1998) illustrates how the Muslim medieval scholar achieved this synthesis by outlining a complex cosmological framework within which the only true and absolute existence of God (*wujud*) is manifested and reflected in the world but only in imperfect and partial forms. For Ibn Arabi, only God and nothing else fully exists as such by Himself. Any other entity in the cosmos, including life on Earth, is at best a "dim reflection" of God's attributes or names (Chittick 1989, 8–9).

A general principle of relativity rules this cosmology, according to which every existent being is part of a hierarchical order (*maratib al-wujud*) in which its position depends on the distance from divine presence. The closer this being is to God, the more it will be a good, though imperfect, approximation of the combination of God's attributes that it reflects. For the sake of simplicity, Ibn Arabi's cosmology can be rendered here in stylized form as being subdivided into three main realms. The world of light is the highest realm. This is where God expresses Himself for what He is. However, the fact that God is revealed in His essence makes it impossible for anybody apart from God Himself to attain this realm. In agreement with the Islamic philosophical assumptions sketched above, nobody can know the essence of God apart from Himself. The effulgent light of God that is found at this level is only vaguely reflected in the lowest and third level: the corporeal world of human existence. Between these two levels, there is another one, the isthmus (*barzakh*) realm of the world of images (*al-alam al-mithal*). Here, God's attributes are manifested in an archetypical form in such a way that they are known unto God, although they are still non-existent in themselves. In his famous account of Ibn Arabi's cosmology, Henri Corbin (1998 [1969]) has named this realm *mundus imaginalis*: namely, the intermediate realm of existence that is not immediately accessible to man and in which other entities exist, such as the angels and other non-physical yet sensory phenomena. According to Ibn Arabi, the *barzakh* is where God's theophany self-discloses itself in its clearest form to humans through the soul. Those aiming to achieve this level can only do so by relying on the faculty of imagination (*khayal*), which I have introduced above.

Ibn Arabi's cosmological framework has often been associated with the theory of the unity of existence (*wahdat al-wujud*)—a simplified interpretation of his work that was upheld by his adversaries to discredit his views. Yet scholars have lately agreed that the theory of *wahdat al-wujud* has not only been frequently misunderstood by his opponents, but also that it was not as central to Ibn Arabi's thinking as it has been portrayed (see Hodgson 1970; Chittick 2011). Yet from an "orthodox" theoretical perspective like that of the medieval Hanbali scholar Ibn Taymiyyah, Ibn Arabi's theory was seen as a form of pantheism which represented a serious threat to the key Islamic principle of *tawhid*. Along similar lines, Nursi has also criticized both this theory and the "unity of witness" (*wahdat ash-shuhud*).[14] Consider this passage from the *Risale*'s *Letters*:

> Yes, the great highway is the highway of the companions [*sahabe*], those that followed them [*tabiin*], and the Purified Ones [*asfiya*]. Their universal rule is, 'The reality of things is constant.' [For every being there is one certain reality/truth (*Varlıkların sabit birer hakikati vardır*).] And in accordance with the sense of 'There is nothing that resembles Him' [Qur'an, 42:11], Almighty God has absolutely nothing that resembles Him. He is utterly beyond being comprehended in place or class and being divided

---

14 This was a variant and corrective of *wahdat al-wujud* that had been more convincingly advanced by the Naqshbandi Indian reformer Ahmad Sirhindi (1564–1624). According to this formulation, the idea of God's association with existence should be ascribed more to human "witnessing" (*shuhud*) than to a real identification of God with nature, namely as something that occurs principally in the human imagination rather than in the real world (Chittick 2011). However, as stressed by successive scholarship, there is no clear opposition between the two theories and Sirhindi's views are meant to actually validate Ibn Arabi's theory (Weismann 2007, 59).

into parts. His relation with beings is Creativity [the divine power of creation (*Halıkıyet*)]. Beings are not imaginings [*hayalat*] or fancies [*evham*] as those who follow the way of the Unity of Existence said. Visible things too are Almighty God's works. Everything is not 'Him,' everything is 'from Him.' For events cannot be pre-eternal.[15]

The position of Nursi on these early debates must be read in light of the intellectual challenges posed by positive philosophy, empiricism, and materialism during his time. In this regard, the main point for him was to clearly and plainly state that worldly reality is an empirically tangible and "real" reality, not a fantasy. As has also been argued by Turner (2013), Nursi's critique of Ibn Arabi was very much the result of the context in which he operated, rather than being a real rejection of his intellectual construct. As noted above, defending Ibn Arabi at a time when materialism was on the upswing and the Sufis were being ostracized within mainstream political discourse was a risk for the Nur movement. Second, as Nursi's declared mission was to define a path for the ordinary Muslim rather than for the refined practitioners of Islamic tradition, the metaphysical elaborations of Ibn Arabi and others did not fit with such a project. As Nursi stated elsewhere about Ibn Arabi's way:

> For the highest of the elite, who pass beyond the sphere of causes and, renouncing everything other than God, sever their attachment to contingent beings and enter a state of complete absorption in God, this way is a righteous way. But to present it in terms of intellectual knowledge to those who are submerged in causes, are enamoured of the world, and are plunged into materialist philosophy and nature, is to drown them in nature and materiality and distance them from the reality of Islam.[16]

However, it is easy to see that Nursi not only often praised Ibn Arabi as a great scholar of Islam and a genius, but also that he relied on many central concepts of his cosmology (Turner 2013, 76–81). As evidenced in the passage above, Nursi refused both the ideas of "unity" and "witnessing," and instead suggested that the relationship between God and the natural world would be better thought of in terms of the divine power of creating (*Halıkıyet*). Interestingly, Nursi was taking this same idea from Ibn Arabi's re-elaboration of the Neoplatonic concept of emanation (Mardin 1989, 207–216).[17] In this vein, Nursi's appraisal

---

15 Nursi 1997, 104.
16 Nursi 1997, 514; also quoted in Turner 2013, 81.
17 Neoplatonism (as Greek philosophy in general) has significantly influenced the evolution of Islamic tradition since its inception. Even Ibn Arabi had internalized some of its

of nature as the expression of God's power, majesty, and creativity reflects a view of the cosmos that is highly indebted to the Andalusian Sufi scholar. Nursi only reproduced it in simpler terms, making it more immediately understandable to the ordinary believer. With this goal in mind, he relied on a more straightforward two-tier cosmological system resembling the one elaborated by al-Ghazali. Instead of establishing a representation of the cosmos on three levels like Ibn Arabi did, al-Ghazali had opted for distinguishing between the two more basic Qur'anic modes of existence represented by the visible world (*al-shahada*) and the hidden world of the unseen (*al-ghayb*) (Turner 2013, 89–90). Following this path, Nursi proposed a more immediate representation of the relationship between human existence and God, between the visible and the invisible worlds. In order to create a link between these two realms, he recurred to metaphors and to a modernist jargon which were more intuitively accessible for the ordinary Muslims whom he intended to address. The metaphor of God as an artist and of creation as His work of art is one of the most effective he used to express this cosmology in immediate and simple terms. The emphasis on God's "creativity" (*Halıkıyet*) indeed reflects a more tangible view than the ideas of "unity of existence" and "unity of witness," providing the ordinary Muslim with an immediate aesthetic concept of God's participation in existence.

Even in this simplified configuration, however, the representation of nature as a continuously functioning miracle and as a theophany of God persists in ways that are very similar to Ibn Arabi. In the Nur eidetic framework, God's powerfulness, majesty, and magnanimity are continuously expressed at every moment by the most basic natural phenomena, as well as by human existence. The "far wider scene" that was mentioned by Ferhat in the opening passage of this section, and from which my interlocutors were supposed to approach their view of existence, can only be seen if one has achieved awareness of this cosmic order and understood the philosophies of life and death that are derived from it. From this perspective, worldly life appears temporally limited, a blink of an eye, when compared to the unfolding mechanisms of the universe. Accordingly, human life must be approached as such: as being part of a wider cosmological order and as being subject to the same laws and conditions of this order, including its ultimate perishing.

---

vocabulary and conceptual frameworks. Yet he has at the same time refuted the interpretation that the philosophers gave of the principle of "emanation." In this regard, Ibn Arabi noticed that for them God's participation in existence was limited to His original act of creation only, and that they did not contemplate God's actual presence in "reality." Instead, he argued that God was not only the Creator of the universe, but also that the world is a constant shadow of His attributes (see Corbin 1993).

6   Reflecting on Death

Since death is related to ideas of judgment and one's destiny in the afterlife, it has always been an issue of ethical concern and theological relevance in Muslim traditions. Following the terrorist attacks of 11 September 2001, the media in the US and Europe have generally presented death in Muslim cultures in relation to acts of martyrdom by Islamic terrorists. Posthumously-released video fragments of jihadists willing to die for the cause of a global "holy war" or videotapes showing terrorist leaders declaring armed struggle against "evil America" are regularly broadcast on Western media, perpetuating the idea that Islam is indissolubly linked with faith, irrationality, violence, and death. By reproducing recurrent biases, these stereotypical portraits prevent us from approaching Islam as a complex and rich tradition dealing with death in the same way as Christianity, Judaism, ancient Greek, Roman, and other religious traditions (MacIntyre 1988, 1991; Hadot 1995).

In his analysis of Muslim homiletics of the Islamic revival in Egypt, Charles Hirschkind (2006) has contended that ideas of death in the Islamic tradition can be better understood if they are thought of as being related to Islamic pedagogical processes that aim to cultivate certain key Islamic dispositions, sensibilities, and feelings, such as sadness and fear. He has shown that the embodiment of these culturally specific dispositions is not only part of the Muslim understanding of death but is also instrumental in providing Muslims with an ethical orientation and a commitment to Islamic conduct. In Hirschkind's words, the remembrance and "tasting" of death is used by Egyptian Muslim preachers "to portray death in its manifold dimensions and ramifications with a vividness and moral depth so as to root it in their sensory experience, to constitute it as a habit of thought, heart, and body" (Ibid., 176). What from a secular modern perspective are generally considered to be negative emotions such as sadness and fear are integral to the process by which Muslims come to inhabit a particular kind of religious life.

Fear of divine judgment was also recalled in many of the meetings I attended within both the *Suffa* and the Gülen communities, especially through the image of *Kiramen Kitabin* (in Arabic *Kiraman Katibin*, "honorable scribes"): the two angels that, according to Islamic teachings, sit on everybody's right and left shoulders, recording people's good and bad deeds, which will then be revealed and weighed on the Day of Judgment (Qur'an 50:16–23, 82:10–12). These and other frightening images often accompanied detailed descriptions of God's steadfastness in punishing the sinful and rewarding the rightful on the Day of Judgment, disincentivizing sinful actions. They were also part of a general eschatological understanding of this worldly life as an examination (*imtihan*) to which God has subjected human beings in order to test their integrity, faith, and obedience, which will be judged in the afterlife. While the cultivation of fear can be included as one of the dimensions of the Nur thanatology, another more harmonious representation of death was prevalent in the view of my interlocutors. Contemplation of death has always been one of the most effective practices within the Sufi path, in particular within the Naqshbandi order in which Nursi had been educated himself (Kuşpınar 2010). In line with this tradition, rather than the harbinger of divine judgment, death was perceived as a mark of the transitory nature of existence and of the passage to a better, more peaceful, and infinite life. Accordingly, death has not generally been seen as something to fear, but to be welcomed with joy and relief. In this light, an overemphasis on the fear of the grave and of the fires of hell would prevent us from understanding how my interlocutors looked at their existence and their death as part of the Sufi cosmology that I have sketched above. In the *Suffa* and the Gülen communities, human life and death were inserted in a cycle of life-seasons which fit with the representation of nature as the reflection of God's creativity in existence, and of humans as an integral part of this cosmology, that is sketched in the *Risale*.

In a passage of the 21st *Lema*—the section of the text that I have previously discussed in relation to the idea of purity and sincerity of faith in brotherhood—Nursi openly explained to his followers how they should reflect on death in ways that are different from the Sufis' "contemplation of death" (*rabıta-i mevt*). The passage is contained in the fourth and final rule that the Nur brothers should follow in order to attain the key virtue of *ihlas*. It is here worth quoting the whole extract:

> O my companions in the service of the Qur'an! One of the most effective means of attaining and preserving sincerity [*ihlas*] is 'contemplation of death' [*rabıta-i mevt*]. [...] Yes, through the instruction the Sufis and people of truth [*ehl-i tarikat ve ehl-i hakikat*] received from verses of the All-Wise Qur'an like, 'Every soul [lower self (*nefs*)] shall taste death' [3:185] and 'Truly you will die, and truly they will die' [39:30, 10], they made the contemplation of death fundamental to their spiritual journeyings, and dispelled the illusion of eternity, the source of worldly ambition. They imagined [*tahayyül*] and conceived [*tasavvur*] of themselves as dead and being placed in the grave. Through prolonged thought the evil-commanding soul [*nefs-i emmare*] becomes saddened and affected by such imagining and to an extent gives up its far-reaching ambitions and hopes. There are numerous advantages in this contemplation. [...] However, since our way is not the Sufi path [*tarikat*] but [perhaps] the way of

reality [*hakikat*], we are not compelled to perform this contemplation in an imaginary and hypothetical form like the Sufis. [...] Our way is not to bring the future to the present by thinking of the end, but [perhaps] to go in [through] the mind [*fikren gitmek*] to the future from the present in respect of reality, and to gaze [*nazaran bakmak*] at it. Yes, having no need of imagination or conception, one may look on one's own corpse, the single fruit on the tree of this brief life. In this way, one may look on one's own death, and if one goes a bit further, one can see [testify (*müşahede*)] the death of this century, and going further still, observe the death of this world, opening up the way to complete sincerity.[18]

In this passage, Nursi establishes a clear distinction between what he defines as the Sufi practice of *rabıta-i mevt*, which to him is based on an "imaginary and hypothetical form," and the exercise of *tefekkür*. As is also revealed by the meaning of *rabıta* as "tie" (*bağ*), "interest" (*ilgi*), and "connection" (*irtibat*) (Yeğin 2005), Nursi understands the technique of imagining (*tahayyül*) and conceiving (*tasavvur*) of oneself as a dead body, and the cultivation of the correspondent emotion of sadness, as being related to the act of creating only an imaginary connection with death. As indicated in the *hadith* that he quotes, this is an exercise of prolonged thought that he interprets as being a form of *dhikr* and that, for this reason, he sees as separate from the path he upholds.[19]

Nursi suggests that his followers should think of death not through an approach based on imagining themselves as lying in the grave, but through reflection, intended as imagination in the sense proposed by Ibn Arabi—namely, by thinking of one's death in relation to the alternation of life and death that also regulates the cosmos. In the passage, *tefekkür* is indicated by using the two verbal forms "going through the mind" (*fikren gitmek*) and to "gaze" (*nazaran bakmak*), both of which imply the idea of acquiring a different sight or gaze (*nazar*) with regard to existence. As Nursi explains, such a method must involve thinking of one's own corpse as the littlest fruit of the tree of life—that is to say, as a tiny point in relation to the wholeness of the cosmos—thus opening up a path to conceiving of its relativity and transitoriness compared to the greater design of God. The "way of reality" that Nursi mentions can be undertaken by reflecting on the fact that the death of a single human being is only a small link

---

18 Nursi 1995b, 217.
19 Notice that, according to Silverstein (2011), meditations about death and other forms of *tarbıta* are still practiced in contemporary Naqshbandi circles in Turkey. However, even in the Sufi brotherhood he studied, these practices have been surpassed in importance by those of a "conversation" on Islamic matters (*sohbet*).

in a much greater chain. If one acquires such a view of life, death, the past, and the future, then all existence is seen from a Godly-illuminated perspective as taking place in an entirely unique moment. Within this framework, death represents the point of connection between this world and the other-worldly reality of God.

To better elucidate this point, consider the following extract, taken from a collective analytic reading (*mütalaa*) of the *Risale*'s seventh *Word* during a student summer camp organized by the *Suffa* foundation in a small village in the province of Manisa. In this passage, Nursi explains the significance of the Islamic core tenets expressed in the sentence "I believe in God and the Last Day" by making recourse to a metaphorical story. The story describes a wounded soldier in a field who is in a desperate condition since he is caught between the gallows in front of him and a lion waiting to attack him from behind. The soldier finds a possible helping hand in "a kindly person shining with light like Khidr"[20] who appears and provides him with medicine and two talismans he might use to turn the two unsettling visions of the gallows and the lion into a "swing for pleasure and enjoyment" and a "docile horse." Ferhat *abi* started the lesson by making the following statement:

> Yes, through the second sacred talisman, death takes on the form of a mastered horse, a steed to take the faithful man (*mümin*) from the prison of this world to the gardens of Paradise and the presence of the Most Merciful One. It is because of this that the perfect and wise (*kamil insanlar*) who have seen death's reality (*ölümün hakikati*) loved it, and even desired it before it came.[21]

---

20   *Khidr* (in Arabic, *al-Khidr*, "the verdant one," *Hızır* in Turkish) is a saintly and mythical figure in Islam who has been identified with various characters of the Old Testament—notably with Elias, of whom he is considered a reincarnation (see Nursi (1997), particularly the first Letter) and with the Orthodox St. George (Irfan 1993). While not mentioned by name in the Qur'an, *Khidr* is assumed to be that mythical figure that Moses accompanies in his travels (Qur'an 18:65–82). Interestingly, in these Qur'anic passages, *Khidr* appears as the bearer of a hidden and divine knowledge that causes his apparently bad and terrifying actions (he first damages the vessel upon which he and Moses are traveling and then he murders a young man) to turn into merciful acts once their real significance is revealed to Moses.

21   This passage is taken from the seventh Word of the *Risale* (Nursi 1993b, 42). At exactly this point of the text a note refers to Qur'an 12:101, where the Prophet Joseph is described as praying to God to let him die as a Muslim who might thus join the righteous people (the very good and saintly Muslims, usually the Prophet's companions and followers).

Ferhat and the other *abi* conducting the lesson, Nimet, then invited a discussion on the meaning of death among the approximately 15 university students who had joined the *mütalaa*. Bekim participated passionately in the discussion, starting the conversation by arguing that they should not fear death or anything bad that may happen in life (sickness or misfortune) because, as Muslims, they know what is waiting for them in the afterlife (the reign of God). For this reason, they do not have to worry about death. In response, another student commented ironically: "Does this mean that since I am part of the *hizmet* I have automatically gained access to paradise and so I don't have to worry about death? [...] This way it would mean that liking death is good (*hayır*)..." As he uttered these words the other students simultaneously exclaimed in a chorus: "No! [*prolonged*] ... *Üstad* says that we do not have to desire death..." Some other comments followed. When it was Bekim's turn to speak again, he said: "When you think about death there is fear (*korku*), but our appreciation for what God has given to us must overcome this feeling of fear." In line with these words, Ferhat *abi* added that they must be afraid of God as Muslims. He was going to say more, but he could not end his sentence because he was interrupted by Nimet, who said: "...but this has to be a compassionate fear" (*şefkatlı bir korku*). Referring to those wise men who have seen the reality of God lying behind this world after dying, Nimet reminded the students that "they have to find pleasure (*lezzet almak*) from that fear." This is explained by the fact that, thanks to the awareness they have gained through *tefekkür*, these men neither have to fear God nor the hereafter. The only thing they have to be afraid of is that the "sincerity of faith could be broken" (*ihlası kırılmasından korkuyoruz*). Nimet stated once more that what they must care about is *ihlas*, because it is when they lose *ihlas* that they will also lose their faith—and if they lose their faith they will start fearing death like any non-believer who sees it as mere nothingness, rather than the passage to a truer reality.

My interlocutors considered the feeling of fear to be part of that emotional repertoire that every Muslim should possess. Such fear comes to define a condition of mind and body—a disposition, as referred to by Hirschkind (2006)—that supports the state of awareness that the Nur brothers have to draw from divinely revealed knowledge, deciphered through the *Risale*. However, in the Nur case, death is not simply used as a dreadful threat to spur those attending the readings to follow a more pious conduct. Rather, practices of meditative reflection on death serve to make people reconnect their personal existence to a broader discourse about the cosmos and the reality of God, an awareness of the profound sense and interconnectedness of existence that they must aim to achieve. In the Nur thanatology, the fear of divine judgment is mitigated by a sense of relaxation and relief from worldly concerns that might even lead to a "wish" for death in some extreme cases. In this perspective, the Nur idea of death seems to be almost totally devoid of any negative connotation or scarecrow role. Rather, it is better understood as one part of a larger idea of wisdom that my interlocutors were expected to attain as they progressed in the cultivation of their Muslim awareness. Whereas they should not be eager to die (suicide being forbidden by Islam), they thought of death as sanctioning the definitive passage from a worldly "non-original" reality to the endless reality of God—which will be manifested only in the hereafter. In this vein, meditative reflection on death is possibly one of the best exemplifications of how my interlocutors grounded their sense of being attentive Muslims on the consciousness that everything in this world is but the reflection of God's existence, namely something ephemeral and transitory, including their lives. The *Risale* guides them through this process of self-realization. By means of its metaphors and poetical representations of human existence, it invites its readers to ponder their life as being part of the larger cycle of creation and continuous recreation of nature that is reflected in the cosmos.

•••

In his seminal work on the paths of man's spiritual self-perfection within the Sunni Islamic tradition, Ira Lapidus (1984) pointed out that the history of Muslim pedagogical endeavors has no unique dominant path and is better described as being based on a complex interrelationship between human intellect, faculties, and deeds. When Islamic and other religious paths are considered, priority can neither be given to bodily practice over mind-based practice, nor to sensory over intellectual faculties, nor to collective over individual performance. Muslim ways of engaging with Islamic tradition differ according to place and time, and must be considered in the context of the dominant political and epistemological conditions. The way my interlocutors linked reading practices of the *Risale* and longstanding Islamic forms of meditative reflection should be read through this lens: as one of the possible ways by which a twentieth-century Sufi-inspired, but reformist-oriented, Islamic scholar willing to engage with new technologies and with the epistemological discourse of modernity has forged a new path to knowledge that was more consonant with the times.

On the one hand, Nur communities like the *Suffa* emphasize reading over oral transmission of the tradition through a master, insisting that reflection is a better way of consolidating Islamic faith than the kind of remembrance practiced within Sufi circles. On the other hand, however, their reading practices induce a form of meditative reflection that is highly indebted to longstanding

Sufi cosmological views. In this case, reflection is not intended to refer to inferential thinking, as is understood in modern scientific discourse, but to a deductive exercise that points to the miraculous character of the mechanisms of nature in order to unveil God's presence behind them. This process involves the "re-enchantment" of one's sight with respect to nature; an intellectual attitude in which the essential organ is not the mind, but the heart. Thought of as the epicenter of the human soul, the heart mediates human rationalist impulses, opening human experience to a broader perspective that includes transcendence. While the mind takes the central stage in post-Enlightenment views of the self, the Nur economy of the self combines the heart and the mind in ways that make it possible to transcend views of nature as consisting of pure materiality. Similar to how Ibn Arabi upheld imagination as the faculty that allows us to reconcile reason and revelation, *tefekkür* allowed my interlocutors to see behind the apparent reality of this world. In this perspective, their emphasis on reflection and mind as the keys to achieving faith in contemporary society does not reflect a departure from Islamic eidetic forms of imagination. Rather, the emphasis they put on reason is the reflex of a semantic alignment of Nursi's discourse with modern epistemological discourse.

These considerations also have significant implications for the way knowledge transmission has been approached in scholarly works on the Muslim world. Whilst anthropological scholarship on the Middle East has generally pointed to the effect of new technologies and media on the consumption of Islamic texts—written or oral—in this chapter I have shown how modern media do not necessarily impact the longstanding practices in a straightforward trajectory of modernization. Although modern means of communication have certainly facilitated the mediatization of religion in ways that imply a reconfiguration of the role of their producers and of their publics, in the case of the *Suffa* and Gülen communities, the consumption of texts remains anchored in a concrete Islamic tradition of intellectual engagement and discernment. While literature on the use of texts in Islamic pedagogy has generally been concerned with the interpolation of textual support with orality and memory, reading may be understood differently and associated with specific intellectual and bodily faculties in different cultural and historical contexts. Far from just being a technical exercise based on decoding written characters, reading engenders multiple and historically specific forms of intellectual engagement. In the case considered here, it stimulates a kind of meditation that is endowed with eidetic goals, that is, which is aimed to achieve a complete reconfiguration of one's ways of sensing the world and constructing its relationship with God and transcendence.

More generally, the Nur case suggests that a reconfiguration of the same idea of knowledge should be undertaken. Such a revision would require a recourse to transcendence to allow us to see our ethical dilemmas and lives from a broader perspective that goes beyond our most immediate worldly concerns. This is the sort of intellectual operation that my interlocutors aimed to pursue. Such an operation was based on a solid idea of transcendence intended not as a sublime and untouchable model of perfection lying beyond this world, but as an actively present and visible principle that shapes our awareness of this world. Contrary to a general view of transcendence impinging upon the idea of a non-human logos or authority—and hence as the source of irrationalism and enchanted forms of life—some authors have recently rehabilitated the notion as a more tangible ground of epistemological, ethical, aesthetic, and political realization (Milbank 2004, 2006 [1990]; Kosky 2004; Schwartz 2004; Taylor 2004). These scholars share the common perception that the underrating of transcendence in mainstream philosophical tradition is not accidental, but an integral and constitutive part of the experience of Western modernity itself, which has also had a significant impact on the reformulation of religious experience within Christianity. For them, it is the definition of transcendence as an ultimate entity existing *beyond* and *independently* from worldly matters—a separation of God's presence from worldly reality that takes place mainly in modern times—that has actually made it difficult for Western philosophers to rely on it as an ethical referent.

Such a clear separation between this world and transcendence has never happened in such radical terms within Islam. As shown, achieving knowledge for my interlocutors did not simply imply learning the technical know-how one needs in order to be able to work upon this world. It meant to achieve awareness about the transitory nature of this world. When compared to cosmic order and time, one's life and death become almost irrelevant and one starts approaching his own existence from a different angle. These considerations have important ethical implications. I will explore these aspects further in Chapter 5, where I will illustrate how a world-renouncing philosophy like this one is turned into a motor of activism in society by my interlocutors. This will also allow me to point, at least in part, to the role of transcendence in redefining Islamic forms of civic engagement in a modern-oriented world.

CHAPTER 4

Putting Islam to Work

At the end of the school-day waves of students flow from Istanbul's highschools, walking or boarding buses to reach home or some public dormitory located in town. Yet some of them are not. They walk alone or in small groups to go to one of the hundreds of houses affiliated with the Gülen community, where "their *abi*s," university students committed to the educational mission of the community, are waiting for them. In an attempt to mark their respect, younger middle and high-school students address the latter as *abi*s, while the university students call them by name. Only when speaking among themselves do the university students refer to the younger students as *talebe*, a word traditionally used by Muslim teachers to name their pupils, conveying a sense of authority. The *abi*s have indeed undertaken the duty of taking care of their younger peers, whom they help to improve their performances at school, but whom they also introduce to the life and ideals of the community. Although an implicit hierarchy separates these two categories of students, the *abi*s are committed to taking care of the *talebe*s as younger brothers in religion rather than as teachers, in line with the pedagogical paths illustrated in Chapter 2.

This vignette depicts daily events taking place until July 15, 2016, before the community was left without the financial support it needed to rent apartments and fund scholarship for students. The *abi*s' dedication to the education of the younger boys responded to a precise call by Gülen, who always invited his followers to invest their time and energies in the mission of raising new generations of educated and pious Muslims who could contribute to the progress of society.[1] The title of this chapter is meant to highlight a precise fact: contrary to what happens in *Suffa*, where a more contemplative approach to living a Muslim life in a "modern" world was promoted, within the Gülen community Islam has always been thought of as a motor for social engagement and put at the service of the community's reform project, as introduced in Chapter 1. The title is a reference to Gregory Starrett's book (1998), in which he has illustrated how the state's encroachment over mass education in modern Egypt was paralleled

---

[1] While since the 1970s pious foundations have generally gathered funds to sponsor the opening of new mosques or *imam-hatip* schools, Gülen has always advised his followers to secure educational facilities for students enrolled in modern secular schools (e.g. see Ünal and Williams 2000, 34, 336).

by a growing interest in religious instruction aimed at instilling a new moral spirit in the citizens. Although Starrett has scrutinized the transformation of religion and its "functionalization" in Egypt within state-sponsored mass education, he has also interestingly acknowledged that a similar program had been put to work for "various types of social and political projects" outside the state's institutions, most notably by the Muslim Brotherhood (Starrett 1998, 10).

As it has been pointed out by Kim Shively (2008), since its foundation the Turkish state has been engaged in a battle to affirm the official view of religion on society. Religious knowledge and education both remain highly politicized and contentious issues to this day. In this light, one of the central ideas of this chapter is to illustrate how the Gülen community has tended to present its activities as an alternative to the national project of education. At the same time, however, this chapter also points to how this and other religious communities' discourses may have partly overlapped with official visions of the place of Islam in Turkey, including a similarly "modern" inclination toward what can be termed as the "moralization of religion." This does not mean that the educational goals of the Gülen community totally matched those of the modern nation-state. For instance, the community did not aim to form a disciplined citizen, but rather a good Muslim dedicated to its religiously-inflected reformist project. Rather, it is my contention that different from the leaders of other Islamic communities of modern Turkey, Gülen has shared the tendency with the modern nation-state to frame its project in a trajectory of progress and to think of Islam in terms of a moral ethos.

What are the social imaginaries and ideals that the community has been able to mobilize to promote such an alternative educational project? To what extent have these imaginaries been affected by broader shifts in twentieth-century discourses concerning the importance of education for national progress? What gaps in national policy has the community been able to take advantage of and prosper through in the last forty years? Through which pedagogical processes were students educated to become responsible and motivated Muslims willing to contribute to the community's mission? In what way do the Nur ontology and cosmology provide the philosophical underpinnings of the community's worldly-oriented project of sociopolitical transformation? These questions are explored in this chapter by means of an ethnographic account of educational practices within the houses and dormitories of the Gülen community.

Life in these places followed a path similar to that described in Chapter 2. However, whereas reading the *Risale* and related contemplative practice occupied a prominent position within the houses at *Suffa*, the enactment of peer-to-peer pedagogies centered on care and exemplariness prevailed in the Gülen houses. The *abi*s had to concretely exemplify to their younger peers how to live a good Muslim life in line with the ideals of dedication and self-sacrifice that were part of their understanding of *hizmet*. The idealized goal was to raise a "golden generation" of educated Muslims willing to join the mission of the community. Showing concern and affection was an important pedagogical strategy through which the university students operated. Meanwhile, taking on increasing educational responsibility was also a way for them to embody those key dispositions of dedication, self-sacrifice, and commitment that are central to the cause of the community, and that they wished to convey to the *talebe*s.

1   Education, the Nation and the Islamic "Ethos"

Beginning with the *Tanzimat* era, the project for the modernization of the Ottoman Empire has gone hand in hand with changes in the education system. Worried by the possibility of foreign military invasion, Ottoman elites urgently implemented institutional reform in order to shrink the technical and intellectual gap they had vis-à-vis the European nations (Bozdoğan and Kasaba 1997; Çınar 2005; Fortna 2002). They were not only challenged from the outside, but also from within by foreign missionaries, highly motivated nationalist educators of neighboring states, and the schools of the non-Muslim, mainly Christian, minorities. Under attack on both the technical and the intellectual fronts, successive generations of Ottoman reformers have opted for gradually introducing European-style schools, foremost in the form of naval (1773) and army (1793) academies, and then of medicine (1827), civil administration (1859), and law (1878) schools.[2]

As shown by Benjamin Fortna (2002) in his study of education reform during the reign of Abdüllahmid II (1876–1909), these transformations were less European-esque than it has been conventionally argued in historical scholarship (e.g. Berkes 1998 [1964]) as they tried to accommodate new political needs while retaining some elements of the past. One of the main problems that Abdüllahmid faced was how to transform a composite ensemble of imperial subjects into a mass of citizens tied together by a shared sense of belonging to an

---

2   The feeling of being permanently under siege has also endured in republican times and has become a constitutive element of Turkish national identity in the form of a real "paranoia" that still influences both internal and external policies (see Guida 2008).

"imagined national community" (Anderson 1991 [1983]). As illustrated in Chapter 1, the assimilation of Islam into public discourse as an element of national unity and identity determined its abstraction from the old ethical and legislative functions it had in the past and transformed it into a subject of ideological confrontation. Although this process took a definitive turn after 1923, it had been underway since late Ottoman times. In the last chapter of his book, Fortna illustrates one manifestation of this process as he points out that in the new Hamidian schools' textbooks Islam was referred to in terms of "morals" (*ahlak*), which were unconditionally shared by the Ottoman citizens. This reference reflects the main goal of Abdüllahmid's campaign to "inculcate [...] students with an Islamic sense of morality" (Fortna 2002, 205) for the purpose of restraining the deleterious effects of foreign educational encroachment on the Ottoman youth by making it loyal to the Empire. Within this program, Islam was treated as a sort of spirit or "ethos" uniting the new generations of Ottoman citizens and dedicating them to the national cause.

The education sector has been an arena of confrontation between internal and external actors since the *Tanzimat* because it allowed for the control of the hearts, minds, and spirits of the new generations (Kaplan 2006). It is no coincidence that the idea of national youth occupied a central place in the collective imagination of both late Ottoman and early Republican Turkish societies. The new generations were indeed seen as the main subject of the scientific and technological revolution that the nation had to undergo to narrow the gap with foreign powers. This was particularly emphasized during Republic times when a veritable "cult of youth" was promoted by the secularist elites (Neyzi 2001). Educated into Republican values and modern science, the new generations represented the hope of the nation, those who would lead the country to the expected social and economic progress upon which the secularization of society would be built. In this sense, the youth became associated with the very possibility of realizing the Kemalist modernization project.[3]

It is in light of the link established between the fate of the new generations and that of the Ottoman-Turkish nation that the proposals of Said Nursi first, and Fethullah Gülen afterwards, should also be read. Whereas during late Ottoman times the class of the *ulema*s and of the Sufi leaders both generally

---

3   The identification of the new generations with the Kemalist revolution and its civilizing project was openly formulated by Kemal Atatürk in the famous speech he delivered at the Second Congress of the Republican People's Party on 15–20 October 1927, in which he directly addressed the Turkish youth. Some of the salient parts of the speech have been condensed in the oath that Turkish schoolchildren still recite every morning at school. Although the AKP administration has recently attempted to remove the oath, its recitation is still widely supported by the people and seen as a central trait of national identity (Altinay 2006).

opposed the modernist turn undertaken by the reformers (Mardin 1989, 110–113), Said Nursi had been an advocate of reform, especially in the education sector (Vahide 2005, 42–49). Before the spiritual crisis he experienced in 1923–1924, after which he decided to write the *Risale*, Nursi had been an eclectic Muslim intellectual and a politically active figure who had supported the introduction of a constitution in the Empire and promoted ideals of freedom that he saw as being entirely in conformity with the *shariʿa*—in line with the position of the Young Ottomans (Vahide 2005, 53, 58). Nursi similarly supported education reform in the Empire, even though this had to be based on the introduction of the modern sciences in the curricula of the *medrese*. His views can be summarized by looking at his proposal for the opening of the *Medresetü'z-Zehra*, an Islamic university which would unite three different educational traditions by bringing together "the most superior *mekteb* by the reason, the very best *medrese* by the heart, and the most sacred *zawiye* by the conscience" (Vahide 2005, 46). In Nursi's vision, the modern sciences like chemistry and physics would have been taught side by side with Islamic sciences and the promotion of Islamic conduct. Although his proposal was never financed by Abdüllahmid—a possibility that waned with the foundation of the Republic—the Nur movement has always upheld an educational philosophy close to this vision, arguing for the compatibility of Islamic teachings and modern scientific knowledge.

Fethullah Gülen was deeply affected by Nursi's teachings in this regard. He had been introduced to them by some prominent Nur brothers like Mehmet Kırkıncı during his youth in Erzurum (Erdoğan 2006 [1995]; Yavuz 2003a, 180–181). While the secularist elites had assumed that there was an inherent conflict between Islam and modernity, Gülen defended the idea that the two could be seamlessly integrated. The schools the community had opened since the 1970s were intended to be a tangible demonstration of this fact (Zengin Arslan 2009; Tee 2016).[4] Different from Nursi, Gülen was advantaged by the much more favorable sociopolitical environment of the post-1980-coup period for implementing his educational project. After spending the first years of his appointment as a state-preacher in Turkey's remote Western province of Edirne, Gülen moved to the more secular city of Izmir in 1966, where he began to volunteer as a teacher in the Qurʾanic school of Kestanepazarı and put effort into

---

4 For more information on the relationship between the community and the teaching of science, see Tee (2016), and especially Zengin Arslan's (2009) argument that the community promotes a project of "conservative modernity" aimed at Islamicizing science rather than trying to genuinely "modernize" Islam.

propagating the Nur ideals in the surrounding region (Erdoğan 2006 [1995]). This first experience as an educator was seminal for the elaboration of Gülen's pedagogical views and methods. In particular, the summer camps that he organized for his students at Kestanepazarı since 1968 functioned as intellectual laboratories for the community.

These camps were a sort of spiritual retreat that took place in isolated locations in the middle of nature. Here, young students had to comply with Islamic rules and etiquette, and spent the day reading and discussing the *Risale-i Nur* under the guidance of Gülen himself. Students conformed to a discipline of time and Muslim socialization that was very similar to that described in Chapter 2. Because these were intensive programs, particular attention was devoted to following a disciplined life, to the extent that even some physical training occurred. In Gülen's own words, the idea behind the camps was to recreate an atmosphere where "the discipline of an army, the good manners of the Sufi lodges and the knowledge of theological schools become a whole" (Erdoğan 2006 [1995], 122). Accounts and memories of the dense spiritual atmosphere of these first camps are still told and remain an important component of the community's self-narrative. Moreover, the camps had a formative role in the consolidation of the first community network, as Gülen established close ties with some of the future leaders of the community in these meetings (Yavuz 2003a, 181–185).

It was during these same years that Gülen elaborated his educational project of forging a "new" or "golden generation" (*yeni nesil, altın nesil*) of Muslims to be educated in modern secular disciplines but who also had to embody Islamic ethics and discipline (see Agai 2003, 2007; Sunier 2014). Gülen first publicly used this expression in a conference in 1977,[5] and then continued to employ it to describe his hopes for raising a new generation of people endowed "with minds enlightened by positive science, with hearts purified by faith, who would be an example of virtue and who would burn with the desire to serve their nation and humanity, and who would live, not for themselves, but for others" (Gülen 1998a; also quoted in Hermansen 2007, 70).[6] The qualities that this new generation should possess included: being motivated by love (*muhabbet*), taking the initiative (*hamle*) in saving others as men of action (*aksiyon insanı*) guided by a true humanist sense (*mürüvvetli hareket*), examining

---
5 The recordings were available at: http://tr.fgulen.com/content/view/7835/108/ (accessed 6 August 2012).
6 Available online at: http://www.fethullahgulen.org/press-room/claims-and-answers/1216-claims-and-answers.html (accessed 6 August 2012).

oneself (*murakabe*) continuously, looking at other brothers as examples, and being ready to suffer and undergo trials (*çile çekmek*) while pursuing ideals of religious service (*hizmet*).

As evidenced by this list of qualities, these new generations of Muslims were expected to be active and dedicated, ready to sacrifice their life for the cause of *hizmet*. According to Gülen's utopian project, they were the long-awaited people who would embody the values of Islam and be actively engaged within society to transform it according to God's will, bringing peace on Earth. In his speeches, the realization of such a project was generally collocated in a distant, indefinite, eschatological future where God's will is finally achieved, and the Earth turned into the hereafter. As also observed by Agai (2003), the golden generation is a metaphorical concept that served the community to express its ideal of educating a new youth that would form the basis for the perfect future, the "Age of Felicity" (*Saadet Asrı*). Yet it is important to notice that the project is also clearly connected to the ideal past exemplified by the pristine community of the Prophet Muhammad and his companions (*sahabe*).[7] In this regard, Marta Hermansen (2007, 71) has stressed how, apart from being drenched in Sufi values, the idea of a "golden generation" was a clear reference to a saying of Muhammad claiming that "the early generations of Muslims were the best and a model for those who come later."[8] In the same conference mentioned above, Gülen referred to this *hadith* and used some heroic stories of the *sahabe*s to exemplify the ideal qualities of the *altın nesil*.[9]

Beyond a strictly Islamic genealogy, the Gülenian project for raising a new generation of educated and pious Muslims is also indebted to debates on the fate of the Turkish nation and the role that the new generations should occupy in it. The pairing of Ottoman-Turkish culture with Islam often found in Gülen's speeches has been generally pointed to as an element that indicates his proximity to the right-wing discourses of the Turkish-Islamic synthesis (Balci 2003; Özdalga 2003; Yavuz 2003a; Bilici 2006; Agai 2007; Turam 2007).

---

7 Not accidentally, the title of one of Gülen's most important books translated into English is *Towards the Lost Paradise* (Gülen 1998d). The book is a collection of his essays on different arguments concerning youth, the new generations and their role as Muslims in the contemporary world.

8 Gülen has designated himself an heir of Sufism. This happened especially after he moved to the United States, where he has perceptively opted for reshaping his image as that of a moderate enlightened Muslim proposing a softened and apolitical version of Islam that is more pleasing to Western ears.

9 This is a recurrent pattern of Gülen's scholarship. His books are replete with stories taken from the first Muslim community (see below). Narratives of the life of the Prophet, a literary genre known as *siyer* in Turkey, have also apparently had a pivotal role in the early education of Gülen as a child (Yavuz 2003a).

Elaborated in the 1960s by the Muslim nationalist think tank *Aydınlar Ocağı*, this theory claimed the existence of a Turkish ethos (*öz*) consisting of a perfectly balanced synthesis between the Turkish cultural element on the one hand, and Islamic civilization on the other. The thesis brought in important elements of novelty. By depicting Islam as the "ethos" of Turkish history, the *Aydınlar Ocağı* put the anti-religious foundations of Kemalism under scrutiny by reintegrating Islamic elements that had been neglected for decades within Turkish identity. It also rejected the excessive functionalism of Ziya Gökalp for seeing religion only as a symbol of collective imagination, rather than the motor of the Turkish civilizational trajectory *tout court* (see Chapter 1). On the other hand, however, as much as the theory integrated a distinctively Turkish kind of Islam into the historical narrative of the nation, it ended by neglecting other versions of Islam, including the history of "Arab people," which were classified as intrinsically incompatible with an allegedly "modern" Turkish identity (Özdalga 2006).[10]

The Turkish-Islamic synthesis has largely been accepted by the official state discourse since the military coup of 1980 and many of its pillars have been included in school textbooks (Copeaux 1998; Yavuz 2003a; Özdalga 2006; Kaplan 2006). Gülen's enmeshing with similar historical narratives, however, dates back even earlier. Since at least the 1940s, other Muslim intellectuals elaborated ideas of a Turkish Islam and promoted forms of activism rooted in an Islamically-grounded moral ethos. Among these intellectuals, there were figures like Necip Fazıl Kısakürek (1904–83) and Nurettin Topçu (1909–1975), who had received their higher education in France and who had been influenced by famous Christian orientalists like Louis Massignon and Maurice Blondel.[11] For a period of his life, Gülen was reportedly a distributor of Kısakürek's *Büyük Doğu* (The Great Orient) (İnsel 1997), a magazine that fostered the romantic conceit that held that spiritualism was a particular birthright of the East as opposed to the materialist West (Guida 2012). Yet Gülen seems to have been more decisively influenced by Nurettin Topçu's philosophy of action (*hareket felsefi*) and his ideas of promoting a civil resistance grounded in moral engagement (*isyan ahlakı*). Topçu's idea that the values of Islamic morality had to be passed

---

10   On the construction of Turkish identity in terms of opposition to a similarly essentialized "Arab identity," see also Bozdoğan and Kasaba (1997) and Navaro-Yashin (2002a).

11   Blondel is the author of the book *L'Action* (*The Action*), a name that probably inspired Topçu when he decided to call his periodical *Hareket* (Action) in 1939. As observed by Guida (2012), with their ideas concerning morality and mysticism, Blondel, Massignon, and Bergson have provided early Republican Muslim Turkish intellectuals with a European avenue for criticizing widespread materialist and positivist ideologies of the time.

on to new generations of "valuable youth" (*kıymetli gençler*) was a clear source of inspiration for Gülen's project to raise a golden generation.¹²

Pointing to the influence that this first generation of Republican Muslim intellectuals had on Gülen is important to shed light on the complex combination of Islam, national identity, and views of progress that are found in his writings. However, I suggest that the convergence of nationalist discourse and Islamism cannot be simply read as the sign of Gülen's propensity toward an over-nationalistic discourse (see also Vicini 2016). From a general Islamic perspective, there is no particular contradiction in promoting a religious view within a national framework. As well-clarified by contemporary scholars of Islam, a good Muslim man will indeed also be a good citizen—whereas it is not certain if a good citizen would also be a good man (al-Attas 1979). Stating this does not deny that the two projects can conflict. They easily do conflict, as I will point to at the end of Chapter 5. However, from the point of view of Gülen, the progress of Islam and that of the nation could also easily collimate.

From an analytical perspective, it is also important to note that these two projects have converged on the point of promoting a sort of moralization of Islam, aimed at responsibilizing new generations of Turkish citizens. The respective goals remain separate, with the community promoting its religiously-inflected program of social reform and the Turkish state a modernizing and mainly "secular" project. Yet similarly to how the national education system has promoted Islam in textbooks as a glue for society and for instilling a sense of commitment of its citizens to the national cause, Gülen has also turned Islam into an inner motivational force, an "ethos," that should inspire the engagement of new generations of Muslims in society and their participation in his reformist project. While the final goals of the two projects remain different, the way Islam has been used as a mobilizing force has some interesting commonalities with the Republican project—and this may also partly explain the dynamics that have led to the excessive idealization of the mission of *hizmet* within the Gülen community, which is also one of the possible reasons behind its late drastic moves (see the end of Chapter 5). In the rest of this chapter, I show how students of the Gülen community were educated into people motivated by such an ethos. In particular, I explore how the main values that the golden generation should embody are longed for and enlivened within the

---

12   Gülen has publicly affirmed his gratitude to Topçu in at least two relatively recent writings (Gülen 2005, 2010c). Another author of that generation that Gülen often quotes is Mehmet Akif Ersoy (1873–1936), the poet and author of the Turkish national anthem, who also advocated the need of educating new generations to the values of technological modernization and cultural authenticity so to shape a Generation of Salvation (*Asım'ın Nesli*)—a concept quite close to that of the golden generation (Bilici 2006).

houses of this community by means of exemplariness and progressive responsibilization.

2 Accessing Quality Education

Although education in Turkey has long been seen as a cornerstone of national progress, great discrepancies in access to quality education have survived until the 1980s. The transition to the Republican system has tended to reproduce the cleavage between a relatively restricted urbanized elite and the large number of people living in the peripheral areas of the country. Over time, a series of reforms have allowed the graduates of religious vocational schools (*imam hatip lisesi*) to climb the social ladder.[13] However, generally coming from conservative and rural families, only a very limited number of these people have been able to gain access to higher education and move up the ladder. The Turkish public educational system is based on a highly competitive and selective process that favors the better prepared students, normally coming from the best non-vocational schools. Middle-school students in Turkey must get high scores on the national exam if they wish to enter the most renowned "Anatolian high-schools" (*Anadolu lisesi*).[14] A similar and even more selective examination (*LYS*, *Lisans Yerleştirme Sınavı*) is undertaken by undergraduates willing to enter public universities or to win a scholarship to attend private ones. Just to give an idea of the selectiveness of these exams, out of a total number of around 1,900,000 students who entered the *LYS* in 2011, only around 750,000 spots were available.[15] For this reason, thanks to their higher economic (and social) capital, the sons of the urbanized and generally secular elite classes have traditionally been privileged in filling these posts.

In Chapter 1, I pointed out how this system began creaking with the economic liberalization of the 1980s. During this time, the emergence of a new conservative bourgeois class of Anatolian origin, backed by newly established

---

13 Moreover, until 2009, when the AKP administration introduced a more favorable legislation, access to university for graduates of the *imam hatip* schools was also limited by the fact that their titles were compared to those of trade high-schools (*meslek liseleri*) and hence given lesser points in the national examination than to the graduates of more prestigious non-trade high-schools (NTV 2009).
14 Today this exam is called *Liseye Geçiş Sınavı* (*LGS*).
15 https://www.osym.gov.tr/TR,1000/2011.html (accessed December 23, 2018). Today this exam is called *Yükseköğretim Kurumları Sınavı* (*YKS*) and in 2018 out of 1,749,144 applicants only 710,982 could enroll in their desired university program (while the spots available were 839,490). See: https://www.osym.gov.tr/ (accessed December 23, 2018).

Islamic foundations, allowed for pious Muslims to pour money in the education sector and give unprecedented educational opportunities to traditionally marginalized strata of society. More than any other religious group, the Gülen community took advantage of these conditions. By offering educational facilities to successful non-elite students, it has grown its investments in education and attracted a progressively higher number of people from diverse groups and classes. As also argued by others, one of the main reasons behind the students' and parents' decision to opt for education in one of the schools of this community was that it offered students concrete opportunities for achieving personal and economic success (Hendrick 2013).

Of particular importance in this framework was the huge investment of the community in the sector of private tutoring schools, the *dershane*s. Until 2016, the country maintained an enormous educational industry. These schools had been growing exponentially in the previous decade and a half, increasing from 1,730 *dershane*s and 174,496 students in 2000, to 4,055 *dershane*s and 1.2 million enrolled in 2012 (*Hürriyet Daily News* 2013). Until a few years ago, these schools competed with each other to attract the best students in the country. This allowed them to create a virtuous circle through which they increased their popularity and, consequently, their incomes. The Gülen community opened its first *dershane* in 1978 and massively invested in this sector after (Agai 2007). Before being closed in 2016, the *dershane*s affiliated with the community were particularly well-reputed for the high results obtained by their students in the national examinations. Consequently, they attracted not only students of conservative families, but also those from middle and high classes of both pious and secular backgrounds, who were ready to pay full fees.

A few months before the coup attempt of July 2016, a leaked governmental proposition planning the closure of all *dershane*s in the country was published by *Zaman*, generating a huge confrontation between the AKP administration and the Gülen community (Vicini 2014b). For the community, these schools had both great symbolic and strategic value. They represented the face of its success and one of its major points of pride. Moreover, they were a major source of income and functioned as an important recruitment channel. Like other regular high-schools run by the community, the *dershane*s followed the national curriculum, their classes were mixed, and they displayed no Islamic symbols in buildings or in the way their staff dressed (see Agai 2003; Balci 2003).[16] Nevertheless, their faculty was mainly, if not entirely, composed of

---

16   This is not just limited to Turkey. The adaptation of the schools to the specific legal and cultural context of each country is also a distinctive character of the community's schools abroad (see Balci 2003; Turam 2007).

community members who saw their work as a mission they had to accomplish as part of their commitment to the community ideals of religious service. The teachers taught according to an "Islamic ethic of education," consisting of a high degree of dedication and care for the students (Agai 2003; Özdalga 2003), that was akin to the one applied by the *abi*s in the houses that I explore below. In addition, they often used to invite their students to visit community places. The director of a small *dershane* located in the neighborhood of Şişli explained to me that the teachers of his school, like all others affiliated with the community, had the duty to encourage the most intelligent students, and those predisposed to moral and religious concerns, to attend the community houses. Alternatively, students could be invited to the *abi*s' houses directly from some of their peers who, *via* their relatives or friends, already attended these places. Very often, the same *abi*s also visited the *dershane*s or offered supplementary lessons to their pupils there, which was another way of meeting new students. The most disciplined of the younger *talebe*s could also go to the *dershane*s to recruit younger middle-school students. This was the case with some of my interlocutors at the house of Şişli who went to a nearby prep-school on Saturdays and Sundays to help tutor younger students.

The importance that teachers at the *dershane*s had in drawing people to the community is also confirmed by the veil of melancholy that shrouded the accounts of my interlocutors about their first encounters with the community. A sense of nostalgia often emerged from the words of the *talebe*s when they told me how they had met "their first *abi*." In most of the cases, this was a teacher at a local *dershane* in their provincial hometown. A sweet and sincere smile lightened their faces when they told me of the afternoons and evenings they had spent together: of when he offered them cola and biscuits, of when they played together, or of when they spent the night awake waiting for the morning to perform the prayer. They often recalled their first *abi*'s kind manners and told of how they had been impressed by his righteous behavior, care, and concern. The *talebe*s generally expressed gratitude for all the teachings they had received from them and for their guidance when they had to choose which school to attend in Istanbul.

If not through the *dershane* system, students might also attend the *abi*s' houses thanks to a reference from relatives, family friends, their own schoolmates, or through other recruitment efforts by the community. Take Ercan's house, for example. Ercan was a university student of literature who managed a community house in the small neighborhood of Feriköy, located in the Şişli district. His task was to take care of as many of the neighborhood middle-school students as possible. He had been able to draw a group of around 20 boys to come to his place, a big flat at the fourth floor of a building located not far from a high-school positioned at the center of the neighborhood. Students were initially invited to come and enjoy the day with their peers and attend some after-school lessons by the *abi*s staying in the house. At this age, they were not expected to perform the five daily prayers regularly and only did so intermittently, usually on the occasional Friday that they would spend the night in the house. Ercan invited young boys he had met in the street and visited their parents to illustrate the community's educational offering for their sons. Even though he was certainly not one of the most devoted brothers that I have met during my research, as he confessed to me, he had been selected by the elder brothers precisely because of his easy-going ways of engaging young-age boys who would be attracted to the house by his personality.

When the pupils are so young, a parent's opinion is crucial in determining whether the students will start attending the houses or not. Most of the families of the *talebe*s I met were pious, either having connections to the Gülen's or other Islamic groups. However, less religiously conservative parents might also send their sons to the *abi*s, either because they hoped to keep them away from bad company and undesirable habits, or because they wanted their sons to receive the free tutoring. Relatives with no previous contact with the community might simply be content with the idea that morally upright university students took care of their sons while they were at work. They were also intrigued by the upward mobility opportunities offered by the community.

This was the case with Ayşe, the mother of Faruk, a 12-year old boy whom she had been raising alone after the father abandoned them some years before. Faruk regularly attended Ercan's house, but on an evening visit to Ayşe's I quickly gathered that he did not come from a conventional religious family. Ayşe made this immediately clear by inviting me to look around and notice that there were no religious symbols in the house and that she did not wear the veil. She feared that because her husband did not visit Faruk often, he could feel the lack of a father figure. Ayşe also acknowledged that she would not have been able to help her son do his homework, both for lack of time and because it had been a long time since she had studied those school-subjects. As she got to know Ercan and started to trust him, she decided to allow her son to go to visit him regularly. The father of another student who attended the same house, who also did not seem particularly pious, told me he was satisfied with the possibilities the community offered his son. The tenant of a small grocery shop in a close neighborhood, he had neither the time nor the capacity to help him, so he was content with the free tutoring offered by Ercan.

Similarly, parents who only knew the community superficially might let their sons decide whether to attend the community's residences or not. This was the case with Ali Eren, one of the high-school students in Şişli. His father was reportedly not very interested in religious matters: he attended the community's meetings rarely and, the student added with a laugh, he even used to swear. Unwilling to make the decision for his son, he left the final decision on whether he would stay in the community housing during his high-school years to Ali Eren. In the end, the student followed the suggestion of his professor at the *dershane* and decided to stay in the community's residence. This option occurred quite frequently when parents living outside of Istanbul were obliged to find accommodation for their sons who moved to a quality high-school in a big city. In these cases, the families might prefer that their sons stayed in one of these or another Islamic community's buildings rather than in public dormitories, where alcohol and cigarette consumption were perceived to be common.

The community worked through both formal and informal channels to attract the highest number of students, but the process also implied a certain selection. Reportedly, teachers had a marked preference for students who had higher performances on the national examinations and good reports at school. Additionally, the student's predisposition toward fulfilling the community's religious standards and rules of conduct was also considered. In short, rather than addressing the neediest people, the community aimed to attract the most successful and devoted students—those who had the potential to succeed in the school or in the community's system. In reverse, it was also possible for some of these same students and their families to strategically use the community to gain upward mobility opportunities and abandon it later. Due to the great diversity of people that frequented the community, this was a concrete possibility, and even older affiliates used the good connections granted by the community to establish business relations (Hendrick 2010, 2013). The few times that I mentioned this aspect to the *abi*s, they smiled at me and added that they had at least "sown a seed" by accomplishing their educational duty and conveying a positive image of the community to society.

3   Modern Times, Docile Methods

While the upward mobility opportunities offered by the community is certainly one reason for its success, another rests on the flexibility of the pedagogical methods implemented by the *abi*s toward the *talebe*s in the houses. As in the case of Ercan above, the educational philosophy of the community prescribed that the *abi*s consistently adapted their demeanor depending on the receptiveness of the students, which changed according to their age and disposition. First of all, the *abi*s approached the *talebe*s with soft words, hoping to introduce them to the community path slowly and patiently. When interrogated about their methodology, the university students generally described their efforts with the idiom "*sahip çıkmak*." This expression can be translated as "looking after," and implies a relation of possession, responsibility, and tutoring toward their pupils. In the *abis*' words, taking care of the *talebe*s did not simply include overseeing them, performing Islamic deeds with them, and checking if they had done their readings. It also encompassed engaging with the *talebe*s by spending time together, asking how their day went at school, and generally "taking an interest" (*ilgilenmek*) in them.

I was conversing with Kamil one night and asked for clarification about what "taking an interest" meant to him. He tried to explain this point by saying: "We warm up their hearts (*kalplerini ısındırıyoruz*). [...] This is the first thing that we do when we meet a *talebe* for the first time." As I asked him what concrete things he did, he answered: "It depends ... You can take an interest in different ways according to the person in question." Kamil used Necmi as an example. Necmi was one of those high-school students who did not stay permanently in the dormitory and who would come and go as he pleased. Though he was in the last year of high-school, he still behaved in a way that was not always conventional for life in the houses. Pointing to Necmi's lack of discipline, Kamil said:

> Take Necmi for example ... How is he? He is one that talks a lot, isn't he? [...] In these cases you don't have to talk to them too much. You have to let them talk ... and let them understand things by themselves. [...] If you're talking with a student who does not conform to Islamic rules of conduct, it doesn't matter whether he's Turkish or not, you'll talk calmly to him, without entering religious arguments immediately. Instead, if he's somebody who already believes and practices Islam, you may pass to a second phase. You can start to make him feel responsible for his basic duties as a Muslim.

Through Kamil's words, it is possible to envisage some of the community's pedagogical principles at work. The first goal of the *abis* was to create a positive relationship with the young newcomer by showing interest, without putting pressure on him, and adapting their requests to his personality and degree of inclination toward life in the houses. This might imply avoiding arguments that could arouse refusal by the youngsters or behaviors that might lead to a dispute with them, such as impeding Necmi from talking too much. At the same time, discussion topics and behaviors had to be modified in accordance with the level of adaptation and the mentality of the pupil. The hope was that once the *talebe*'s heart was "warmed up," the student would retain the educator's teachings and the tutor would be able to increase his expectations.

A similar point was raised by Enes, a university student responsible for another house located in the neighborhood of Fatih. In a conversation we had about educational processes within the houses, he made a point of distinguishing between their educational enterprise and that of the school. He explained that, while students are required to go to school and respect their teachers, it was the *abi*s' duty to establish and maintain a respectful relationship with the *talebe*s in the houses and to motivate them to come over and study rather than stay at home relaxing or playing video-games. Expanding on this point, Enes said that the first time a young student comes to the house, he is usually not required to do anything: "If he does not want to pray he is not obliged to do it [...] Since if he is satisfied by his visit then he will come back. [...] The *talebe*s 'warm up' [they become sensitive to things] over time."

Noting the similarity between Enes' words and those I had heard from other *abi*s, I asked him to clarify in concrete terms what he did to "warm up" the *talebe*s. He answered: "With goodness and love." Then, to further explain the point, he described a scene which I had observed repeatedly in the houses:

> For example, we wake up in order to prepare breakfast. [...] If the *abi* stayed in bed yawning and said 'why should I care?' then the *talebe* would go outside hungry ... or he'd arrive at school late. Then how would he feel? [...] Instead we wake up. We wake them up. They find a good breakfast ready ... and then we accompany them to the door and we tell them 'May God protect you' (*Allah'a emanet ol*). [...] So the students go outside and go to school happy. You have to make them like things here. Otherwise nobody would come. [...] There's only one thing: love (*sevgi*). That is the thing that keeps everything together here.

It is only by making students fond of the house's atmosphere, showing them interest and love, that the *abi*s might be successful and hope that their pedagogical efforts will be effective in the long run. The words of Enes recalled many memories of behaviors I had observed within the houses and dorms during my stay. Every day the *abi*s awoke at dawn to get the *talebe*s performing the morning prayer. Meanwhile, another brother prepared breakfast for everybody. During and after breakfast the *imam abi* entertained the young students until it was time to leave for school. He accompanied them to the door, waiting until they slipped on their shoes to wish them God's protection for the day. When the *talebe*s returned from school in the afternoon, the *abi*s were ready to welcome them, to ask how they spent their day, and whether everything went well. Then they all prayed together, after which the *abi* prepared dinner. In some cases, the *abi*s paid a very maternal kind of attention, displaying palpable apprehension and concern for the younger students and their doings. They dedicated considerable time to answering *talebes*' school-related questions or other issues that might arise. They showed concern for their problems and tried to help in many ways, never scolding or making the students feel guilty about their wrongdoings; always answering with a smile, showing understanding, and not letting any sign of impatience be seen.

The reliance on "docile methods" by the *abi*s is part of a community pedagogical path that they have embodied during the years they spent in the community houses since they were teenagers. Throughout this time, they had been gradually given greater responsibilities, eventually becoming *abi*s themselves, and they had been taught how to fulfill their educational duties. There were no technical discussions on the topic among the *abi*s other than in specific seminars that they were asked to attend in preparation for fulfilling their role. These pedagogies, indeed, were part of a tradition that had been handed down through successive generations of students and that the *abi*s had learned through direct experience in the houses. Yet its theoretical underpinnings are the outcome of intellectual elaboration by Gülen. In the late 1970s he was convinced that if the community wanted to be attractive to a world where religious institutions had lost most of their influence, their methods had to be at peace with the changed conditions of the time. The following section is dedicated to exploring the theoretical roots of this pedagogical stance.

4 From *Jihad* to Reforming Society

Debates concerning children's education are centuries old within Islamic tradition. They form an integral part of the corpus of Qur'anic and *hadith* tradition which, during the medieval period, was integrated with discussions contained in Ancient Greek texts, most notably by Ibn Khaldun (Giladi 1989, 125; Ay 1993, 56). However, since the late nineteenth century, new educational theories derived from the Enlightenment have been added to this tradition. Although it is difficult to prove that late-Ottoman Muslim intellectuals actually read the works of the European philosophers, they were most certainly exposed to several French sources. Many of their writings were inspired by Rousseau's highly-influential novel *Emile* (Zachs 2014), but also by other European works such as those of the Swiss pedagogue Johann Heinrich Pestalozzi (1746–1827), who is famous for having put Rousseau's philosophy of education into practice (Ay 1993, 35–36). It is within this framework that Gülen's rejection of what he calls traditional methods, which is explored below, acquires meaning. Similarly, the Muslim scholar was certainly influenced by early Republican discourses cursorily dismissing the Ottoman education system as unfit for educating new generations of citizens given its inclination to uphold the absolute authority of the master over the pupils and its occasional prescription of corporal punishment (Yilmaz 2016, 55).

Gülen first outlined his pedagogical philosophy in a series of articles tellingly entitled "The Problems of Youth" (*Gençliğin Problemleri*). Appearing in *Sızıntı* between March 1981 and July 1982, these writings were a direct attack against the Kemalist project. In line with the critiques of previous generations of Muslim intellectuals such as Nurettin Topçu (1997, 75–104), Gülen depicted modernization as a process of cultural deprivation leading to the Europeanization of Turkey's customs along the French model (*alafrangalaşma*) (Gülen 1981a, b). In order to reverse this process and return to a model consistent with the country's historical and religious traditions, he suggested the need for reforming new generations by educating them (*terbiye etmek*) according to Islamic views. This would initiate a double and interrelated process of cultural re-appropriation and moralization of society, which he saw as two indivisible aspects of the same civilizational project. Given the centrality taken by this pedagogical enterprise in the Islamic reformist project, Gülen claimed that the education of the new generations could be considered as one kind of *jihad*, and maybe even one amongst the greatest kinds (Gülen 1981c).[17] In these passages, he makes reference to a classical distinction in Islam between "lesser" and "greater" *jihad*. The former (*al-jihad al-asghar*) was the kind of struggle that early generations of Muslims conducted as they fought for the survival of the community and the conquest of new lands. Greater *jihad* (*al-jihad al-akbar*), instead, was meant to be the ethical struggle with one's self, an understanding of *jihad* that was closer to the original meaning of the Arabic word encompassing "struggle" or "striving" (Renard 1988; Cook 2015). While the Qur'an is quite clear about the fact that "lesser *jihad*" is the most valuable of the two (see 2:218, 8:72, 9:20, 49:15), some passages (e.g. 22:78) use the same term to describe a more spiritual kind of striving. Therefore, it is possible to argue that the development of the idea of a "greater *jihad*" is a later development that dates back to the end of the ninth century, when those who could not take part in the Muslim conquest (in what had become far-away lands) had to find legal grounds to justify their involvement in some sort of *jihad* (Cook 2015, 32 ff).[18]

---

17 "Actually, the education of the children is also a kind of *jihad*. Maybe, since it is related to the goal of making the inner self righteous, it is one of the biggest struggles (*cihadların en büyüğü*)" (Gülen 1981b).

18 While there are a few *hadith*s that can be used to justify this use of the term, the practice was inspired by one in particular which, however, is not included in the main *hadith* collections: "A number of fighters came to the Messenger of Allah," and he said: "You have done well in coming from the 'lesser *jihad*' to the 'greater *jihad*.'" They said: "What is

In one of his most important books on the topic, *I'la-yi Kelimetullah veya Cihad*, Gülen embraces this later interpretation of *jihad* and stresses the importance of reforming oneself before engaging in preaching activities (Gülen 1996). More strikingly, he stretches the meaning of the word to include all the efforts aimed at reforming society through education and preaching. Gülen extends the term so far that it overlaps with the idea of Islamic proselytizing (*daʿwa*), aimed at reforming society, a mission that is very akin to that of *hizmet* (see Chapter 1). In line with reformist Islamic projects elsewhere (Hatina 2006), Gülen established a strong link between the moral reform of the individual and that of broader society. Rather than in instructing people in the subjects taught in a classical *medrese*, he was indeed more interested in instilling a broad public of ordinary Muslims with basic Islamic dispositions and eventually involve them in *hizmet*. While his emphasis on character formation is a longstanding trait of education within Islam (Halstead 2004; see also below), the notable difference here is that Gülen sees such formation as preparatory to Muslims' active involvement in the reformist project of the community.

In order to achieve this goal, Gülen saw the need for a great change in pedagogical methods. To this end, in his seminal articles in *Sızıntı* (but see also Gülen 1998b), he proposed a technique for educating new generations that was based on love (*sevgi*) and endearment (*okşamak*). He claimed that educators must show "total dedication" to students and their concerns, always addressing them with a "positive attitude" and "modeling self-sacrifice." Ideas of love and affection are central in this pedagogy because an educator's demonstration of these feelings are more effective (*tesirli, müessir*) in evoking positive responses than harsher methods based on discipline. For Gülen, discipline (*tedip*) and corporal punishment (*dayak cezası*) should be the very last resort in the educational enterprise. Although they may appear to achieve some result, they only pacify (*müsekkin etmek*) and do not provide a real and lasting effect. As he stated: "to stabilize the spiritual condition of the young person [...] situations which lead to the arousal of his negative reaction must be avoided." Instead, the most "effective weapons" (*müessir silah*) to arouse positive responses from others are good works (*iyilikler*), benevolence (*ihsan*), and smiles (*güler-yüz*), because "if you enter their hearts with love, presents, and prizes, then they will show respect to your thoughts and suggestions" (Gülen 1981c).[19]

the 'greater *jihad*?'" He said: "For the servant [of God] to fight his passions" (quoted in Cook 2015, 35).

19 Other specific behaviors suggested by Gülen included: teaching things gradually (*tedricilikle*) by adapting to the nature (*fıtrat*) of the young student; being tolerant (*müsamaha*) toward pupils' shortcomings, which also means, illustrating things collectively (*toplum içinde* or *umumi olarak*) and talking privately to the students only if they persist in error;

What Gülen defines in these writings is a positive pedagogy based on principles of mutual respect and adaptation to the needs of the *talebe*s, in which love, concern, dedication, and self-sacrifice occupy a central place. For this reason, I have elsewhere defined these attitudes "pedagogies of affection" (Vicini 2013). As it will be shown below, the love and dedication that the *abi*s showed toward the students were pivotal in leading them to emulate their tutors through a process of progressive adaptation to life in the houses. In these pedagogies, the emphasis is on the relational dimension of the educational enterprise. For this reason, they may sound similar to those defined in pedagogical works that have attempted to isolate a "care ethics" as distinct from virtue ethics (Noddings 1984, 2002). However, no distinction between care and virtue ethics could be found in the educative interactions that I observed in the houses. Within the Gülen community, care and affection were the means that allowed the activation of other pedagogies based on exemplariness and emulation, through which the embodiment of key virtues and principles took place. In this light, the "pedagogies of affection" circumscribe the relational process by means of which more powerful emulative mechanisms based on exemplary conduct were reproduced among the students.

5 Life and Tutoring in the Gülen Housings

Before considering the place of exemplary conduct in the pedagogical path of the community, it is useful to pause for a moment to consider what the educational goals were for the *talebe*s and how their maturation process was managed by the *abi*s in the separate environments of the dormitories and the houses. To introduce this aspect, let me quote the words of Mustafa, the director of one of the two main dormitories of the community that I regularly visited during fieldwork. Well-shaven other than a thin, small moustache, he was a twenty-six-year-old graduate in mathematics from the prestigious Boğaziçi University. One night, when asked about what they wished for the *talebe*s, he answered:

> We want them to learn to live their religion [...] In the dormitory students spend most of their time studying school-related subjects. Some other time is dedicated to social activities. Then for the remaining time, we try to remind them of their religion. [...] As is explained also by psychology, in this period of their life boys experience a process of radical change

---

using good and beautiful words (*iyi ve güzel sözler*) and a balance of love and fear; and establishing an harmonious (*uyum*) relationship with the young person.

during which their character (*karakter*) is formed. In this period religion has to provide the foundation for this process.

Relying on a rhetoric rooted in Islamic views but saturated with references to Western psycho-pedagogical theory, Mustafa pointed out how adolescence is a very important time to instill the basic Islamic dispositions that will shape the character of the young boys in the long run. In line with a tradition of virtue ethics that goes back to Aristotle, the development of intellect and character cannot be separated in Islamic education (*terbiye*, in Arabic *tarbiya*) (Boyle 2004; Halstead 2004). Accordingly, when Mustafa envisages religion as the necessary solid ground upon which character can be formed, he is driven by the usual concern within this and other religious traditions of how to initiate pupils into faith.

According to Mustafa, there were two basic dispositions that the *talebe*s had to embody at this age. First is the habit of regularly performing the daily prayer out of the key virtue of *ihlas*. The second is the disposition to behave in accordance with what he called "good morals" (*güzel ahlak*); the etiquette of righteous behavior and moods better exemplified by the exemplary conduct of the Prophet Muhammad (see Chapter 2 and below). At this age, the community was very much concerned with the acquisition of these two basic habits because they were considered the basis upon which other key community virtues, such as responsibility, self-sacrifice, and dedication to the cause of *hizmet*, could be progressively embodied by the *talebe*s. Prayer occupied a special place in this regard. Not only was it considered to be the first and main duty students had to undertake as pious Muslims, it was also seen as important in instilling in them the discipline necessary to be successful at school today and active people in society tomorrow. During my frequent visits to the dorm in the course of two academic terms, I could observe how several lessons by the elder brothers were dedicated to explain questions related to the performance of the prayer in some detail to the younger brothers: how to make the ritual purification that preceded it, how to catch the right time-slot, and even how to bend the back so as to not invalidate the prayer.

The dormitories were considered better places than the houses to instill these two main dispositions in the *talebe*s because a disciplined environment could be recreated more easily. This became clear to me when, in correspondence with the opening of the new academic semester, the group of six high-school students that I first met in the house in Şişli moved to the newly-opened nearby dormitory managed by Mustafa. Kamil was asked by the community to move with the students in order to facilitate their integration in the new place and to assist Mustafa in accomplishing his task. A white sheet headed by the parenthetical word "program" was posted at each floor of the structure, which indicated the strict schedule students had to follow for each hour of the day. As for the houses, the schedule was set according to the five daily prayers. It started before dawn with the morning prayer, which was followed by breakfast. Then the students went to school. When they were back in the early afternoon, they spent the rest of the day until sleeping (planned for 11 p.m.) by taking three one-hour studying sessions (*etüd*) distributed before and after dinner. One final time-slot was dedicated to reading religious texts, which generally occurred after they performed the last prayer. Exceptions were made for visits by elder brothers who regularly came to conduct collective readings (*sohbet*), which took place in the big salon that occupied the last floor of the building, according to a community custom.

There were ways for the students to evade the austere discipline of the place and engage in some entertaining activity, however. During breaks, especially after dinner and before going to bed, they generally spent some recreational time in the leisure area adjacent to the small cafeteria located in the basement. Here they could play ping-pong, have some sweets, watch TV, and even use one of the computers to surf the internet, though always under the supervision of the *abi*s or of more experienced *talebe*s. In extraordinary circumstances, the community also organized special recreational activities like football matches or video-game tournaments. These were considered breaks from the discipline of the place that eased the feeling of excessive oppression, facilitating the students' process of adaptation. The collective play also had an important educational dimension, as it was conducted in accordance with the community's morals. In the football matches I watched, for example, I never saw a young boy boast about his own skills or make fun of another who played poorly. The level of competitiveness was purposefully kept low, and rivalry and disputes were avoided. This was done in order not to compromise, and rather foster, a sense of harmony and brotherhood among the youngsters. Collective recreational activities were important ways of constructing an alternative normality drenched with Islamic morals and love for the brothers, which was in opposition to the competitiveness, individualism, and bullying that the students had to face at school and in outside society in general.

In the dormitories, the *abi*s were referred to as *beletmen abi*s. Like Kamil, they had been appointed to ensure that the younger students conformed to the dormitory rules. They were also responsible with providing them with assistance in accordance with the pedagogies of affection that I have detailed above. As such, the *beletmen abi*s were the first to be held responsible for the education of the *talebe*s and could even be scolded by their superiors if they did not sufficiently dedicate themselves to the cause (see below). Nevertheless, they were outnumbered by the students, whom they could not always monitor properly. Their main duty was to maintain the order and discipline within the dorm with particular regard to the conduct of the prayer, study hours, and reading of religious texts.

The real tutoring of the *talebe*s was assigned to the *abi*s staying in the houses. In line with a longstanding Nur tradition, the houses were indeed the original laboratory of the community and the places where core teachings were passed down to the new generations. In Gülen's vision, the community houses had to radiate a spirituality and energy like the one present in the first Muslim community under the guidance of Muhammad, because this would be conducive to the accomplishment of the community's preaching mission (*tebliğ, irşad*) (Gülen 2008, 11–16; Gülen 1992a, b). Once called among themselves "houses of light" (*ışık evleri*), corresponding with the more transnational and missionary character that the movement took since the late 1990s, they have been renamed "houses of service" (*hizmet evleri*). The *talebe*s were divided into small groups of around three or four people, generally of the same age and possibly attending the same school, but not necessarily staying in the same dormitory. Each group regularly visited one house every week where they spent time with "their *abi*." Working as a tutor to them, the *abi* provided help and assistance, but overall, he supervised the students' progress both at school and with regard to their spiritual growth. This also implied the duty of regularly taking note of the number of pages the students read during the week for the *Risale*, Gülen books, and the Qur'an, in addition to the portions of the Qur'an and of the prayer formulas (*cevşen*) they had memorized, and the number of minutes of Gülen's sermons they had listened to.[20] All this information was registered in Excel files named *çtl* and reported to upper-echelon brothers who could monitor the most disciplined students and select the potential future *abi*s among them.

Apart from these checking-and-reporting tasks, the tutoring *abi*s also showed a serious concern for the students' problems and the challenges they might face during their maturation process. They paid regular visits to the students at the dorms, took part in common activities organized by the *beletmen abi*s, and actively participated in the summer camps or other activities, including trips abroad, that the community organized at least once per semester. As their spiritual guides, they had to convey the habit of praying, to introduce them to fundamental readings, and to behave as role models by exemplifying

---

20   The sections of the Qur'an had to be memorized in Arabic. At this age, the students were expected to be able to read it. For this purpose, the middle-school *talebe*s were sent to summer courses organized at local mosques either by their parents or by the *abi*s.

the best virtues and etiquettes. This was in line with the key pedagogical principle of exemplariness that I will illustrate below, but can also be read as the reflex of a specific pedagogical strategy of the community based on the use of subtle techniques aimed at disguising *abi*s' surveilling duties under the appearance of care and concern for their problems.

The *talebe*s generally visited their *abi* on Friday, the holy day of Islam and the day marking the beginning of the weekend, when they could study more intensively. They arrived in the afternoon after school and would stay overnight in order to spend a good amount of time with their tutor and perform the entire ritual of the two most important prayers of the night and the morning. The key moment of the meeting was the approximately 30-minute reading of a portion of the *Risale* or a book by Gülen. While at this age the *talebe*s were already expected to read these books by themselves, the *abi*s' explanation was very important, as many of the terms and nuances used in the texts were difficult for them to grasp. Since I have already explored the reading practices of key religious texts in the previous chapter, it suffices to say that, at this age, readings mainly focused on basic themes like the importance of regularly performing the prayer and taming the lower self. Alternatively, they provided students with some first teachings about the transitoriness of life and the need to locate one's own life within the Nur ontological framework. According to the aforementioned principle of exemplariness, another important topic was the life and accomplishments of some important and exemplary religious figures, a discussion of which occurs in the next section.

6   Romanticizing Prophethood

In the Gülen community, the life of Muhammad or other prophets was often highlighted to exemplify an ideal virtuous life. This is in line with Gülen's preference for emotional accounts of the life of the early Muslim community over complex theological discussions in his sermons. The narration of stories about the first generation of Muslims has indeed been a distinctive character of the speeches through which Gülen became known to the large public in the 1990s, which were later published in what is probably his most famous work: the three-volume *Sonsuz Nur* (The Infinite Light) (Gülen 1999).[21] *The Infinite Light* is a passionate account of the life of the Prophet and his companions that sets

---

21   Before 2016, in the community's *NT* stores it was also possible to find the whole collection of videotaped sermons gathered in a DVD box set. These DVDs were often watched together by community members during meetings.

out their distinctive virtues and qualities, thereby presenting Muslims with a model of ideal piousness, through which they should be inspired. The text extensively relies on authoritative *hadith*s, but also on biographical accounts of the Prophet Muhammad (*siyer*, or *siyar* in Arabic).[22] These are not accepted as part of the legal corpus of *fiqh*, but they offer insights and anecdotes about the Prophet's life that have often been used by Muslim preachers to report and convey exemplary expressions of pious demeanor. Gülen's sermons have generally been filled with stories, historical accounts, and legends about the formative period of Islam. By drawing upon the *siyer* literature, in *Sonsuz Nur* he narrates the Prophet's life in a dramaturgical form filled with romanticized details to better convey the Islamic message of piety to a public of ordinary Muslims. To this end, when he spoke in public, he reported these stories using highly-emotional tones and postures, in ways that contravened conventional masculine gender models that in Turkey forbid men to cry in public (Özyürek 1997).[23] One of the most distinguishing traits of these sermons was indeed Gülen's recourse to tears and shouts regarding the piety and devotion through which the Prophet and his companions endured adversity and trouble during the early years of Islam.

Similar narrative strategies were also used by community brothers to instill in the students those dispositions of patience, dedication, and self-sacrifice that are considered to be central to the ideals of *hizmet*. Sunier and Sahin (2015) have reported how weeping sessions took place during collective meetings of the community (*sohbet*). They have also argued that, rather than as simple emotional performances, these meetings can be better understood as

---

22   *Siyer* literature is a quite popular genre in Turkey (e.g. Sarıçam 2004; Topbaş 2006; Köksal 2013), whose origins go back to the first fourteenth-century Ottoman-Turkish version of Mavlid poems dated around 1388, when Yusuf of Erzurum (also known as Darir (blind) as he indeed was) wrote the *Siyer-i Nebi*. The manuscript is a translation, both in prose and verses, of *Siret in-Nabi*, written by the well-known Arab historian Ibn-i Hisham. Another famous old *siyer* is the *Vesilet ün-Necat* of Süleyman Chelebi (1364–1422 circa) which soon became widely diffused. Recited in the Ottoman courts since the fifteenth century, it was later translated into the languages of all the nations under Ottoman dominion including Arabic, Persian, Bosnian, Albanian, and Greek (Çağatay 1968).

23   In his speeches and books, Gülen often also refers to the more recent Ottoman past. In the above-mentioned conference on the golden generation, for instance, he tells a story about Sultan Fatih Mehmet II, the conqueror of Istanbul, to exalt the idea of Islamic justice. This legendary account was also reported to me by more than one of my interlocutors. It narrates how even the Sultan had offered to have his hand amputated after a judge considered him guilty according to Islamic law for having unjustly ordered the cutting of the architect Atik Sinan's hands. At the end, Sinan dropped the charges and the Sultan's hands were saved, but only after the latter had agreed to submit to the judge's decision.

"sensational forms" (Meyer 2008) and processes of "moral attunement" (Hirschkind 2006) during which community members embody key community dispositions. Because these rituals are probably performed more frequently in the higher echelons of the community, I have only occasionally seen some *abi*s gently weeping while watching one of Gülen's old speeches. Given their young age, the *talebe*s still tended to experience their participation in these meetings with joy and lightheartedness, and I never saw one of them crying due to emotions evoked by one of these speeches. In addition, the *abi*s generally preferred to show their students *Bamteli*, the weekly sermon that the leader of the community released every Sunday on the community website *herkül.org*. In these more recent sermons, Gülen tends to maintain a more scholarly stance and is seldom emotional.

However, narratives of the prophets, including those belonging to the other monotheistic traditions, were still relied upon by the tutoring *abi*s to provide the *talebe*s with examples of virtuous conduct. Take as an example what Halil, a young *talebe* from the house in Şişli, told me about one of these readings. The day before they had read the first section of the second chapter of "The Flashes"—a comment on Qur'an 21:83—with Canan *abi* (Nursi 1995b). In the passage, Nursi comments upon the story of the Prophet Job (*Eyüp*), a figure whose unshakable faith is put to test through hopeless illness by God and who hence is seen as an example par excellence of the pious man in all three monotheist traditions. Halil recounted:

> Job was seriously wounded and for a long time he was not healing. However, he did not complain about his condition to God. He was very patient (*sabır*) ... But he could endure only until the day when his suffering was so great that the pain did not even allow him to pray. Only at this point and only for this reason, he finally decided to ask God for help. Then God caused the miracle and Job was finally healed.

Like Nursi's writing, Halil emphasized the sincerity—*halis*, a term coming from the same root of *ihlas*—with which Job submitted his request. Indeed, it is only when praying for help moved by the sincere desire to be able to pray again, and not to bring an end to his suffering, that God healed him. Then Halil repeated to me the comment made by Canan *abi* during the reading session: "And sometimes we even complain when the *abi* is late preparing our dinner," and acknowledged how right the *abi* was in remarking this aspect as a good example of the impatience they sometimes manifest. Finally, Halil remembered one of the comments Nursi made in the *Lema* about this story:

> Every sin is a sort of wound we have in our inner soul. Even if apparently we are not wounded, not on the outside at least, on the inside we are. On the contrary, the Saint Job had many wounds on the outside but he did not have any on the inside [in his soul].

As Nursi concludes in the text, each committed sin and every single doubt that may arise in our mind about God's existence opens a wound in the heart and the soul. Whereas the wounds of Job were so deep that they threatened his worldly life, one's inner wounds threaten one's access to the Qur'anic message in this world and to an infinite life in the hereafter.

By way of short, simple, and effective exemplary stories like this one, Canan gave his pupils a lesson about being more patient in small everyday acts, such as waiting for dinner or for a friend. If Job was so patient in front of the great adversities he had to face, the students should find it comparatively easier to be a little more patient in their daily occurrences after listening to this story. In the meantime, the reading also allowed Canan to introduce deeper teachings about the human soul, its fragility, and how sins can easily insinuate themselves and take root in it, no matters whether one's sins are visible on the outside or not. Although this and other passages from religious texts were not read in full and with the insight that was requested at a later age, they already made it possible for Canan and other *abi*s to convey some basic teachings and principles to the *talebe*s. But if the exemplifying narratives of holy and pious figures were considered to be particularly effective in conveying fundamental demeanors and values at this age, it was also because the pedagogical technique fit into a more general educational and preaching principle of the community: exemplary conduct.

7 Learning by Example

Apart from community narratives, it is in the concrete practice of everyday life in the houses and dorms that the *abi*s had to exemplify the ideal form of Muslim conduct proposed by *hizmet*. In *İrşad Ekseni* (the Axis of Guidance), considered one of Gülen's most important and original works along with *Sonsuz Nur* and *I'la-yi Kelimetullah veya Cihad*, he talks of living an exemplary Muslim life (*örnek olmak, temsil etmek*) as a fundamental principle of Islamic conduct. Gülen traces the origins of this principle back to the Prophet's leadership over the first Muslim community and insists that every person of service should abide by it (Gülen 1998b, 167–191). This book is taken from a series of speeches that Gülen gave in the 1980s and whose main topic was the method of predication within Islam (*İslam'da tebliğ usulü*). In *İrşad Ekseni*, parallels are drawn between the preaching method of the prophets of the three monotheist traditions. For this reason, the book is a very important reference and motivational source for community members. In it Gülen invites his followers to preach Islam according to the Qur'anic injunction [3:104] "ordering the good and forbidding the evil" (*emr-i bi'l-maruf nehy-i ani'l münker*). Not to be simply seen as an individual path, adherence to an exemplary conduct should be approached as an integral part of the community's broader project for reforming society.

Accordingly, the *abi*s had to maintain an exemplary conduct in the houses in order to inspire the *talebe*s. Such conduct did not only consist of the performance of key Islamic obligations, but also of the students' conformation to all the community's more important virtuous behaviors, including self-sacrifice, dedication, care for others, and a strong sense of responsibility for and commitment to one's duties. One of Gülen's oft-repeated sayings is a good illustration of the emphasis put on exemplariness within the community: "How can you teach the things you don't live?" As Gülen had explained in his early writings in *Sızıntı*, if the educator wants to see his pupils animated by sincere and pure faith (*samimi inançlı*), this same kind of sincerity has to become apparent in everything he does. To cultivate a genuine Islamic commitment in young people, the educator must perform every act—eating, drinking, sleeping, getting up, and dressing—with a "formative meticulousness" (Gülen 1981c).

As for the many pedagogical issues discussed in this work, the issue of exemplariness was also rarely, if ever, discussed among the brothers. Rather, it was actualized by them in daily life. It was only during a conversation with Kamil one evening at the dormitory that the issue was made explicit to me. I had just asked him what he thought was the best way of approaching the *talebe*s given their young age. After thinking his reply over for a moment, Kamil advanced the idea that the best thing to do after establishing a positive relationship with the young person is:

> Explaining myself through my own actions, that is to say: setting a good example, explaining the good qualities of Islam by living them. [...] Explaining things verbally to the *talebe*s is not so important. For sure you explain, but then if you don't perform the prayers, you don't fast, etc., you are telling lies...

Words cannot effectively influence the students if they are not followed by action. There are two lines of argument in Kamil's answer. The first is the rather obvious observation that if a tutor does not comply with certain rules, it would be unreasonable to expect his pupils to do so. The second concerns the efficacy of the pedagogical intervention. Saying things is not enough. If one really wishes to have a strong imprint on the formation of his students' character, he has to exemplify the values he wants to convey in his daily attitudes and behaviors. It is for this reason that, if the *abi*s hoped to be successful as educators, they first had to be successful in the "greatest *jihad*"—in reforming themselves by taming the lower self and embodying the dispositions prescribed by the community. Only after this process has been accomplished, completely or in part, might they hope to positively affect the *talebe*s.

According to dynamics that resemble those described in the second chapter, the experience of cohabitation and daily socialization within the housings served the goal of making exemplariness an effective method of pedagogical intervention. The embodiment of community etiquettes and principles inspired by the *sunna* unfolded through a gradual process of adaptation by the students to the rhythms and discipline of the houses. As I have discussed extensively elsewhere (Vicini 2013), studies on daily socialization (Ochs and Shohet 2006; Gaskins and Paradise 2009; Paradise and Rogoff 2009) and legitimate peripheral participation (Lave and Wenger 1991; cf. Boyle 2004) provide valuable insights for illustrating the progressive nature of the process. The *talebe*s embodied the dispositions that were required by a disciplined Muslim life dedicated to *hizmet* through daily socialization in the houses. However, I have also explained why this scholarship is limited when it comes to accounting for the role of educators in pedagogical processes.

It was indeed the flexible nature of the *abi*s-*talebe*s relationship that made socialization particularly effective in these contexts. This relationship was characterized by both proximity (in terms of age) and distance (in terms of authority), a fact that allowed the pedagogical enterprise to function more naturally than with school teachers or parents. In line with seniority rules of this and other Islamic communities in Turkey, the *talebe*s were expected to address the *abi*s respectfully and, more importantly, to be willing to follow their suggestions. At the same time, the proximity of age among the two allowed for the conveyance of the teachings in ways that made authority less of an imposition on the students. It was this proximity which made the *abi*s role models that the *talebe*s were willing to follow in their path toward a full Muslim maturity. For them, the *abi*s worked as guides to be emulated along their own personal path toward maturation as both adults and professionals. They might also have an impact on the *talebe*s' willingness to commit to *hizmet* in the near future and become *abi*s themselves when they start attending university.

To illustrate these aspects, take as an example the words of two high-school students. Toward the end of my fieldwork, when the *abi*s' trust toward me had grown, I decided to interview a dozen of the *talebe*s among those whom I had interacted with most during fieldwork. One of the things I was most interested in was to understand the extent to which they had been affected by their tutors. With this goal in mind, I asked them if they had a favorite *abi* and what they liked most about him. When I posed this question to Hamza, a seventeen-year-old devout student who attended the German high-school (*Özel Alman Lisesi*) and who was tutored by Enes in the Fatih house, he answered:

> Do you know the *öss* [now *YKS*] exam? He [Enes] knows everything about it ... And whatever kind of question you ask him, he's always there to help us. For example, he reads the Qur'an very well ... and he's really a very conscientious *abi*. He really understands spiritual matters ... Despite the difficulty of our lessons, he takes an interest in us. He works with us so much ... five or six days per week. He helps us, he calls us ... Therefore, some days he only sleeps three or four hours. Sometimes he sits on the chair and he sleeps there ... because there isn't any space. I mean, he really gives his commitment its full due. This is the thing I like the most about him.

The other extract is from Necmi, the undisciplined *talebe* of whom Kamil spoke. Also seventeen-year-old, he went to the very prestigious French-language *Galatasaray Lisesi*. Although Necmi was a more vivacious boy than Hamza, and he still seemed not to take *hizmet* too seriously, when asked about what he liked most of his *abi* Talat, he gave a similar answer to that of his peer:

> First, his patience ... second, he really makes an effort to work with us. [...] The *abi* [...] got the degree from our same school and he is studying what I want ... I mean, he followed the same life-path I want to follow, and he is an *abi* whose example I have to take seriously. I mean, for me, he is a sort of role-model. [...] From the point of view of the university ... of the school ... Talat *abi* is really a good *abi*. [...] When you look at him, you can't see anything bad.

While the two *talebe*s emphasized different qualities of their *abi*s, both positively evaluated the fact that their tutors were committed to their educational duties and that they made the maximum effort to help them day and night. Such an appraisal was accompanied by a palpable sense of admiration for the knowledge and capacities they exhibited. According to what both Hamza and Necmi say, the fact that their *abi*s demonstrated a genuine interest in them, that they were helpful, and that they dedicated their time altruistically, aroused esteem and awe towards their *abi*s. In this sense, the *abi*s' effort in keeping up with the community's educational model appears to be not only functional in establishing a positive relationship with the students, but also a way to display the same qualities and values the *abi*s uphold as both educators and adults. A nearly maternal kind of concern, dedication, and commitment to their own responsibilities, matched with an embodied piety, made the probability of affecting the *talebe*s higher than in other pedagogical circumstances, especially when a chain of positive evaluation-admiration-emulation was activated. When this mechanism succeeded, the *abi*s became models worthy of emulation by their pupils, who may desire to internalize these same qualities in the long run.

At the same time, the *talebe*s saw the *abi*s as inspirational people. This aspect clearly emerges from the words of Necmi, for whom Talat was not only an example in his moral conduct and commitment to the ideals of service, but for a whole life-path as well. Necmi wanted to pursue the same studies at the university and to be as academically successful as his *abi*. He expressed an appreciation for Talat's qualities and for his life-choices. He wanted to emulate him in his life in an entirety that included both being educated and being a good Muslim. The effect of the *abi*s' example on the students goes beyond the contours of simply committing to a specific religious path. It also influences the *talebe*s' will to emulate them toward a successful Muslim maturity. While neither the *abi*s nor the *talebe*s ever used this word, the notion of maturity seems to be relevant here. By functioning as role models for their younger brothers, the *abi*s offered them a horizon, a life-perspective, on how to become both good Muslims and successful individuals. They were a model the *talebe*s could follow as they were caught in the difficult and intricate path leading to adulthood. For a young Muslim in a society where Islamic forms of expression were stigmatized until recently, to undertake a pious life-path probably appeared more difficult than following other paths. For this reason, the *abi*s' success in matters both of life and spirit was a powerful source of inspiration for the pupils as it presented them with a concrete option for their future.

8 Embodying Responsibility

Being an *abi* was not an easy task. After all, the university students were only a few years older than their pupils and they were also in the process of learning how to comply with the norms and values of community life. They had a great responsibility. The *beletmen abi*s were the first to be held responsible for inculcating the fundamental habits of the community in the *talebe*s. As part of their duties they had to wake up the students in time for the morning prayer, lead the recitation of the *tesbihat* afterwards, accompany them to the cafeteria for breakfast, welcome them when they returned from school in the afternoon, check that everyone joined the *etüd* and did not stay in their room, and help them with schoolwork or preparatory tests for the national examination. However, there was no guarantee that the *abi*s would be successful in their endeavors. This often caused a sense of frustration in the university students. Yet it was a calculated risk by the community. Learning how to deal with the burden of responsibility was part of the same process through which the *abi*s embodied the sense of commitment required of its members by *hizmet*. At the same time, it was a way for the elder brothers to test whether they were able to keep up with their expectations and, eventually, to select the most committed ones for directive roles within the hierarchy of the community.

To explore this aspect and give an idea of the kind of dedication that was requested of the university students, consider the words of Erdem, the *abi* supervising all the educational activities of the community in the northern part of Istanbul European side—one of the three main administrative districts (*bölge*) into which the city had been divided by the community. With a thin moustache and a stern look, Erdem always seemed to be in a rush. He came to the dorm regularly, at least a couple of times per month, to talk with the *beletmen abi*s and meet the students. I had been struck by his awkward manners, in particular by the severity with which he addressed the personnel at the dorm, as well as by the sharp replies he gave to the students on some occasions.[24]

When Erdem entered the room, the atmosphere was already tense. Before I had time to open my mouth, he had caught my eye and waved his hand to signal that I could stay. Among those present, there were the *beletmen abi*s of this and other dormitories located in the nearby neighborhoods of Şişli, Beyoğlu, and Beşiktaş. After learning that one of them could not come to the meeting nor join the following evening program at a local school of the community, Erdem became more on edge than usual, and began rebuking the students with his proverbial severe tones:

> How is that possible? Didn't I tell you that you shouldn't take any appointment for today until midnight?! [...] We are people of service ... We

---

24 For example, when one student asked him about the theory of Darwin (a quite controversial matter within the community) Erdem reacted by abruptly rejecting the theory as an attempt by their secular teachers to impose their values upon them. Raising such a topic during a reading was considered a sign of defiance toward authority, and it was always addressed with some embarrassment and bitterness by elder brothers. However, Erdem's attitude exceeded this general attitude to such an extent that his reaction sounded at odds with the principles of the pedagogies of affection that I have described above.

don't have private lives ... It's not allowed for us to have private lives! [...] Eating, sleeping, going to the bathroom ... all these are physiological needs that it isn't possible to abstain from. But for the remaining 18 hours of the day, we've got to fully dedicate ourselves to *hizmet*, we've got to be always ready and available. [...] There is only one certain truth and that's the afterlife, but in order to enter paradise there are some duties (*vazife*) we must accomplish, some responsibilities (*sorumluluk*) we must take upon ourselves. [...] It's as if we were in a movie ... as if we were actors in a movie: our goal is to create a happy world, to make it blossom like a rose. It is in order to achieve such a goal that we've got to be permanently active ... Only in this way can we spread the beautiful model of the Prophet everywhere. [...] In order to achieve this goal *hizmet* needs disciplined people in its ranks.

Erdem's outburst was intended to remind those present that they had some duties to fulfill as people who had decided to join the cause of *hizmet*. Not all those who stayed in the Gülen facilities as teenagers became *abi*s later, and if they did, it is because they had accepted the responsibility that accompanied this choice. Their duties and responsibility were put by Erdem in a teleological perspective, in which the ideal society dreamed by the community is realized. But he also presented the *abi*s with a price they had to pay to be rewarded with paradise in the afterlife. His rebuke was a reminder to the students that they had to devote themselves entirely to the education of the *talebe*s in order to achieve both goals. Erdem implied that he knew that some of them were undisciplined and used to go late to bed, but this did not matter much. As for the community, they could even go back to bed once the students had left for school. The important thing was that they would be ready to welcome the *talebe*s when these were back in the afternoon, to ask how the day had gone and help them with their homework. At the same time, the *abi*s had to be a role model for their younger brothers:

You've got to take your duties more seriously, including the way you dress, the shoes you wear and your appearance more in general ... Because anything you do wrong may influence the students negatively. [...] It's particularly important that you give the best example. [...] Because one day these boys will represent *hizmet*. Example ... example ... you have to be an example for them. [...] This is the religious legacy that has been bestowed upon you; the legacy of our Prophet, of Mevlana, of Said Nursi, of Hocaefendi ... the legacy of the martyrs of Gallipoli. [...] It may be that you will not see the results of all your efforts. It may happen that you will not see your own students become şakird [abis].²⁵ But even if it isn't you, others will be successful in this work.

In this passage, Erdem softened his tone. I read the link he traced between the *abi*s' efforts and a chain of Muslim saintly people going back to the Prophet Muhammad as an attempt to motivate his audience. Erdem's mention of Gallipoli, which echoes reports of war and martyrdom, may have served to remind the *abi*s about the need to maintain the discipline and commitment of an army. The final note, suggesting that even if they fail other *abi*s would succeed, was most certainly meant to lighten their burden of responsibility and to conclude the speech with a comforting message. However, for most of the talk, Erdem had been quite harsh with the students. He even sounded insulting when—with a light complacent smile on his face—he told them he was aware that they were not very successful students, but that they had not to worry about it since the community would take care of them one day. What really mattered was that they focused on the *talebe*s, even if this meant they had to fall behind in their own studies.

When the *abi*s emptied the room at the end of the meeting, some grumbles were heard in the background. Not without embarrassment, I asked Kamil what he thought about Erdem's speech. With a melancholic face, he said he was disappointed because he knew that the *abi* was right. Kamil acknowledged that there was a malaise in *hizmet* that had to be eradicated. He implied that some of the *abi*s lacked the discipline necessary to accomplish their duty properly. His words confirmed the existence of some possible weaknesses in the functioning mechanisms of the community. At the same time, they pointed out the more basic fact that no matter how the community tried to deny it, the *abi*s were young and still in the process of (only eventually) becoming fully dedicated to *hizmet*. Being responsible for the *talebe*s was not only their duty. It was also part of the path through which they embodied the sense of responsibility and dedication that the golden generation, envisioned by Gülen, had to possess.

Kamil's comment reflects this twofold condition, of both educators and apprentices, which the university students had to juggle while residing in the community's housings. Specific readings were done by the university students to reflect on their ambivalent status. Their commitment to *hizmet* had not only

---

25 From the Persian word for "disciple" (*shagird*), şakird is a term that is colloquially used within the Nur movement to indicate the students of the *Risale-i Nur*. In this specific case, it is contextually used to indicate the person who will embody the main values of the community and commit himself to the ideals of religious service.

taken most of their time and energies since a quite young age, but had also meant renouncing many of the liberties that their peers could enjoy. These and other aspects related to their status as *abi*s were addressed in specific meetings. Take the case of a reading attended by the five *abi*s who supervised the group of *talebe*s going to the *Galatasaray Lisesi*. The meeting was led by Talat, who was also the supervisor of this group of *abi*s. Given the nature of the meeting, Talat had chosen the fifth topic of the first section of *Asa-yı Mûsa*, a passage of the *Risale* that is entirely dedicated to discussing youth.[26]

> [*text*] There is no doubt that youth will end. Like the summer leaves space to the winter, and the day to the night, so also youngness will ineluctably turn into oldness and death. If you will spend that ephemeral [*fani*] and transitory [*geçici*] youth accomplishing good and rightful actions, then [...] you will gain an endless and permanent youth [in the afterworld].[27]

The passage recalls usual Nur cosmologies and related views concerning the transitoriness of worldly life. Adding to this, Talat commented:

> Although this world is ephemeral, people continue to commit sins. The *Risale* is seen by Nursi as a cure (*tedavi*) against this kind of sickness. [...] If you look around, indeed, there's a lot of wasted time ... If you look at other university students they are aimless, without a goal. [...] By involving us in *hizmet* God is saving us from this emptiness. For this reason, you should not see the time you spend in service as a loss of something else, but as an enrichment. [...] Indeed, these other people are not happy in their heart. [...] We may often feel tired, but what we do gives a special taste to our life.

The *abi*s nodded in silence at the words of Talat. This was not the first time they had pondered their situation as young *abi*s. Yet the reading served as a reminder of the philosophical underpinnings of their sense of commitment. With that in mind, Talat added a comparison between their life and that of other people of their age. While it may be hard to take the responsibility that *hizmet* requires, being engaged in religious service confers a special quality

---

26   The *Asa-yı Mûsa*, also known as *Meyve Risalesi* (The Fruits of Belief), is one of the shortest books of the *Risale-i Nur*. Nursi wrote it around 1944 as he was secluded in the prison of Denizli waiting for a trial by the state. In the text, he addresses the condition of the prisoner, which he mainly describes in the terms of the transitory nature of worldly life if compared to the infinite life in the hereafter.
27   Nursi 1995a, 22.Translation by the author.

and direction to their lives. Rather than a burden, their engagement in educational service conferred an additional and enriching trait to their existence: it filled the void left by the sense of idleness that new generations may feel in modern consumerist society. As said, these sorts of reflections about the meaning of life and the sense of being involved in *hizmet* were not new, but part of larger discussions they had been involved in for a long time. When they were still *talebe*s, the university students had already tasted what dedication to others implied in terms of sacrifice. They did so gradually, by taking responsibility for some small duties such as assisting younger peers or helping the *abi*s implement order in the dorms.

The fact that gradual responsibilization was part of the educational path of the students since quite a young age was not only explained to me by some of the *abi*s in the field, but I could witness it in some of the most disciplined among the *talebe*s I met, such as Halil, Lütfi, and Deniz. With their commitment to following rules and disciplining themselves to the required conduct, they were the high-school students who tried hardest to set a daily example for the others and helped keep order in the dorm. As their tutor Canan told me one day in their regard, "they are boys who want responsibility." For this reason, they had the potential for scaling the ranks in the community. If they could continue to meet the expectations of the community, they would one day become good *abi*s, and good representatives of the kind of educated and dedicated Muslim that *hizmet* intended to raise.

∙ ∙ ∙

Taking responsibility was not simply an additional character trait among others that students of the Gülen community had to cultivate. It was an integral part of the path leading to dedicating one's entire life to *hizmet*. It was the quintessential trait of a process of internalization of the sense of commitment and ethos that distinguished this community from the *Suffa* and other Islamic groups in the country. Not content with merely asking his followers to comply with Muslim basic conduct, Gülen asked them to embody a sense of responsibility for the poor state of the world and engage in religious service spurred by the will to change the dim state of things. The *talebe*s began this path at a very young age, when they were still teenagers. They were usually drawn to the community's ranks through their family connections or by means of the capillary network of *dershane*s. Offered upward mobility opportunities and linked to the *abi*s by specific relations of affection, they were gradually fascinated by the ideals of the community. In time, they socialized together with other young members and became increasingly involved in *hizmet*. If they decided to remain committed to the community's project once they had completed their studies, they could either join the community's ranks or participate in its mission as persons operating in different spheres of society. Yet this was dependent on the degree of dedication and obedience they had demonstrated along the years. Only the most devoted students could enter the community's decisional structure.

Commitment to the community takes such a central place in the Gülen case that one may wonder about the entire enterprise of *hizmet*. Several traits of the educational practices illustrated in this chapter seem indeed to contradict appraisals that depict the community as an expression of an "Islamic Enlightenment" in the community, aimed at shaping new generations of educated, critical people willing to advance the communal good (Yavuz 2013). What was the real goal of the community? Was it to raise new generations of educated and pious Muslims able to engage in society freely and contribute to the collective well-being? Or, rather, was it to shape a crew of trusty people dedicated to the expansive goals of the community? Where does the border between these two orientations lie? How is the balance maintained between an original civilizational impetus rooted in the Islamic tradition and the more self-referential need to advance the agenda of the community?

Additionally, one may speculate whether the Gülen community has been affected—more than other religious groups in Turkey—by a modern tendency to see in Islam an aggregative and motivational force more than anything else. Although community members remained focused on conventional Islamic practices, their conduct seemed to be subordinated to what is a more "modernly-fashioned" inclination to push individuals to become loyal to a sociopolitical entity (the community in this case) and move in a coordinate way to achieve such entity's goals. In the framework of modern politics, this sense of commitment is generally reserved for loyalty to the nation-state, while in the Gülen case it was oriented toward the expansion of the community and the promotion of its ideals throughout society.

As the following chapter will show, a combination of responsibility and activism in a modernizing society is a component of both the *Suffa* and the Gülen communities. However, since the beginning, a more radical tension permeates the Gülen community, both from within and from the outside. From within, the ideals it promotes clashes with its own concrete policies. On the outside, the community has always been in competition with the secularists for the control of the state. This irresolvable tension is what lies at the basis of the conflictual relationship it developed with the AKP administration in the last years, which is explored further in the following chapter.

CHAPTER 5

Politics of Brotherhood

Chapter 3 explored the nuanced process by which Nursi reinterpreted the intellectual repertoires of the Islamic tradition to offer his followers a new method for the cultivation of their faith under the changed epistemological and social conditions of modern times. In this chapter, I look at how these forms of reflection provide people in the *Suffa* and the Gülen communities also with ways to think about human freedom, responsibility, and engagement in society from a specific kind of Muslim perspective. Although they are two distinct offshoots of the Nur movement, the *Suffa* and the Gülen communities shared a view of *hizmet* that did not see a contradiction between commitment to social reform and service to the state within the contours of modern Turkish society. This comes at some costs, however, as the swinging between religious ideals and mundane goals created a state of permanent tension within these communities, as well as between them and the surrounding political order. On the one hand, their driving logic was indeed grounded in a longstanding path of Islamic civility that goes "beyond secular reason" by appealing to a universal call to human brotherhood. On the other hand, however, especially in the Gülen case, different mechanisms pulled members back toward the community-centered goal of increasing the reach of *hizmet*.

In order to address this conundrum, I first explore the genealogy of Muslim ideals of responsibility and action, and subsequently shed light on how they have been re-evaluated within the *Suffa* and the Gülen communities in response to modern liberal views of human agency, as well as in the specific context of modern Turkey. The chapter will address questions such as those that follow. What societal ideas of human freedom, responsibility, and action animate Muslim forms of civic engagement in these two groups? To what extent do these ideas present an alternative to homologous secular modern views that began circulating in late Ottoman times? What is the nature of the tension that permeates the enactment of Islamically-grounded forms of civility in a context dominated by other non-religious logics? In what ways does the realization of a religious ideal eventually clash with the contingency of life and politics both in the past and in modern times?

These questions interlace with two other main aspects. The first is the scholarly issue of whether we can think of these forms of Islamically-inspired civic engagement as this-worldly oriented in the Weberian sense, and hence deemed to lose their original transcendent projection in the long term. Can we really, as some scholars claimed in regard to the Gülen community (Özdalga 2003; Yavuz 2003c), use the ideal type of inner-worldly asceticism to understand them? Although inner-worldly asceticism offers a metaphorical parallel with similar transformations in the Christian tradition, my general answer is that insofar as it suggests that a sort of secularization-cum-rationalization of Islam is underway, this ideal type remains largely unsatisfactory to describe the intertwining of activism and transcendent projection within Islam. In this vein, this chapter explores Muslim forms of civic engagement by looking at their more fundamental Islamic civility impulses and at how these have been refashioned in relation to broader structural and epistemological transformations during the modern era. A specific understanding of transcendence continues to uphold views of the self, individual responsibility, and action within the two communities under study and the Nur movement at large. Accordingly, rationalization-cum-secularization remains, at best, a very specific product of European history, which is not easily reconcilable with other contexts (Asad 2003).

The second more political aspect concerns whether the intermingling of Islam with this-worldly oriented logic may have had an impact on the communities under study in ways that limit the sincerity and disinterestedness of their forms of civic engagement. This question is especially pressing given the allegations claiming that the Gülen community played a decisive role in the perpetration of the coup attempt of July 15, 2016. As also determined by some recent studies, this community has always sought to expand its influence both at home and in other countries where it has become established (Hendrick 2013; Dohrn 2018). The prominent role that public officers linked to the community have allegedly played in the political events of the last ten years in Turkey is another indicator of its involvement in the fight for power. Relatedly, some of the following questions may cross the reader's mind: To what extent has the Gülen community operated based on a sincere commitment to raising new generations of educated and pious Muslims? Was the community's real goal to offer educational opportunities to these young people or was it to accumulate power? In other words, has the Gülen community sought to gain sociopolitical influence and take control of the state since the very beginning or was this only a later development?

While the community's intention to increase its influence in the country has been proven by its story of success and progressive occupation of spaces in the media, the economy, and the governmental institutions, it is difficult for a social scientist to grasp what are the "real intentions" of the interlocutors he meets in the field and link them to a specific programmatic goal. This is particularly true for this study, which focuses on young students who were members of the community only *in potentia* and who may have left it soon after. It follows that this work is unable to offer clear and definitive replies to these sorts of questions. What this chapter may help elucidate, however, is how my interlocutors believed there was no contradiction between their commitment to living their faith and their involvement in a project of social reform, including their attempt to get appointed to positions within state institutions. From this perspective, it is evident how a permanent—and inevitable—tension strained the relationship of the *Suffa* and the Gülen communities with the institutional framework in which they operated. It is to such tension between this-worldly and other-worldly orientation that I will draw attention in the concluding part of this chapter; a tension that is rooted in the inherent opposition between religious and secular domains and that has taken new forms under the conditions created by the political project of secular modernity.

1 "You'll Be of Service to This Country"

At the student meeting marking the beginning of the new scholastic year, the head of the Istanbul branch of the *Suffa* foundation, Muharram *abi*, was listing the community's initiatives to an audience of around 60 university students. The students were residents of the community's houses and had been gathered to learn about the expectations that the elder brothers had for them in regard to their own maturation as young participants in the life of the community. Muharram had just pointed to the successes the foundation had achieved over the last few years in spreading the *Risale-i Nur* through the opening of new internet sites and reading centers. He concluded his speech by addressing the students in a solemn voice:

> ...But you are indeed our greatest service. [...] Without forgetting your own culture, you will be successful in your work and morally upright. This is how you are going to be of service to this country. There is a person that was in these houses and that today is an associate professor ... Both Islam and culture ... Only so can *Suffa*'s existence be worthwhile. God willing one day you will support this *hizmet* too ... God willing one day our service will spread to the entire world. [...] Whatever work you do, you'll do it the right way ... You'll be a Muslim and you'll be someone who is dutifully working. Maybe one day you will be a doctor in a hospital ... If it is so, then surely you will not explain the contents of the *Risale* to the people. But by showing that you are both a good Muslim and a person doing

his job well you will be doing an important service. You will be representing *hizmet* in an appropriate way. [...] Because if some people oppose religion, this is due to our own shortcomings in representing it. This means you'll be doing an important service because you'll be demonstrating the value of Islam. [...] Persons endowed with the right manners, views, and understanding will have come from this very place.

Before uttering these words, Muharram had emphasized how the students had to take complete advantage of their university years. Echoing words I had already heard within the Gülen community, he warned his audience that while they now had plenty of time to dedicate themselves to cultivating their intellect and spirit, this would no longer be possible once full-time work began (see Vicini 2016). Studying was essential for the students' careers and for their development as individuals, but also for the community, as highlighted by Muharram's reference to them as their "greatest service." For brothers at *Suffa*, the students were indeed the greatest contribution that they had to offer to society. In this regard, like in the Gülen community Muharram also recognizes that the Islamic civilization project is interlinked with the national one of educating new generations of people into good citizens (see Chapter 4). In the same way, he rejected any presumed incompatibility between the community's intentions and the nation's project. His words were intended to persuade the students that they could better serve their country from a religious perspective if they became successful people professionally.

A pious Muslim becoming a good doctor is not only a way of contributing to the wellbeing and progress of society, but also of demonstrating that religion and modernity can go hand in hand. It is by becoming such a kind of person that students at *Suffa* can accomplish the best possible service to Islam. However, this must be done with the maximum care. Indeed, Muharram argues that the rejection of religious worldviews can derive from the students' own limitedness in representing Islam correctly. By claiming this, he entrusts the students with a very high dose of responsibility for the destiny of Islam. Charging them with such a responsibility should not be seen only as a burden, however. It is also a way of motivating them to give their maximum effort to the task at hand by extolling their central role in the community's mission for social reform.

Muharram's speech is only one example of the many ways in which students of both the *Suffa* and the Gülen communities were charged with the responsibility and sense of mission of *hizmet*. Although these ideals have a longstanding trajectory within Islam, they have acquired new meaning and importance in the context provided by the modern nation-state and the underlying ideas about people's participation in society. Before exploring this aspect, however, it is first necessary to further examine the origins of Islamic views of individual responsibility. This operation entails taking into account community views of the self and related ideas of will, freedom, and action in society.

2 The Nur Self's Spaces of Will and Freedom

A good starting point for discussing ideas of the self in relation to notions of will and freedom within the *Suffa* and the Gülen communities is a meeting of a Nur study group that I visited a few times along with some of the students of *Suffa* in the neighborhood of Fatih. This was not a conventional reading of the *Risale*, but a monthly appointment that the group had set up, in which one or two students addressed a particular topic in front of their fellow brothers. There were eight people attending in addition to me, of whom six were university students and two were elder brothers. A second-year university student in the Faculty of Law at Istanbul University, Arslan had decided to discuss the idea of freedom in Islam, with the intention of differentiating it from what he perceived as mainstream concepts of liberty intended as "total freedom."

Arslan began his lecture by observing how freedom appears in many slogans and is often upheld as a central value of our times. He then quoted one sentence of Dostoevsky and one of Said Nursi, both of which exalted the concept.[1] However, he quickly clarified that embracing an excessively glorified view of liberty as "total freedom" could conceal a certain degree of danger. Arslan argued that the exercise of freedom by one person may hinder other people's freedom, even potentially hurt them, and liberty should not simply be thought of as a "lack of any sort of restraint" (*başıboşluk*). Leaving an uncertain concept like freedom to decay may open the way to despotism and tyranny of men over other men. In line with Islamic views of justice that are frequently heard within Turkish conservative Islamist circles (Vicini 2018), Arslan elaborated that Islamic civilization upholds a message of universal justice resting on the basic principle that any sort of abuse of a fellow brother by another must be avoided, thereby seeking a communal fraternity in submission to God instead.

Arslan closed the first part of his speech with an old quote taken from Nursi's autobiographical account *Tarihçe-i Hayat*, in which he suggested to his followers: "Do not misinterpret freedom; so that it will not escape from our hands and that they [the misbelievers] will not make us suffocate by making us drink

---

1 For example: *Ekmeksiz yaşarım, hürriyetsiz yaşayamam* (I can live without bread but I could not live without freedom) (Nursi 1995d, 470).

worn-out old forms of captivity from another glass" (Nursi 1995d, 57). Here, the oppressor is the external enemy and misbeliever, but Nursi warns that if Muslims are infected with foreign views of freedom, then disharmony and disunity could emerge among them. In this warning, one can easily hear the echoes of late Ottoman times when Muslim intellectuals, bewildered by the supremacy of European powers, envisaged the reason for their political and military failure as their alleged moral decay. It is no accident that the only writings in which Nursi directly addressed the issue of freedom (*hürriyet*) were those that he authored prior to 1923 or in which he recounted his life before that date. These include texts such as the *Damascus Sermon*, that Nursi wrote during that period, or *Tarihçe-i Hayat*, in which he talks at length about his life before writing the *Risale-i Nur*. At that time, he mainly thought of *hürriyet* as civic and political freedom within the constitutional system that he was advocating for, along with other Ottoman intellectuals, as a political solution to the many problems of the Empire.[2]

It is by drawing upon these few scattered passages that Arslan built his talk on freedom, a goal he pursued in the following way:

> Because in Islam it is freedom which is the preliminary condition allowing one not only to accept but also to acquiesce to faith and good ethical actions (*salih amel*). Those who don't understand that freedom must have limits, given that they cannot really comprehend freedom anyway, also lose the ability to understand responsibility. [...] Since human beings are responsible to God, the fact that they are really free stems from their relationship of trust with Him. [...] To be free consists of liberating oneself from serving the objects of this world. "He who is a true servant of God, cannot be a servant of someone else" (*Allah'a hakiki abd olan, başkalarına abd olamaz*).[3] [...] Said Nursi recognized that slavery comes from a negation of Islamic truth, and freedom from faith. To explain how true freedom consists of being faithful and being affiliated with Him, he says: "Freedom is increased to the degree faith is strengthened" (*imana ne kadar kuvvet verilirse, hürriyet o kadar kuvvet bulur*).[4]

---

2 The *Damascus Sermon* (*Hutbe-i Şamiye*) is a speech that Nursi delivered in the Umayyad Mosque in 1911. It is part of a series of speeches about constitutionalism he delivered during a short winter journey to the "Arab lands" (Diyarbakir, Urfa, Kilis, and Damascus) (see Vahide 2005, 94).

3 Nursi (1995d).

4 This last sentence is quoted from the section titled "Reddü'l Evham" of the *Damascus Sermon*. It is taken from Said Nursi's reply to what he called the sixth "groundless fear" (*vehim*), which in its English translation is rendered as "the true believer is truly free." For the original

Freedom, according to Arslan, is the first condition that allows an individual to commit to faith and pursue a life in tune with Islam and its ethical teachings. As such, he takes it into the highest consideration. In order to be conducive to faith, however, limits must be put on liberty in accordance with one's relationship with God. Similar to how reason has to be mediated by the heart within *tefekkür* (see Chapter 3), an excessive reliance on individual freedom as the cornerstone of human action would cause human beings to forget about others and the natural world. For this reason, the exercise of freedom should be restricted within the limits marked by revelation.

Arslan's Islamically-grounded view is in critical dialogue with the Western philosophical tradition best represented by the German philosopher Immanuel Kant (1724–1804). Kant is commonly considered the paradigmatic thinker of the Enlightenment, an intellectual movement that sanctioned human reason has to be exercised independently from any kind of religious foundation or subordination to authority. This does not exclude a transcendent principle from Kant's formulation. For Kant, human freedom could only be theoretically inferred, and thus practically preserved, through moral laws that were to be found in a transcendent realm. However, these superhuman laws could only be determined by means of human reason itself (Guyer 2010, 2–7), as epitomized in one of his most famous statements: "Enlightenment is man's emergence from his self-incurred immaturity. Immaturity is the inability to use one's own understanding without the guidance of another" (Kant 2009, 1). According to Kant, the bedrock of the highest human ethical standards is the free exercise of the human intellect, which must not be subordinated by any other authority, such as a ruler or God. Without freedom from the constraints of authority, no independent exercise of the mind is possible in his view. In this regard, paradoxically, it may be said that freedom was even more central than reason to Kant's ethics, since there would not be the latter without the ontological premises of the former (Guyer 2010; see also Hallaq 2013, 58–62).

To the Kantian view of transcendence, Arslan opposed an alternative perspective in which freedom of will was still valued as one of the fundaments of faith, but where the source of ethical deliberation could only be found in a transcendent entity. In this configuration, the transcendent external Other, or God, allows for a smoother articulation of inter-individual human relations than the one based on individual reasoning. Individual reason and freedom remain within the broad picture, but they are subordinated to a more fundamental search for human solidarity sealed by God as a mediator of human

---

Turkish, see this Nur website dedicated to the *Risale*: http://www.sorularlarisale.com/index.php?s=modules/kulliyat&id=7344 (accessed June 19, 2017).

relations. What in Kant's view is the transcendent moral law, in Arslan's view is the transcendent figure of God, whose laws have been revealed to humanity and are reflected in the Qur'an and in the Islamic tradition. In this configuration, there is no contradiction between reason and revelation. Rather, according to Arslan, the revealed message offers a valuable basis for thinking about human freedom, though this must be exercised according to "reasonable" principles.

To many readers, Arslan's views may exemplify an obsequious deference to an all-embracing Islamic logic that is in contradiction with reason, considering how it has been conceived since Kant. Any reference to God when talking of freedom resembles claims that tie human life down to an all-encompassing and unique set of normative propositions that are epitomized in the Islamic tradition by the *shari'a*. For this reason, Arslan's words might sound like an acrobatic effort at qualifying a set of disciplinary practices as an exercise of freedom when they are, in fact, not. However, interpreting his views in this way would mean favoring a modern liberal perspective of freedom and related notions of reason and agency, which is the outcome of a specific European history, no matter how universal it claims to be (Asad 2003).

In his comparative study of the public sphere in Christianity, Islam, and modernity, Armando Salvatore (2007) has illustrated how, in pre-modern times, views akin to those exposed by Arslan were the norm within both Islamic and Christian traditions. Combining the work of civilizational studies by Shmuel N. Eisenstadt and Johann P. Arnason with that of virtue ethicists like MacIntyre, Salvatore has illustrated how earlier and alternative formulations of the public sphere are as old as human civilization. In order to envisage the presence of proto-versions of the public sphere, Salvatore points to how the social bond, the basic relationship permitting communicative action, was constructed in these other contexts. He thus illustrates that inter-subjective relations in axial traditions were articulated through binary relations bonding self and other (*ego* and *alter*), but only through the mediation of a third point of reference, which was represented by the superhuman instance of God in the three monotheistic traditions. In these traditions, common faith in God did not merely represent a transcendent principle of order to which humanity had to submit because ordered to do so, as modern secular readings of religion would make us to believe. Rather, transcendence was the fundamental external reference that allowed the mediation of human relations and the articulation of the bond between *ego* and *alter*. As such, God was the third element of the triadic relationship bonding *ego* with *alter* horizontally and had a central place in the formulation of religiously-grounded ethical frameworks. In such a pyramidal structure, God served as the central axis of a hierarchy of goods that sealed the social pact and represented the essential prerequisite for people to reason about these goods (Salvatore 2007, 33–67).

The articulation of the concept of freedom elaborated by Arslan reflects a specific contemporary reformulation of these axial traditions. I will trace its specificity in the rest of the chapter, particularly in relation to the two interrelated notions of responsibility and brotherhood in the framework of community religious service. For the moment, it suffices to say that sharing faith in God allowed my interlocutors to know better themselves, along the lines delineated in Chapter 3. By projecting their own actions and will onto the wider cosmological framework offered by the *Risale*, they were able to transcend all those perspectives that place human rational faculties at the center of ethical deliberation. By thinking of their life as ephemeral and contingent, they were prepared to rethink and put limits on the exercise of a liberty intended as "total freedom" and to forge relationships with their coreligionists.

In other words, my interlocutors' willingness to put themselves fully in God's hands did not necessitate their dis-empowerment or loss of "freedom." Rather, as stressed by Arslan toward the end of his speech, "True freedom finds its full manifestation only in the realization of the highest ideals." For them, maintaining a relationship with God is a prerequisite to enter in harmony with a view of the good on Earth, of which dedication to high ideals like those of *hizmet* represents one of the noblest options. In their perspective, only when men are moved by lofty sentiments and projects can they really feel liberated from worldly concerns and become "full human beings." Yet in order to transform these ideals into concrete forms of activism in society, they have to link them to a palpable sense of responsibility for their community's mission. Although Said Nursi had not introduced the concept of responsibility in his discourses about freedom, it was Arslan himself who did so in his speech. Before considering this point, however, I will dig deeper into the secular liberal understanding of the self and show how it contradicts views that were defended by my interlocutors.

3 The Relativity of the Good: On the Modern Liberal Conception of the Self

Not belonging to a civilizational trajectory exclusive to Western modernity, the idea of the self as a subject of will, freedom, and responsibility has a long genealogy in the pathways of world civilizations. There is indeed a common Platonic-Aristotelian root to the concept of the self in the three Abrahamic monotheistic traditions (Judaism, Christianity, and Islam), as well as in the so-called Western modern liberal tradition (Salvatore 2004; see also Asad 2003; Dupret 2004; cf. Mauss 1985). This is because all these different civilizational trajectories have historically interacted and intertwined with each other. However, practitioners of each tradition have reinterpreted the jargon to fit specific sociohistorical and cultural circumstances by developing alternative solutions for solving the problem of how to link personal responsibility, morality, and action. Ideas of the self have been developed in each context with particular regard to legal discourse.

It was Marcel Mauss who first brought the cagetories of the person and the self to the fore of socio-anthropological inquiry and who attempted a historical reconstruction of their origins since the times of "primitive societies." In his seminal 1938 lecture, Mauss traced back to Roman law the first emergence of a conception of the self in terms of individual consciousness distinguished from the idea of a person intended as the expression of prescribed social roles. The distinction is all-important, because if the self was previously thought of as indistinct from the role and function that a person had in society, it had since been associated with the idea of a nominal person. This represented a radical anthropological change sanctioning that a person was now no longer identified with her social role, but with an alleged "true" and enshrined self, with its desires and will. Maybe for the first time in history, Roman law made people individually responsible, and hence accountable, for their own actions, by introducing the distinction between *personae, res,* and *actiones* (Mauss 1985, 17). According to the French sociologist, this initial shift in the category of the person was just the prelude to successive evolutions within Western civilization trajectory. The idea of the "moral person," developed during Roman times, was indeed still partly cast in a social role. It successively became the "metaphysical being" of Christianity (the idea of Man), in which the self was completely unbound from any such role. Later, the Protestant idea of liberty of conscience would bring about the emergence of the modern notion of the self, understood as an equivalent to conscience—the innermost being of Fichte. At this juncture, the idea of the person no longer pertained only to the legal domain but became part of common views in society about individual identity and agency in the world (Dupret 2004, 10).

Mauss certainly deserves credit for having been the first to highlight the culturally and historically constituted nature of the idea of the self and for opening the way for successive explorations. However, scholars today agree that Mauss's reconstruction was simplistic at best, and loaded with evolutionist and Eurocentric vestiges. When elaborating on all the successive stages in the transformation of this idea—from the legal person of Rome to the view of the conscientious self of the seventeenth-century European philosophy—Mauss was reproducing a specifically modern liberal trajectory that envisages a continuous and ineluctable progression from a collective and shared identity, the Roman proto-notion of the person, to the view of the individual autonomous self of European modernity (cf. Taylor 1989). In other words, the Maussian formulation of the person rested upon Eurocentric views that saw the autonomous self as the apex of modern civilization, an ineluctable destiny to which any other civilization was destined.

Contrary to these assumptions, more recent explorations have persuasively demonstrated how the idea of the "moral self," intended as an autonomous subject unencumbered from power, instead reflects the expression of modern secular articulations of political power which are a specific product of European history. Notably, the work of Talal Asad has been seminal in mapping the genealogy of such views and demonstrating how they continue to underlie scholarly representations of human agency (see also Mahmood 2005; Hirschkind 2006). Asad has traced the origins of the "moral self" back as far as the writings of the Scottish philosopher John Locke (1632–1704), the first for whom the person begins to designate a conscientious subject immunized from sociohistorical forces and possessing "a continuous consciousness in a single body" (Asad 2003, 74). Accordingly, it was again Locke who introduced for the first time the fundamental and radical opposition between human reason and passions. In pre-modern understandings of the self, the capability of expressing emotions publicly was thought to be normal and integrally linked with one's ethical dispositions, hence central for the construction of one's identity. To the contrary, in seventeenth-century Atlantic-European formulations of the self—which were later developed by Locke's successors of the Scottish Enlightenment among which was David Hume (1711–1776)—the expression of passions and emotions was thought of as abnormal and ostracized as highly inappropriate social conduct.

In this eminently Atlantic-European tradition, emotions were seen as something to be tamed and secluded in the privacy of the inner self (Asad 2003, 73–79). Asad linked the relegation of emotions in the inner forum to the parallel emergence in modern continental philosophy of public reasoning, a deliberative process that rests upon the mere exercise of human reason. As shown above, Immanuel Kant notably formulated the idea that moral reasoning can be considered such only when associated with the freedom of the individuals to employ their intellectual potential independently from any form of external pressure or authority, including passions which he saw as the expression of the imperatives of the desirous soul. Asad remarks that such an understanding of rationality as being disconnected from one's passions significantly impacted legal formulations of the subject of law in seventeenth-century Europe. It is at that historical juncture that one's degree of accountability in front of the law was no longer seen as depending solely on the nature of the committed crime, but also on the degree to which the crime was the result of one's own individual and *subjective* intentions—where subjective meant intentionally (read rationally) willed actions, sans obfuscation from one's passions. To illustrate this aspect, Asad uses the insightful example of how "crimes of passion" are considered less culpable than premeditated crimes in modern liberal legal doctrines because the reasoning of the defendant in the former case would have been hindered by his passions. On this secular formulation of moral agency, Asad states:

> Now that emotions are generally thought of as part of the internal economy of the self, the notion is reinforced that agency means the self-ownership of the individual to whom external power always signifies a potential threat.[5]

Talal Asad's critique of secular agency is extensively indebted to the work of Alasdair MacIntyre (1988, 260–280), particularly to the latter's account of the emergence of the idea of "moral sense" among other Scottish Enlightenment philosophers such as Anthony Ashley Cooper, third Earl of Shaftesbury (1671–1713), and Francis Hutcheson (1694–1746). MacIntyre is a Marxist-turned-Catholic virtue ethics philosopher who has been advocating an Aristotelian-cum-Aquinas view of ethics based on reasoning around a socially shared hierarchy of the goods—something that he sees as being completely lacking in modern capitalist society. In *Whose Justice? Which Rationality?*, he details how ways of reasoning around a shared view of the good have long been dominant, beginning with the ancient world until the Middle Ages, before they were replaced by secular modern views. In the pre-modern world, the recognition of what was "good," right or wrong, depended on socially shared hierarchies of goods. However, beginning with Shaftesbury and Hutcheson, ethics has been grounded on the idea that human beings share a natural desire for reciprocal recognition, which is engendered by the natural passions of self-love and benevolence toward other fellow human beings.

The ascription of these sentiments to essential traits of human nature laid the groundwork for the elaboration of "moral sense," intended as the natural human faculty which monitors and limits the individual's will to dominate others, providing the basis for morality and sociality (MacIntyre 1988, 267–270). The switch from "virtue" to "morality" is not accidental, because it parallels a

---

5 Asad 2003, 75.

shift from ethics intended as a way of life that one cultivates through a long process of embodiment of dispositions of good character (and of the related ability to reason in accordance with such goods), to morality originating from "natural" human sentiments which do not need any training. In this latter philosophical framework, moral reasoning is disconnected from higher ideas of justice and shared views of the common good (but also from Kantian views of the higher moral law) and transferred to the immanent stage of individual moral senses.

In his reading of the work of MacIntyre, Armando Salvatore has aptly defined Scottish moral philosophers' moral sense in terms of:

> an inner, basically passive capacity of discerning good and bad based on a mildly reflective kind of sentiment [...] naturally possessed and developed by the human self [that] allows man to know what is good, and to orient and order one's actions toward the good on the basis of the impulses determined by rightly guided passions and sound interests.[6]

Unlike Asad, Salvatore does not envisage a total neglect of the passions in the moral self, but their taming through an emphatic and "mild" kind of reasoning based on immanent inter-individual (*ego*-to-*ego*) relations. Adding to MacIntyre's analysis, he argues that moral reasoning is redefined as a prudential kind of sentiment (*prudentia*) in this configuration. Drawing upon Axial Age theory, he clarifies that as long as *prudentia* is based on people's innate and natural capacity for identifying themselves with others, it implies the divorce of moral reasoning from a transcendent and trans-individual hierarchy of goods, a role that was fulfilled by God in those traditions. As Salvatore puts it, in the thinking of Scottish moralists: "The premises are laid for turning the sharp triadic engagement [of *ego-alter*-God] into a mild dyadic game where Alter [God/*telos*] is given a somewhat honorary, basically functionless (yet often symbolically overloaded [...] and potentially ideological) position" (Salvatore 2007, 221).

The best exemplification of this philosophical trend is David Hume's vision of the "rational agent." In Hume's view of the self as being guided by a self-centered, interest-based, idea of reasoning, only a very residual function is left to higher conceptions of the good. In contrast to how mechanisms of intersubjective mediation worked within axial traditions, the individual and his reasoning capacities are definitively detached from any idea of God and the related hierarchy of goods. In this modern liberal configuration, moral agency

---

6   Salvatore 2007, 220.

depends on the individuals' capacity to anticipate the consequences of their actions, and thereby choose to avoid those that could hurt others' interests. Completely detached from the idea of public interest (Salvatore 2007, 223), this view is based on "instrumental action":

> [...] a type of action that is built on a different apprehension of the goods, usually one dictated by some notion of interest, and privileging goods of effectiveness over goods of excellence. Reasoning is applied not to the dialogical and/or agonic ordering of the goods, but to the calculation of the best means to achieve any ends contingently dictated by interest. [...] [T]his kind of instrumental action was reformulated in the course of the eighteenth-century metamorphosis of *phronesis/prudentia* into the Anglo-Scottish "prudence," which denotes exactly this kind of prudential-calculative rationality.[7]

Since the reasoning faculty of the individual is reduced to a prudential-calculative kind of rationality directed toward a set of worldly "goods of effectiveness" (as distinct from the "goods of excellence" ingrained in virtuous dispositions), the notion of moral responsibility also has an essentially prudential-calculative nature. In this modern liberal formulation of the self, one's forms of reasoning around the good, and hence one's conception of one's own freedom, responsibility, and accountability, are no longer framed in a perspective that transcends the individual, including his interests and passions. Instead, they are based on an *ego*-centric subjective perception of the good, where priority is given to everybody's right and freedom to achieve individual empowerment as long as this does not clash with the rights of others.[8] Relatedly, one's feeling of responsibility is not the consequence of an act of reflection through which one frames his actions in a higher and shared hierarchy of goods. Nor—and not accidentally—has the agent been trained to cultivate those ethical dispositions requested of him to reason morally according to such higher principles. Prudential calculation consists of one's capacity to

---

7   Salvatore 2007, 78.
8   In his last book, Talal Asad associates the emergence of secular, calculative reason to an eminently European program of expansion and domination of both natural phenomena (through modern science) and foreign populations (*via* colonization), that is based on the principle that "chance can be tamed [...] by minimizing loss and maximizing gain" (Asad 2018, 152). Basically, it is a form of reason in which there is no space for even a spark of morality as everything is reduced to calculation. If this analysis may have some utility for defining logics of domination and expansion, however, it seems to fit much less our goal here of defining how secular morality articulates solidarity and connectedness in modern liberal Western thought.

anticipate the interventions of the law, but also of shared moral judgment, by preventing any action that can run counter to this moral sense. In other words, in such a formulation, people avoid wrong behaviors because doing so would mean having to face social disapproval or legal punishment, not because they are discordant with socially shared ethical principles.

Clearly, the description offered so far of the modern liberal understanding of the self is an abstract and theoretical reconstruction which does not find an exact correspondence in people's ethical comportment. In the real world, it is indeed hard to find people whose behavior is strictly based on prudential calculation. Fragments of ethical systems based on the virtues survive beside more recent secular formulations (MacIntyre 1984 [1981]). Furthermore, as observed by MacIntyre (1988), the calculation of one's own "interest"—what he calls the "goods of effectiveness"—is an ever present anthropological condition of moral systems that must be taken into account. However, it should be noted that secular modern formulations of moral agency have become quite influential in Europe since the eighteenth century and, as remarked by Asad, that they still consistently affect scholarly representations of human agency. More importantly, the way in which representations of the interest-based self have long shaped Muslim perceptions of Western people should not be underestimated. As it happened in the case of Nursi, these models have indirectly influenced Muslim scholars when they attempted to rebuild religiously-grounded forms of solidarity and action for their societies.

4   Being an Aware and Responsible Muslim

It is now time to go back to how Arslan's words point to the sense of responsibility for, and commitment to, the religious mission of the *Suffa* and the Gülen communities. Of particular relevance is the connection Arslan established between freedom and responsibility in his lesson. According to Arslan, if people lose the real value of the will and freedom that God has bestowed upon them, then they "also lose the ability to understand responsibility." His words reflect the shared view within the Nur movement that good Muslims must feel and nurture a sense of responsibility to prompt their commitment to *hizmet*. As illustrated in Chapter 4, within the Gülen community, responsibility is a disposition that the *abi*s were expected to embody through their daily engagement in the educational activities within the houses. University students at *Suffa* followed a less demanding path, oriented toward instilling in the residents a sense of commitment to spread the message of the *Risale* in society. In both cases, however, responsibility was upheld as a key value that sustained the students' sense of dedication to the cause of *hizmet*, both in the present and in the future—might they decide to pursue their connection with the community after the university years.

Just as ideas of individual freedom, will, and conscience are not the exclusive product of Western liberal modernity, the same is true for personal responsibility, which has been a subject of reflection within the Islamic tradition since seminal debates regarding human accountability. This fact is particularly important given how Muslim societies have been described, at least since Weber, as dominated by a collectivistic ethos in which individuals submit themselves either to collective norms or to charismatic leaders (Martensson 2007). Yet it must be noted how this idea of individual responsibility has developed and taken different forms and meanings across time. In particular, it has received a new emphasis and taken on a partially new connotation since the late-nineteenth century, in connection with the rising importance that commitment to preaching the Qur'anic message has taken within Muslim reformist discourse. The link that was established by my interlocutors between responsibility and commitment to a mission of religious revival is a common trait between these communities and other reformist-oriented movements, including the Muslim Brotherhood, both in Egypt and in other countries of the Middle East (al-Anani 2016; Kandil 2016), or the *Tablighi Jamaat* in Asia (Ali 2012; Noor 2012).

It is no coincidence that the contemporary Muslim intellectual who dedicated the most attention to the place of responsibility in Islam is a modernist scholar of Islam. In a paper delivered in 1964 at the East-West Philosophy Conference, Fazlur Rahman (1919–1988) argued that the idea of personal responsibility in Islam finds its roots in the view that a person is accountable for how he has behaved in life, as supported by some Qur'anic injunctions related to the Day of Judgment. To demonstrate that it is the individual himself, and not the entire Muslim community, who is considered accountable for his own sins, he quotes verses such as "Today (on the Day of Judgment) you have come to Us as individuals (*furada*) just as We created you in the first place" [6:95] and "Every soul earns but for itself, and no soul shall bear the burden of another, and even thus shall you return to your Lord" [6:165] (Rahman 1966, 320). Following a recurrent theme in Islamic reformist discourse, Rahman adds that Muslim responsibility is also rooted in the trust that God bestows upon human beings as the only creatures endowed with potentialities—among which there are will, conscience, and responsibility—which confer them the ability to choose between obeying or disobeying His prescriptions. For example, in what is a widely shared view that I have also heard from my interlocutors, what distinguishes human beings from the angels is that the latter do not possess the human qualities of reason and will. Since they have neither the intellectual faculties that would allow them to discern between proper and improper behavior nor the free will necessary to be able to choose between the two, they cannot act outside the limits that are set by God's commands. In other words, without such qualities angles simply *cannot* disobey God. Will and reason are distinctive traits of human beings and it is this ontological condition that implies their accountability in the afterworld.

At the same time, however, this condition also makes human beings representatives or vicegerents (*khalifa*) of God on Earth, a view that has gained wide acceptance in today's Muslim world.[9] Such a view has been upheld by several Islamic reformers, including Rahman himself, to advocate for the more active involvement of individual Muslims in mass movements supporting the religious reform of society. Conversely, it has been contested by more traditionalist scholars, who have highlighted how Islamic reformists like Muhammad Abduh, Said Qutb, and Mawdudi distorted the sources (in particular Qur'an, 2:30) to make them fit a modern secular worldview (Idris 1990). Certainly, this emphasis on the idea of *khalifa* can be related to the trauma generated by end of the Caliphate, which determined the passage of the responsibility for upholding Islamic civilization from the Caliph to all Muslims. As observed by Robinson (2004), the tension between this-worldly and other-worldly piety did not begin with modern reformist-oriented Islamic movements. The change in emphasis from one pole to the other has been constant throughout Islamic history and has manifested in different expressions of Islam over time. In the last two centuries, however, a marked swing of the pendulum toward a this-worldly focus and the realization of God's will on Earth has taken place. Appeals to Muslims' sense of responsibility have dominated in the nineteenth and twentieth-century Islamic reformist discourse, from Muslims scholars such as Sayyid Ahmad Khan (d. 1898), Muhammad Ilyas (d. 1944) and Muhammad Iqbal (d. 1933) in the Indian continent, to Muhammad Abduh (1849–1905), Rashid Rida and Hasan al-Banna (1906–49) in Egypt, or Ayatollah

---

9 Inspired by Ibn Arabian narratives concerning paths for spiritual perfection, Gülen has stressed how, by complying with God's requirements, human beings can fully realize their nature and potentially attain a status higher than that of the angels (while if they do not, they may fall to a level lower than that of the animals). Gülen attributes this idea to a saying of Ali ibn Abi Talib, the son-in-law of the Prophet and forth Rightly Guided Caliph: Ali "is reported to have said: God has characterized angels by intellect without sexual desire, passion, and anger, and animals with anger and desire without intellect. He exalted humanity by bestowing upon them all these qualities. Accordingly, if a person's intellect dominates his or her desire and ferocity, he or she rises to a station above that of angels, because this station is attained by a human being in spite of the existence of obstacles that do not vex angels" (Ünal and Williams 2000, 308).

Morteza Motahhari (1919–1979) and Ali Shariati (1933–1977) in Iran (Robinson 2004; cf. Smith 1977). All these scholars have called on believers to engage in society with the goal of diverting the course of their countries away from Western influence.

On this point, it is possible to speculate that a call to ordinary Muslims to engage in preaching activities is a general response from practitioners of religious traditions to the progressive advancement of modern forms of power and related secularized understandings of public life. In the case of Turkey, the establishment of modern political configurations in the region has progressively deprived Muslim scholars of their power and influence in society (see Chapter 1), calling up ordinary believers to carry the burden of bringing forth the Islamic civilizing mission. Therefore, the internalization of responsibility by the ordinary Muslim may also be seen as a mirror image of the modern idea of active citizenship, intended as the outcome of new forms of governmentality that delegate to individuals the internalization of the same rules and principles that determine their subjection to power (Foucault 1991). Since the emergence of modern nations, people have been held responsible for the advancement, prosperity, and defense of their states. From a mass of politically passive subjects they have been turned into active and committed citizens. Likewise, in modern times, religiously faithful people have been called upon to engage with this world with the intention of transforming it into a place that can accommodate their eschatological project.

Given these premises, how can we position the activities promoted by the *Suffa* and the Gülen communities along this reformist trend? What is the exact place and role of my interlocutors within this trajectory as Muslims educated in both secular subjects and religious values? In their discourses, university students often established a specific link between their commitment to *hizmet* and the status of aware and educated Muslims they aimed to attain (see Chapter 1). Relatedly, they stressed that only they, as a generation of "aware Muslims" who were cultivating their faith by means of the *Risale*, could be held fully responsible for the mission of *hizmet*.

Consider the following conversation with Halim, one of my main interlocutors from *Suffa*, and his friend Shakir, an ex-resident of the Gülen houses who had recently moved to a dormitory managed by another Islamic foundation. After attending the Saturday evening reading at *Suffa*, I was invited by Halim to go out for tea in *At Pazarı*, a small street with a high concentration of teahouses and shisha places located in the neighborhood of Faith. When introducing himself, Shakir explained that he was still a practicing Muslim and a person concerned with the mission of *hizmet*, even though he had decided to leave the Gülen houses after a quarrel with some elder members. To illustrate his dedication, Shakir made an argument based on the difference between his understanding of what a committed Muslim life should consist of and that of his parents, but also of most of his peers:

> My parents are believers. They perform the daily prayers, they fast during Ramadan and do all the things that Muslims should do, but they are part of the group of Muslims who are only concerned with these kinds of things. [...] Once they have kept the commandments, they do not become interested in what all the others around them may or may not believe. This instead is the mission of *hizmet*. This is *hizmet*.

These words remind of Bekim's distinction between "true" (*hakiki*) Muslims and Muslims by imitation (*taklid*) reported in Chapter 1: new generations of Muslims educated in the Nur houses feel better prepared than others to represent and carry out Muslim life in the way required by the times. As educated people who are also enlightened by an updated understanding of Islam, they have a better knowledge of how to behave in this era.

Adding to the conversation, Halim said, "In fact, it is our duty as Muslims to explain Islam to others." He immediately quoted the Qur'anic verse "Are they ever equal, those who know and those who do not know?" [Qur'an 39:9].[10] He interpreted it as an invitation for educated Muslims to teach others and then added:

> But in order to explain Islam to others, you have to know it yourself, and you have to be conscious. You can't explain what you don't know... Because you wouldn't even understand what you have to explain. [...] Instead, we know that we have the duty of performing this service. [...] In contrast to our parents, who practiced Islam out of imitation (*taklid*), we are aware. [...] Whereas *hizmet* should be the duty of everybody, only those who are aware are considered responsible for it.

Halim's words stood on a precise juridical distinction between actions that are mandatory for every Muslim (*farz-ı ayın*), like the five pillars of Islamic conduct, and other actions from which the majority of Muslims are exempt but that must be accomplished by some (*farz-ı kifaye*). The demarcation has been addressed in theological terms by both Said Nursi (e.g. Nursi 1995c) and Gülen. Not by accident, Gülen (1998b) uses the expression *farz-ı kifaye* in *The Axis of*

---

10 In Turkish the verse is, "*Hiç bilenle bilmeyen bir olur mu?*" Then, the verse continues, "Only the people of discernment will reflect (on the distinction between knowledge and ignorance, and obedience to God and disobedience), and be mindful" (Ünal 2008, 788).

Guidance to define all those obligations that are usually related to the wellbeing of the community, including the responsibility of preaching Islam (*tebliğ*, *irşad*), which should be upheld by at least one part of the Muslim community. In similar fashion, long before in the *Damascus Sermon*, Nursi had observed how the goal of striving for Islam (*jihad*) in modern times has passed from being *farz-i kifaye* to being mandatory for every Muslim.

As noted in Muharram's words at the opening of this chapter, the mission of *Suffa* is to raise students who will one day engage in this kind of social mission. Through their words and actions, they will represent Islam at its best, showing the compatibility of Muslim and modern life. It is at this juncture that the embodiment of a sense of responsibility is intertwined with a sense of realization for having achieved their full potential as human beings and as good Muslims. The high position that responsibility takes in the *Suffa* and the Gülen communities' hierarchy of goods is in line with the ideals of freedom elaborated upon by Arslan. As he said, if one is to be "fully free," he must see the limits of his freedom in the responsibilities he has to shoulder for the realization of higher goals, hopefully leading to the betterment of life in this world. From such a perspective, Muslim responsibility is not a hindrance to the exercise of freedom. Rather the opposite, it is the sphere within which Muslims can fully realize themselves by aiming to achieve greater ideals such as those brought forth by the community they belong to.

5 On Brotherhood and Moral Reasoning

In Chapter 2, I have looked at brotherhood as a matrix of Muslim civility, functioning as both a model of comportment and sociality and an organizational form for members of the *Suffa* and the Gülen communities. As shown, Nursi highlighted the principle of unity in brotherhood because it provided his followers with the necessary shield for organizing and defending Islamic life against the threats posed by the secular order established by the Republic. Accordingly, brotherhood was sought through the constant practice and experience of the cardinal virtue of sincerity in religion (*ihlas*) within the houses. As mentioned, however, community life was also conducive to a "non-heroic" kind of virtuous path that stressed self-sacrifice and dedication toward others, and that rested on a conception of inter-human relations that operated "beyond secular reason" (Milbank 2006 [1990]). This section explores this alternative logic and points out how the ideal of brotherhood provided my interlocutors with a civility matrix that opens space for imagining forms of human relations and solidarity beyond community boundaries.

Within the Islamic ecumene, the idea of brotherhood has historically provided a pattern of civility through which Muslims have thought of the articulation of the social bond in society in forms that precede, and hence elude, modern liberal secular formulations (Salvatore 2016). The idea has great potential indeed, insofar as it rests on a call for an "ethic of brotherliness" and "world-denying love" that was the original incipit of all salvation religions emerging from the axial breakthrough (Bellah 1999; cf. Weber 1978). My suggestion is that my interlocutors are the bearers, *via* Nursi, of this alternative tradition for thinking of human relations. This is a tradition that transcends ethical models structured around the idea of individual interest that have developed in secular liberal modernity.

At the same time, however, a perennial tension also exists within the *Suffa* and the Gülen communities between such a religious universal call to fraternity and their engagement in a modern secular order. To introduce how Nursi advocated brotherhood as an alternative to the idea of moral sense proposed by secular liberal European philosophers, it is worth quoting a short passage from the 20th chapter of the *Lema*s. This and the following 21st chapter are the only other sections of the *Risale* in which Nursi talks about brotherhood in explicit terms, by elaborating a proposal that sounds much like a critical response to utilitarian European models that had been spreading in Ottoman lands since the second half of the eighteenth century. Although he does not make explicit mention of these concurrent moral theories, the reference is clear when he talks of people of neglect and misguidance who are motivated by individual interest:

> In just the same way that rivalry and disagreement among the people of guidance do not arise from failure to foresee consequences or from shortsightedness, so too wholehearted agreement among the people of misguidance does not result from farsightedness or loftiness of vision. Rather the people of guidance, through the influence of truth and reality, do not succumb to the blind emotions of the [lower] soul [*nefs*], and follow instead the farsighted inclinations of the heart and the intellect. [...] [Similarly,] [d]ispute and rivalry among the people of truth do not arise from jealousy and greed for the world, and conversely union among the worldly and neglectful does not arise from generosity and magnanimity. As for the people of neglect and misguidance, in order not to lose the benefits with which they are infatuated and not to offend the leaders and companions they worship for the sake of benefit, in their utter humiliation, abasement and lack of manliness, they practice union at all costs with their companions, however abominable, treacherous and harmful they

be, and wholeheartedly agree with their partners in whatever form may be dictated by their common interest. As a result of this wholeheartedness, they indeed attain the benefits desired.[11]

Here, Nursi clearly distinguishes between faithful Muslims and people of misguidance. Yet this is not to say that the former are in greater agreement among themselves than the latter or vice versa. In his view, both groups can either be internally divided or united. What differs is that, for people of misguidance, agreement is not attained as the result of their orientation toward the higher good or "loftiness of vision," but moved only by the search for personal benefit, for which they are ready to humiliate and abase themselves at a level lower than that of animals (showing a "lack of manliness"). Although unity based on common interest may appear as repugnant—and even harmful to the welfare of the collectivity—Nursi recognizes that these self-interested people are still able to wholeheartedly agree with their partners for the sake of their mutual interest. Echoing his own words about corporate personality (see Chapter 2), Nursi argues that these people may even be—and indeed often are—more successful than others in finding a unity of spirit. The difference is that their unity is not sealed by the sharing of a common view of the higher goods, but rather by the search for individual benefit. In this regard, they are opposed to rightly guided people who do not succumb to the inclinations of the lower self and are able to follow the "farsighted inclinations of the heart and the intellect" to achieve sincerity and true unity of spirit within brotherhood.

This blunt appraisal of the apparent success of the forces of modernity is revelatory of the different premises upon which Islamic forms of civic engagement have been elaborated upon by Nursi. This contrasts the modern liberal assumption by which people are seen as subjects of action only if they are able to use their shrewdness to cooperate with others for the search of mutual benefit. The ideal of brotherhood upheld by Nursi presents his fellow Muslims with an upturned perspective within which the search for unity is the real goal, whereas the search for individual benefit is the last resort. There is no reason for *ego* to compete with *alter* in this configuration. The principle of brotherhood works at a pre-calculative stage, at which every single individual is preemptively asked to renounce his own desires to prevail over others in the name of higher goods held to have transcendent authority. By taming the egotist impulses of their lower selves, Muslims are invited to renounce competition and disputes, offer themselves up in complete self-sacrifice for the realization of a higher ideal of the good, and live in solidarity with other fellow brothers under the aegis of God.

---

11   Nursi 1995b, 209.

These ideals were enacted in daily life within the two communities under study and talked about repeatedly during the reading meetings. My interlocutors were often reminded by their elder companions that nobody should feel envious of other brothers, either because of their success in ascending the community's ladder or because, for example, one of them had done better in an act of service. Rather, they were invited to appreciate what other brothers had accomplished and to congratulate them on the work they had done. While this was partly due to their search for unity of intents with the goal of fostering *hizmet*, it was also spurred by a more primordial and genuine call for universal brotherhood. Consider the following words of Yusuf, a twenty-six-year-old member of the Gülen community who kept a weekly *sohbet* in the house of Mecidiyeköy for a group of his peers, most of whom worked in white collar occupations. Responding to my request of clarification about the relationship between purity of faith and brotherhood that is stated by Nursi in the *Risale*, Yusuf stated:

> In order to be really sincere in our commitment and disinterested in the service we accomplish for God's sake, that is, in order to attain *ihlas*, it is necessary to be able to renounce this world and not find any kind of interest in it. Then, if we are really able to renounce to the pleasures of this world, there is no reason to enter in competition with our brothers over any sort of things.

The words of Yusuf agree with those of Nursi, pointing to the need to prioritize collective over individual interests. This is an inclination that members of the *Suffa* and the Gülen communities learn through meditative reflection as they comprehend that this world is transitory and therefore not worth fighting for. Competition and rivalry increase when people fail to realize that this life is transient, and nothing is worth being desired from it. To the contrary, the members of both the communities were expected to learn to downplay their interests to establish stronger relations among themselves. In relation to this point, later in the conversation, I asked Yusuf to clarify the idea contained in the fourth rule of the 21st chapter of the *Lema*s, according to which Nur brothers should self-sacrifice for their fellow brothers to the point where they have to annihilate their selves in the brotherhood (*fena fi'l-ihvan*), in a way similar to how the Sufis seek for annihilation in the master (*fena fi-ş şeyh*).[12] In response,

---

12   This is the passage: "This [fourth rule] is to imagine your brothers' virtues and merits in your own selves, and to thankfully take pride at their glory. The Sufis have terms they use among themselves, 'annihilation in the shaykh,' 'annihilation in the Prophet;' I am not a Sufi, but these principles of theirs make a good rule in our way, in the form of 'annihilation

Yusuf told me that Nursi had taken this idea from that of self-annihilation in the Prophet (*fena fi'r-resul*) and added:

> Said Nursi has put the issue in these terms. If he, *Allah Resulü* [the Prophet Muhammad], was here among us how would we talk? How would we behave? [...] Thus, for example, when the Prophet performed the prayer he did it together with his brothers. All together ... Or, again, when somebody was lacking food a brother gave him what he could ...

As he had uttered these words, a Prophet's *hadith* came to his mind: "Without faith you will not be allowed to enter paradise, and if you do not love each other you cannot fully reach faith." Yusuf's reference to the early times of the Muslim community is not accidental. Just as Muhammad's original call was uttered in the name of a unity that cut across differences of lineage, ethnicity, and place of origin, so my interlocutors grounded their ideals about reconstructing human relations in a modern world on similar primordial assumptions. Love for their fellow brothers is the matrix of a message of civility upholding fraternity and solidarity among human beings independently from what their class, status, or origins are. In this configuration, the idea of brotherhood is extended beyond the limits of the community and absolutized to include humanity *tout court*. Such a call for universal brotherhood contains the seeds of what Max Weber once named "world-denying love:" a core input within axial salvation religions to love fellow human beings regardless of their identity or belonging (Bellah 1999). As specified by the German sociologist, all salvation religions have historically been distinguished by a radical and utopian impulse to transcend social and political differences. This is a distinctive trait that put them in a state of conflict and tension with the contingent social and political order. While such tension has always been present, it has become even more evident as a consequence of the recent processes of modernization and secularization. By determining the further separation of the mundane order into the clearly distinct domains of politics, the family, the secular intellectual sphere, and the aesthetic and erotic orders, such processes have indeed determined an even more marked detachment of the in-worldly realm from the transcendent domain.

---

in the brothers' [*fena fi'l-ihvan*]. Among brothers this is called '*tafani*'; that is, 'annihilation [*fani olmak*] in one another.' That is to say, to forget the feelings of one's own carnal soul, and live in one's mind with one's brothers' virtues and feelings. [...] Our way is the closest friendship. This friendship necessitates being the closest friend, the most sacrificing [*fedakar*] companion, the most appreciative [*takdir edici*] comrade, the noblest brother. The essence of this friendship is true sincerity [*samimi ihlas*]" (Nursi 1995b, 216).

Since its origins, the ideal of universal brotherhood has aspired to transcend all social divisions. As such, inevitably, it has ended up clashing with a modern political order that is built upon the separation of different ethnic and national groups and which pretends to relegate the religious search for transcendence to the private sphere. In this sense, the original impetus of Nursi's call consists of an invitation to rethink human relations beyond modern secular assumptions. My interlocutors' appeal to a sense of brotherhood under the aegis of God echoes such a call for love and fraternity among human beings whose potential is found in their propensity for reconstructing social solidarity upon a different basis. This view also loudly resounds as a critique of widespread political and societal models that are centered on fostering competition among nations, rather than establishing a more equal and harmonious global order. References to love and heart are not accidental. They are, rather, the indication that religious approaches to reconstructing solidarity at a translocal level are grounded on a view of rationality that must be mediated by human sentiment if the desire is to create a better and more just society.

It is based on these intellectual premises that people of the *Suffa* and the Gülen communities developed an Islamically-grounded view of human relations intended as an alternative to modern secular logic. Yet because these premises are at odds with how society is ruled and governed in the contemporary world, a question remains as to what extent such a program can be activated without conflicting with the present order. An inevitable tension permeates universal calls for human brotherhood insofar as they clash with the loyalties that are requested by modern secular institutions. This is true for both cases considered, but especially for the Gülen community, whose project of social reform has also rested on a strong sense of loyalty to the community, and to its expansive goals, by its members. In light of these considerations, what are the external, but also internal limits that the two communities encounter in the promotion of a call to human universal brotherhood? How is the permanent tension between this-worldly and other-worldly order negotiated within them and with the outside? How is balance maintained between the commitment to a mission aimed at the promotion of universal brotherhood on the one hand, and the parallel need of fostering the community project, on the other?

•••

As shown, the *Suffa* and the Gülen communities' world-renouncing views of human life as transient are redirected into this-worldly activism through a complex process of recovery and re-assessment of Islamic ideas of freedom, responsibility, and action to make them fit the needs of their reformist project.

The words of Muharram, Arslan, and others show how Muslim forms of civic engagement within these communities find their ground in a framework dominated by God's sovereignty, but one that simultaneously overlaps with the contours of the modern national project. Students are taught to think of their role in reassessing the place of Islam in the country, as well as in the world, and helping to shape the fate of the nation toward new unexplored directions. For them, there is no contradiction between taking part in a movement of Islamic revitalization and contributing to the well-being of the country. Quite the opposite, they aim to instantiate Islamic values of responsibility and civic participation to the core of the state-led modernization process—a process from which they feel they have been excluded for too many years. In their perspective, the country will benefit from them as people who are both enlightened by modern secular knowledge and moved by a religiously-grounded sense of dedication to the realization of lofty ideals.

As they read their existence through a reformist puritan lens highlighting their role as vicegerents of God on Earth, my interlocutors thought of their freedom within the limits set by their responsibilities as human beings devoted to such higher goals. Whereas in the modern secular tradition responsibility is generally seen as a burden, students of the *Suffa* and the Gülen communities figured it as a privilege they had, as chosen people, to live a full Muslim life and take an active role in such an elevated project. With this view in mind, they set out for a pathway that weaves together freedom with the assigned duty to transform this world into a better place, as opposed to one based on a search for "total freedom" intended as the narcissistic satisfaction of one's personal interests and desires.

From this standpoint, their forms of civic engagement openly defy modern secular liberal views of religious life. As shown, within secular modern liberal thought, one's subjection to God's sovereignty has, since Kant, been thought of as a waiver of human agency and a mark of submission and obedience to the divine will. Yet similar representations of religious commitment are largely inaccurate and reductive. While complying with religious obligations does occupy an important place in the lives of my interlocutors, the meaning of their subjugation to God covers other meanings as well. It is the basis for dealing with the fundamental ontological question concerning how human beings can mediate their relationships with others; of how they should regenerate the social bond and overcome the limits imposed by secular modern systems that highlight a strong sense of individualism and rivalry.

Saying that my interlocutors base their civic participation on assumptions that contradict secular modern logic does not mean that they are completely at odds with the project of Turkish modernity or with a more general modern focus on the worldly realm. Both communities want to shape lay Muslims who may find an occupation in private enterprises or public institutions to conduct their *hizmet* from that position. As such, the worldly renouncing perspective they cultivate by reading the *Risale* provides them with the philosophical ground upon which they build their desire to engage in this world. Borrowing classic Weberian vocabulary, it is possible to say that while my interlocutors are inclined to re-enchant their views of this world in order to find God in it (by seeing this world as a reflection of God's existence), they are also ready to measure themselves within it—within a "disenchanted" world ruled by the logic of the market, state bureaucracy, efficiency, and which endorses other values. As sanctioned by the words of Muharram that opened this chapter, community brothers want students to "be of service to this country." While the idea of service has a religious connotation, for them it does not contradict modern secular views of progress. Rather, it projects ideals of service within an eschatological time where God's plan will be realized; a time that, in their minds, coincides with that of the destiny of the nation.

Although my interlocutors did not see a contradiction between their faith and their participation in state institutions, however, their views collide with those of their secular rivals who see religious loyalty as a hindrance to their full and sincere participation in the republican project. More importantly, this conflict of power is reflected in the civility program of the two communities under study. Both, but particularly Gülen's, seem to be straddled by an inner tension. This becomes evident when one juxtaposes their promotion of a message of universal brotherhood with the strategies of survival and advancement of *hizmet*, intended as expansion of the community and of its influence in society. As stated by Weber, the tension is not only a matter of a religious sphere conflicting with the other progressively rationalizing and distinguishing spheres of worldly affairs, such as the political or the aesthetic. It also concerns the inner contradiction that emerges from the existing conflict between ultra-mundane and mundane issues, between ideal lofty propositions and the contingency of worldly politics.

Not being exclusive to the religious sphere, the detachment between ideals and human affairs is a common trait of all sociopolitical projects, including those drawing upon secular ideologies. However, within movements grounding their forms of civic engagement on a transcendent order of things, it takes a specific form. This is especially true in the modern context in which, as illustrated in Chapter 1, Islam has been progressively detached from its legal forms and turned into a symbolic normative referent used to catalyze political consensus. Not remaining limited to the political sphere, the ideologization of Islam is a process that has affected religious movements including the *Suffa* and the Gülen communities, though in a different way. In these communities, Islam is not ideologized with the goal of creating a political consensus. Rather, it is turned into a utopian and eschatological goal, which is offered to their members to justify the expansion of the community and the rise of its power in society.

As mentioned in Chapter 2, the germs of such an inclination can be found in Said Nursi's stress on the need to recreate a sense of unity in brotherhood resembling that of modern corporate personalities. In his own explanation of how Muslims should come together into a solidarity of hearts to face the challenges of secularization and modernization, the emphasis swung between a universal call and an inter-communal impetus. In this regard, one may argue that the need of safeguarding the movement from external enemies has contributed to raising a certain degree of self-centeredness of the Nur communities at the expenses of their intellectual openness. This risk has been lamented by authoritative figures of the movement, such as Metin Karabaşoglu, who has openly criticized the inability of the last two generations of followers of the *Risale* to build a "dynamic intellectual and religious community," thus transforming a wide transversal network into a closed one (Karabaşoğlu 2003).

It is true that people at *Suffa* tend to idealize Said Nursi's message and to think of their understanding of Islam as superior than that of other Muslims. However, this attitude has not led the community to overstep the limits set by a mission centered on the goal of spreading the message of the *Risale*. The discourse is different for the Gülen community, insofar as the latter went quite far in terms of using a complacent Islamic discourse to catalyze a large following of people and convince them to penetrate institutions to increase its presence and power in society. Besides, the community has often done so by being irrespective of some institutional rules, and sometimes even at the cost of infringing upon some of its own foundational principles. For example, in Chapter 4 I have noted how elder members of the Gülen community asked some university students to sacrifice their own university career to look after their younger brothers. As recent events in the country have sadly revealed, the community's goal of shaping loyal and dedicated people seems to have prevailed over the original civilizational impetus they claimed to strive for. Even if one were to assume that this is not an original trait of the community, but instead a later development, it is one that has become prominent in the last ten years, at least since the time of the *Ergenekon* and *Balyoz* trials, when some of its members allegedly made recourse to all available means to conduct a series of arrests against prominent people from the military and the old Kemalist apparatus. Following the collision with the AKP administration in 2013, the situation has rapidly degenerated. The community seems to have completely lost a realistic view of facts on the ground and entered a clash of power that has led it further astray from the genuine motives that had originally animated many of its members and sympathizers in Turkey and across the world—a drift which ended in the tragic events of July 15, 2016.

Conclusion

Two main questions have guided this work. Firstly, how have long-standing processes of reinterpretation of the Islamic tradition been taken over within the *Suffa* and the Gülen communities as they faced the challenges posed by the changing epistemological and sociopolitical conditions of modern times? Secondly, how have reformed streams of the Islamic tradition been rethought and empowered by these two communities to involve a large number of ordinary Muslims into a project of social reform rooted in a strengthened sense of religious awareness in a modernizing world? These questions have provided the background for addressing different aspects concerning the reconfiguration of pedagogical paths, forms of meditative reflection, and patterns of civic engagement within the two communities. While I have envisaged an Islamic genealogy for all these dimensions, I also observed how they have been reformulated through a delicate process of re-balancing of Islamic repertoires of thought and action in order to make them consonant with the needs and the challenges posed by contemporary times.

Disappointed by the radical secularist turn taken by the national project after 1923, Said Nursi attained a synthesis of the Islamic tradition aimed at harmonizing it with modern epistemological assumptions and scientific descriptions of the natural world. Even if the social and cultural context has changed significantly since early Republican times, many of the answers and solutions that Nursi suggested remain valid for a large number of Muslims in Turkey today. Members of the *Suffa* and the Gülen communities continue to read the *Risale-i Nur* cyclically and think through its poetically dense metaphors to discern God's presence in every moment and aspect of their lives. In their meetings, they continue to warn each other of the devilish inclinations of their carnal souls and to mitigate its temptations by cultivating their spiritual dimension. At the same time, they continue to remind themselves of the need they each have to pursue their Muslim life and cultivate a sense of unity in brotherhood. They also recall the responsibility they have, as aware Muslims, of engaging in society moved by a religiously-grounded sense of sincerity and commitment.

To many readers of both academic and nonacademic background, the reliance that my interlocutors put on the *Risale-i Nur* as their main guidance may appear to reveal how their intellectual practices are still largely dependent upon religious authority and hence unsuitable to modern life. Against this perspective, *Reading Islam* has illustrated that the *Suffa* and the Gülen communities uphold reading religious texts as key to revitalizing Islamic repertoires of thought and action in a way that suits the modern condition. In such a perspective, far from being an unshakable sign of religious vacuity, the fact that the *Risale-i Nur* retains a consistent following today is symptomatic of how many Muslims in Turkey are still dissatisfied by the fact that Islam has lost centrality in shaping the worldview and direction of their society. Despite the general relaxation of secularist policies in the country in the last fifteen years, my interlocutors still struggled with the dominance of modern secular views emphasizing individualism and obscuring Muslim perspectives on human life. No matter how religion is being reintegrated in contemporary public discourse, the overarching worldview in Turkey, as elsewhere, remains that of a disenchanted and economic oriented society in which religious values have only a corollary and accessory role in the life of the majority of the people.

However, contemporary readers of the *Risale* do conform to modern life and views in many ways. For instance, they neither resist the separation of the state machine from the religious sphere or the country's participation in a global economy, nor do they reject modern life intended as involving urbanization and modern forms of employment. Rather, they question the idea that modern forms of power and knowledge are sufficient in guaranteeing the full development of human potential. For this same reason, their critique is also directed against those Muslims who do not show the same awareness of the present condition of society and do not share the same desire to reform it. Indeed, in their view, living a Muslim life in such a society requires a higher level of concern and commitment than that of previous generations, an aspect that points to their emphasis on Islam as a tradition based on reflection and rational scrutiny.

With their stress on reading and related practices of reflective meditation, indeed, the two communities put the image of Islam as a tradition of intellectual engagement into the foreground. When practicing *tefekkür* members of the *Suffa* and the Gülen communities evoke ontological religious views that see human beings as being in a constant state of tension between a transcendent cosmic order and their mundane life. During their reading meetings, they do more than simply embody those dispositions that are at the core of their understanding of a correct Muslim life. They also engage in a process of intellectual discernment that elicits a set of ethical considerations regarding their place and responsibility as Muslims living in the contemporary world. In this vein, reading practices of the *Risale* exemplify how the Islamic tradition can be reinterpreted within contemporary movements to provide Muslims with valuable answers to new questions about their place and role, as faithful people, in society—questions that emerged with major force following the global affirmation of a secular order which sharpened the existing tension between this-worldly and other-worldly domains.

As mentioned throughout this work, the exploration of forms of meditation based on the *Risale* offers insight for rethinking Islamic practice in ways that diverge from how this has been conceived in important studies in the anthropology of Islam. The contributions of Mahmood (2005) and others (Asad 1986, 1993; Hirschkind 2006) have been groundbreaking in terms of opening new directions of research, not only in anthropology but also in other cognate fields such as sociology, religious studies, and political science. This scholarship has been particularly effective in sanctioning the latent Western-centrism that characterizes the social sciences, which has often obscured our capacity to comprehend human experience beyond the categories we have inherited from European historical experience. More specifically, it has succeeded in reintegrating the place of emotions and feelings such as piety, humility, and fear—which are conventionally categorized as passive in the modern liberal universe of sense—in the study of religious experience, and Muslim life in particular. Additionally, these works have pointed to the essentially political nature of the religious phenomena in a modern setting. As Soares and Osella (2010) have observed, the scholarship inspired by Asad has been determinant for revealing the micro-politics of Islamic practice beyond the confines of party politics and the state, which have occupied most of the attention of political scientists. By relying on the use of fine-tuned ethnographic inquiry, this scholarship has given voice to local interlocutors and provided descriptions of Muslim life that are highly attuned to local views and sensibilities.

Yet it is the representation of Muslim life as bound to a set of "practices" these works offer that the cases of the *Suffa* and the Gülen communities call into question. In their accounts, Muslim life is figured in the image of a training, namely of a disciplinary process imprinting its marks on pious bodies—the embodied dispositions—by means of constant repetition of deliberate exercises over time. Although neither Mahmood nor Hirschkind deny reflection its place in the no-better-defined domain of Islamic practice, they both present their interlocutors as primarily engaged in a process that draws its efficacy from reiteration. It is indeed repetition itself, and not the acts of intellectual discernment related to religious practice, that allows for the settling of ethical dispositions in the body of the women of the mosque movement of Mahmood. The same can be said for the listeners of the cassette-sermons of Hirschkind, with the only notable distinction that in his account repetition also serves to cultivate an openness, an attunedness to receiving the divine speech, which is aurally conveyed in the sermon (Mittermaier 2012). As a consequence, the role of Islam as a tradition oriented toward a transcendent plane which provides Muslim practitioners with imaginative repertoires to connect their ethical endeavors to a broader religious design is marginal, if not absent, in these works. In their accounts, tradition is mainly understood as discursive in the strictest sense of the term, namely as a source of authoritative discourses that prescribe to pious Muslims the set of practices they have to obey in order to attune their sensory and emotional apparatuses to the standards required by virtuous Muslim conduct.

The limitations of these approaches seem to be rooted in their basic inability to overcome some of the debates about social structure and human agency that have haunted the social sciences since the 1960s (Ortner 1984). It is indeed possible to read the insistence of Mahmood and others on reiteration as the symptom of a latent Bourdieusian view of human life, understood as the expression of a process of internalization of (and almost imperceptible deflection from) an overdetermined social structure. In their accounts, a view of *habitus* reproduction persists, which mainly conceives embodiment as a sort of mechanic process by which Muslim practitioners learn to live a virtuous life by soberly abiding to authoritative religious discourse. In this way, they reproduce a circular understanding of Muslim life as "practice," namely as the actualization of overdetermined social structures—here epitomized by religious discourse—at the expense of a full consideration of the place of intellectual discernment within it. Since there is no possibility of escaping the grip of the imperatives of religious discourse, there is neither space for factors external to the determination of social structure, for a *telos* transcending the contingent imperatives of social order, in their accounts. It is this conception of practice as the actualization of authoritative religious discourses that occludes the possibility for these approaches to explore Muslim life beyond the contours of self-imposed discipline.

In contrast, my interlocutors' path to inhabiting a Muslim life involves the exercise of meditative reflection: a process of intellectual discernment about their role as human beings who relate themselves to a transcendent order of things, and which has clear ethical and political implications. An understanding of the Islamically-informed worldviews that underlie these intellectual practices is essential to appreciate the formative path of the two communities under study. Highlighting the place of reflection in religious practice does not belittle the importance of repetition. After all, reflective practices within the *Suffa* and the Gülen communities were also based on the reiterated reading of the same religious texts over time. In this light, repetition is an important dimension of meditative reflection too. However, it is not considered by my interlocutors to be sufficient for the development of the Muslim person.

Embracing the ontological and philosophical perspectives disclosed by the *Risale* is more important than reiterated engagement with the text or, to state it differently, the latter is the means to the former.

The exploration of the reading practices of the *Risale* suggests that an account of intellective practice within Islam is desirable to enlarge our perspective on Muslim life beyond the contour of reiterated compliance with a religious discipline. Such an exploration invites us to deflect our attention from Islam as consisting mainly of compliance with a set of "practices," and redirect it toward Muslim life, intended as engagement with the questions that guide religious practitioners' sense of commitment and their desire to live such commitment by participating in the world surrounding them. In this vein, the cases explored in this work push us to consider Muslim life not as an answer to the question: through which exercises, efforts or training do I make myself into a virtuous subject in a society dominated by secular modern logic? Rather, it invites us to look from a different perspective, which asks: how can I attain the full state of human being, which I can only truly achieve by transcending my own earthly existence and thinking of myself as part of a wider principle of reason and truth that guides the reality of this world? The implication for an alternative theory of ethical formation in Islam is not just whether people can find in their body a potential instrument for attaining a state of freedom from secular power, but how far they can keep their own intellectual and bodily practices consistent with a theory that concerns their sense of humanness and their understanding of their role in the world beyond the constraints of such power.

Replying to these questions requires the invocation of a transcendent referent that provides grounds for speculation about the place and role of humanity in this world. The Nur cosmologies that the readers of the *Risale* ponder represent a horizon of meaning and ethical attachment that helps them address both the theological and the more contingent mundane issues. In this regard, they are a clear invitation to shift our attention toward the place of God and transcendence in Muslim life. The role that teleological imaginaries and the "metaphysical elsewhere" occupy in Muslim life have recently received growing attention in the scholarship on Islam (Meyer 2008; Mittermaier 2011, 2012; Abenante and Vicini 2017; Vicini 2017). Inasmuch as these studies open new promising venues for exploring Muslim life beyond the strict contours of "Islamic practice," they also push the field to think beyond a latent immanent perspective that continues to pervade the academic understanding of religion. Still too often, religious life is approached as the simple expression of powerful human discourses, rather than as a force for articulating forms of ethical commitment and solidarity that presuppose the existence of vertical relations with a transcendent plane. Only by further developing such a perspective can this field of research develop a more comprehensive understanding of religious life which may attempt to go beyond the contours of "secular reason" (Milbank 2006 [1990]; Kahn 2016).

Because religious life in Islam as well as in other traditions is seldom disconnected from forms of engagement in the surrounding world, the analysis should not be confined to disciplining processes in secluded spaces. As shown, forms of meditative reflection prompted by reading practices of the *Risale* underlie also the forms of civic engagement of members of the *Suffa* and the Gülen communities. And the motivations and ideals that these groups uphold essentially contradict conventional understandings of social behavior as the reflex of means-to-ends logics. This brings us to the second major point of this work, namely that an inclusion of a transhuman dimension also enriches our understanding of religiously-grounded forms of sociopolitical participation. As also suggested by the subtitle of this book, these communities promote a form of politics that is rooted in ideals of universal human brotherhood, which supersede dominant secular modern logic and have a radical subversive potential. Inasmuch as my interlocutors' practices of intellectual discernment were oriented toward the realization of what they saw as a higher good, they escaped categorizations that are commonly used to define political behavior as oriented toward the achievement of personal ends. It is for this reason that I have opted for investigating the *Suffa* and the Gülen communities from the perspective of their inner motivations and ideals, rather than seeing them as the expression of deeper structural transformations in a neoliberal age (e.g. Tuğal 2009). The attempt has not been made to deny the affinity that has existed between Muslim activism and neoliberal dynamics since the 1980s, nor out of a unique anthropological taste for cultural relativism. Rather, it reflects the conviction that by sticking to a socio-anthropological perspective, attentive to the connection between contemporary forms of Muslim engagement and longstanding trajectories of the Islamic tradition, allows for a fine understanding of the motivations and inner dynamics that lie behind Muslim participation in contemporary societies.

An exploration of the ethical considerations foregrounded by the idea of Islamic brotherhood has been central in this enterprise. Following Salvatore (2016), brotherhood has been first approached as a matrix of civility offering my interlocutors patterns for reconstructing social cohesion and mobilization beyond the contours of modern, state-centered models. Later, the concept has been pushed further into the domain of ethics, showing how it helped my interlocutors to link their forms of civic engagement with a non-contingent transcendent order. This perspective was especially useful to illustrate how contemporary members of the *Suffa* and the Gülen communities are guided by views, motives, and sentiments that are rooted in their world-renouncing philosophies. As shown, my interlocutors' forms of civic engagement are grounded on a subtle, yet pervasive, conversion of paths aimed at achieving awareness of the transitoriness of worldly existence into an engine for in-worldly activism. For them, taming the lower self is not just an end that they have to pursue to maintain a proper Muslim conduct. It is also the precondition for a life spent in self-denial and self-sacrifice in order to realize community goals that they consider to be higher goods than others. It is such ingraining of religiously-inspired worldly-renouncing philosophies into forms of social activism that explains the mobilizing potential of these two communities.

Yet as they have ingrained their civic potential into new power dynamics, these Islamic forces have intertwined their projects with that of the post-Ottoman Republican order. For instance, the call of the Gülen community for new generations of young Muslims to receive a good education and play an active role in society in the name of Islamic reform has many common traits with a Republican project that based its success on the education of the nation's citizens. While the two logics, "transcendent" and "mundane," that orient these two projects are opposed, they overlap on several points. Pupils educated in the houses of the community were seen by Gülen as the sons of modern Turkey—as people who would contribute to the country's progress by supporting its technological, economic, and moral advancement. On this point, views of the social good promoted within this and other Islamic communities dovetail with those of more recent national manufacture.

As a corollary, however, the promiscuity of Turkish Islamism with the project of political modernity has also sanctioned its partial assimilation of a corporative understanding of the brotherhood that is more oriented towards the realization of communitarian goals than by a genuine attitude for achieving the common good. While Islamic forces are the bearers of an alternative project of civility, their engagement in politically sensitive fields such as education and public employment has generated an inevitable conflict with other forces that aim to shape politics in the country. As shown, this conflict was already inherent in a tension between mundane and transcendent orders that permeates these forms of Muslim civility. The roots of such a clash can be found in Nursi's partial reinterpretation of the brotherhood *via* a new corporative understanding of social relations, which has been inspired by Western modernity. This suggestion has been later translated into concrete organizational forms when what originated as a dynamic network of Nur circles promoting intellectual speculation and discovery was fragmented into a myriad of isolated and self-enclosed communities, in which the Nur message has been dispossessed of its original intellectual vitality (Karabaşoğlu 2003).

CONCLUSION

Following their expansion in the 1970s, the Nur communities, as well as other Muslim groups, have progressively transformed into catalyzers of economic and human capital and been able to expand their activities throughout society. As distinctly shown by the case of the Gülen community, Islamic communities have over time developed into sociopolitical forces whose main goal has become to pursue such expansive policies and possibly extend their grasp on institutions. While it seemed natural to define the relationship between the state and these groups as confrontational when the institutions were mainly controlled by secularist elites, it may seem less obvious to do so for the last fifteen years, as the power has switched in the hands of political forces that have emerged from a similar Islamic impulse. The reckless clash between the Gülen community and the AKP administration that dramatically resulted in the coup attempt of July 15, 2016 is a clear indicator of how, for this particular community, the expansion of Islamic ideals into the public arena has not simply been motivated by a desire to effuse an alternative message of civility. Rather, its project has always rested also on the more immediate political goal of replacing the secular elites and increase the presence of pious Muslims in the cultural and educational sectors, as well as in the economy and the bureaucracy—including academia, the police, and the army—with the consequent exacerbation of the existing tensions crossing both the religious-conservative camp within, and the relations between this latter camp and the rest of society.

Turkish society today is in a period of renewed polarization along the conservative-secular divide; between supporters of the AKP administration and those who totally oppose it. As observed by Jenny B. White (2012) already before the political shifts of the last five years, Turkey is overwhelmed by a mounting wave of Muslim nationalism. Turkish society is today in a standoff between those defending a religious conservative view of how the country should evolve and those who wish for a return to a political project which would pursue a program of modernization and secularization in line with that inaugurated by Atatürk ninety five years ago. This climax, combined with the progressive assimilation of many Islamic communities into the state machine after the coup attempt of July 2016, do not bode well for the emergence of a genuine project for the revitalization of the Islamic civic tradition in the near future. Rather, the current situation seems to pave the way for a process of further crystallization and disempowerment of the civic potential of the Islamic legacy, which is once again sacrificed on the altar of more stringent political issues. If until 2013 there was hope for the development of a more dynamic relationship between Muslim forms of civic engagement and formal politics, such a possibility has now waned, at least temporarily, as it is subordinated to other more contingent needs.

Yet the integration of long-standing alternative patterns for the organization of the social and political orders in Turkey seems more urgent today than ever. In a world where modern liberal paths have shown their inability to provide social integrity, solidarity, and justice, taking into account the grasp that Islamic civility still maintains in Muslim-majority societies seems to be particularly timely and necessary. The revolts that spread across the Arab World a few years ago are but a further demonstration of the incapacity of old models to provide effective answers for these societies, and they urge us to take into serious consideration the way Muslims think of themselves as sociopolitical actors of the modern world. This seems to be particularly critical outside of the Middle Eastern region as well. Today, as the global crisis is straining modern liberal forms of public governance and related ideas of representativeness to the limit, it may be the right time to rethink these models through alternative patterns. If, as I believe, one of the aims of analytical inquiry should be that of opening up new ways of thinking, and if the anthropological enterprise has traditionally been committed to do so by looking at traditions alternative to the dominant ones, I hope that this work represents a contribution in this direction.

References

Abenante, Paola. 2013. "Inner and Outer Ways: Sufism and Subjectivity in Egypt and Beyond." *Ethnos: Journal of Anthropology* 78 (4): 490–514.

Abenante, Paola, and Fabio Vicini. 2017. "Interiority Unbound: Sufi and Modern Articulations of the Self." *Culture and Religion* 18 (2): 57–71.

Acar, Feride. 1991. "Women in the Ideology of Islamic Revivalism in Turkey: Three Islamic Women's Journals." In *Islam in Modern Turkey: Religion, Politics and Literature in a Secular State*, edited by Richard Tapper, 280–303. London and New York: I.B. Tauris.

Agai, Bekim. 2003. "The Gülen Movement's Islamic Ethic of Education." In *Turkish Islam and the Secular State: The Gülen Movement*, edited by M. Hakan Yavuz and John L. Esposito, 48–68. Syracuse, NY: Syracuse University Press.

Agai, Bekim. 2007. "Islam and Education in Secular Turkey: State Policies and the Emergence of the Fethullah Gülen Group." In *Schooling Islam: The Culture and Politics of Modern Muslim Education*, edited by Robert W. Hefner and Muhammad Qasim Zaman, 149–171. Princeton: Princeton University Press.

Agamben, Giorgio. 2013. *The Highest Poverty: Monastic Rules and Form-of-Life*. Stanford: Stanford University Press.

Ahmad, Feroz. 1993. *The Making of Modern Turkey*. London and New York: Routledge.

Ahmad, Irfan. 2017. *Religion as Critique: Islamic Critical Thinking From Mecca to the Marketplace*. Chapel Hill, NC: The University of North Carolina Press.

Ahmed, Shahab. 2016. *What Is Islam? The Importance of Being Islamic*. Princeton: Princeton University Press.

Aishima, Hatsuki. 2016. *Public Culture and Islam in Modern Egypt*. London and New York: I.B. Tauris.

Akşit, Bahattin. 1991. "Islamic Education in Turkey: Medrese Reform in Late Ottoman Times and Imam-Hatip Schools in the Republic." In *Islam in Modern Turkey: Religion, Politics and Literature in a Secular State*, edited by Richard Tapper, 145–170. London and New York: I.B. Tauris.

Al-Anani, Khalil. 2016. *Inside the Muslim Brotherhood: Religion, Identity, and Politics*. New York: Oxford University Press.

Al-Attas, Syed Muhammad Naguib. 1979. "Preliminary Thoughts on the Nature of Knowledge and the Definition and Aims of Education." In *Aims and Objectives of Islamic Education*, edited by Syed Muhammad Naguib Al-Attas, 19–47. London: Hodder & Stoughton.

Alatas, Syed Farid. 2017. "Said Nursi (1877–1960)." In *Sociological Theory Beyond the Canon*, edited by Syed Farid Alatas and Vineeta Sinha, 205–236. London: Palgrave Macmillan.

Algar, Hamid. 2001. "The Centennial Renewer: Bediüzzaman Said Nursi and the Tradition of Tajdid." *Journal of Islamic Studies* 12 (3): 291–311.

Ali, Jan A. 2012. *Islamic Revivalism Encounters the Modern World: A Study of the Tabligh Jama'at*. New Delhi: Sterling Publishers.

Altinay, Ayşe Gül. 2006. *The Myth of the Military-Nation: Militarism, Gender, and Education in Turkey*. New York: Palgrave Macmillan.

Anderson, Benedict. 1991 [1983]. *Imagined Communities: Reflections on the Origin and Spread of Nationalism*. London and New York: Verso.

Angey, Gabrielle. 2018. "The Gülen Movement and the Transfer of a Political Conflict from Turkey to Senegal." *Politics, Religion & Ideology* 19 (1): 53–68.

Anjum, Ovamir. 2007. "Islam as a Discursive Tradition: Talal Asad and His Interlocutors." *Comparative Studies of South Asia, Africa and the Middle East* 27 (3): 656–672.

Anscombe, Gertrude E. M. 1958. "Modern Moral Philosophy." *Philosophy* 33 (124): 1–19.

Asad, Talal. 1986. *The Idea of an Anthropology of Islam*. Washington, DC: Georgetown University Center for Contemporary Arab Studies.

Asad, Talal. 1993. *Genealogies of Religion: Discipline and Reasons of Power in Christianity and Islam*. Baltimore and London: Johns Hopkins University Press.

Asad, Talal. 2003. *Formations of the Secular: Christianity, Islam, Modernity*. Stanford: Stanford University Press.

Asad, Talal. 2015. "Thinking About Tradition, Religion, and Politics in Egypt Today." *Critical Inquiry* 42 (1): 166–214.

Asad, Talal. 2018. *Secular Translations: Nation-State, Modern Self, and Calculative Reason*. New York: Columbia University Press.

Atasoy, Yıldız. 1997. "Islamic Revivalism and the Nation-State Project: Competing Claims for Modernity." *Social Compass* 44 (1): 83–99.

Ay, Mehmet Emin. 1993. *Din Eğitimi ve Öğretiminde Mükafat ve Ceza*. Izmir: Uludağ Üniversitesi Basımevi.

Babou, Cheikh A. M. 2007. *Fighting the Greater Jihad: Amadu Bamba and the Founding of the Muridiyya of Senegal, 1853–1913*. Athens, OH: Ohio University Press.

Bacık, Gökhan. 2018. "How Has the Gülen Movement Ended Up Where It Is?" *Ahval*, May 9, 2018. Accessed July 17, 2018. https://ahvalnews.com/gulen-movement/how-has-gulen-movement-ended-where-it.

Baker, Barbara G. 2018. "Erdoğan Demands Gülen Extradition for US Pastor's Release." *World Watch Monitor*, April 23, 2018. Accessed July 17, 2018. https://www.worldwatchmonitor.org/2018/04/erdogan-demands-gulen-extradition-for-us-pastors-release/.

Balci, Bayram. 2003. *Missionnaires de l'Islam en Asie Centrale: Les Écoles Turques de Fethullah Gülen*. Paris and Istanbul: Maisonneuve & Larose–Institut Français d'Études Anatoliennes.

Balci, Tamer, and Christopher L. Miller, eds. 2012. *The Gülen Hizmet Movement: Circumspect Activism in Faith-Based Reform*. Newcastle upon Tyne: Cambridge Scholars.

REFERENCES

BBC. 2013. "Turkey Ministers Caglayan, Guler and Bayraktar Resign Amid Scandal." *BBC News*, December 25, 2013. Accessed June 14, 2018. https://www.bbc.com/news/world-europe-25514579.

Bein, Amit. 2011. *Ottoman Ulema, Turkish Republic: Agents of Change and Guardians of Tradition*. Stanford: Stanford University Press.

Bellah, Robert N. 1999. "Max Weber and World-Denying Love: A Look at the Historical Sociology of Religion." *Journal of the American Academy of Religion* 67 (2): 277–304.

Berkes, Niyazi. 1998 [1964]. *The Development of Secularism in Turkey*. London: Hurst.

Bialecki, Jon. 2014. "Does God Exist in Methodological Atheism? On Tanya Lurhmann's *When God Talks Back* and Bruno Latour." *Anthropology of Consciousness* 25 (1): 32–52.

Bialecki, Jon. 2018. "Anthropology, Theology, and the Challenge of Immanence." In *Theologically Engaged Anthropology*, edited by J. Derrick Lemons, 156–178. Oxford: Oxford University Press.

Bilici, Faruk. 1993. "Sociabilité et Expression Politique Islamiste en Turquie: Les Nouveaux Waqfs en Turquie." *Revue Française de Science Politique* 43 (3): 412–434.

Bilici, Mucahit. 2006. "The Gülen Movement and Its Politics of Representation in Turkey." *The Muslim World* 96 (1): 1–20.

Birgün. 2017. "FETÖ'den Boşalan Yerler Yeni Tarikatlarla Dolduruldu." *Birgün*, August 11, 2017. Accessed July 17, 2018. https://www.birgun.net/haber-detay/feto-den-bosalan-yerler-yeni-tarikatlarla-dolduruldu-174268.html.

Birnbaum, Michael. 2013. "In Turkey Protests, Splits in Erdogan's Base." *The Washington Post*, June 14, 2013. Accessed June 14, 2018. https://www.washingtonpost.com/world/erdogan-offers-concessions-to-turkeys-protesters/2013/06/14/9a87fff6-d4bf-11e2-a73e-826d299ff459_story.html?noredirect=on&utm_term=.6caf10f546d5.

Bowen, John R. 1993. *Muslims Through Discourse: Religion and Ritual in Gayo Society*. Princeton: Princeton University Press.

Boyle, Helen N. 2004. *Quranic Schools: Agents of Preservation and Change*. New York and London: Routledge.

Bozdoğan, Sibel, and Reşat Kasaba, eds. 1997. *Rethinking Modernity and National Identity in Turkey*. Seattle, WA: University of Washington Press.

Bruinessen, Martin van. 2009. "Sufism, 'Popular' Islam and the Encounter with Modernity." In *Islam and Modernity: Key Issues and Debates*, edited by Masud M. Khalid, Armando Salvatore and Martin van Bruinessen, 125–157. Edinburgh: Edinburgh University Press.

Bulaç, Ali. 2007. *Din, Kent ve Cemaat: Fethullah Gülen Örneği*. Istanbul: Ufuk Kitap.

Butler, Daren. 2012. "Turkish Spy Row Hits Kurdish Peace, Democratization Move." *Reuters*, February 17, 2012. Accessed June 14, 2018. https://www.reuters.com/article/us-turkey-kurds-idUSTRE81G0HT20120217.

Calverley, Edwin E. 1943. "Doctrines of the Soul (Nafs and Ruh) in Islam." *The Muslim World* 33 (4): 254–264.

Casanova, José. 1994. *Public Religions in the Modern World*. Chicago: The University of Chicago Press.
Cebecioğlu, Ethem. 1997. Hizmet. In *Tasavvuf Terimleri ve Deyimleri Sözlüğü*, edited by Ethem Cebecioğlu. Ankara: Rehber.
Chih, Rachida. 2007. "What is a Sufi Order? Revisiting the Concept Through a Case Study of the Khalwatiyya in Contemporary Egypt." In *Sufism and the "Modern" in Islam*, edited by Martin van Bruinessen and Julia D. Howell, 21–38. London and New York: I.B. Tauris.
Chittick, William C. 1989. *The Sufi Path of Knowledge: Ibn Arabi's Metaphysics of Imagination*. Albany, NY: SUNY Press.
Chittick, William C. 1998. *The Self-Disclosure of God: Principles of Ibn al-Arabi's Cosmology*. Albany, NY: SUNY Press.
Chittick, William C. 2000. *Faith and Practice of Islam: Three Thirteenth Century Sufi Texts*. Kuala Lumpur: S. Abdul Majeed & Co.
Chittick, William C. 2007. *Sufism: A Beginner's Guide*. London: Oneworld Publications.
Chittick, William C. 2011. "Wahdat Al-Shuhud." In *Encyclopedia of Islam*, 2nd Edition, edited by P. Bearman, Th. Bianquis, C. E. Bosworth, E. van Donzel and W. P. Heinrichs. Leiden: Brill.
Coleman, Janet. 1994. "MacIntyre and Aquinas." In *After MacIntyre: Critical Perspectives on the Work of Alasdair MacIntyre*, edited by John Horton and Susan Mendus. Cambridge: Polity Press.
Cook, David. 2015. *Understanding Jihad*. Oakland, CA: University of California Press.
Cooper, John. 1999 [1993]. "Rumi and Hikmat: Towards a Reading of Sabziwari's Commentary on the Mathnawi." In *The Heritage of Sufism*, Vol. I, edited by Leonard Lewisohn, 409–433. Oxford: Oneworld Publications.
Copeaux, Etienne. 1996. "*Hizmet*: A Keyword in the Turkish Historical Narrative." *New Perspectives on Turkey* 14 (Spring): 97–114.
Copeaux, Etienne. 1998. "Ahmed Arvasi, un Idéologue de la Synthèse Turco-Islamique." *Turcica* 30: 211–223.
Corbin, Henry. 1993. *History of Islamic Philosophy*. London and New York: Kegan Paul International.
Corbin, Henry. 1998 [1969]. *Alone with the Alone: Creative Imagination in the Sufism of Ibn Arabi*. Princeton: Princeton University Press.
Cornell, Vincent J. 2010. "Reasons Public and Divine: Liberal Democracy, Shari'a Fundamentalism, and the Epistemological Crisis of Islam." In *Rethinking Islamic Studies: From Orientalism to Cosmopolitanism*, edited by Carl W. Ernst and Richard C. Martin, 23–51. Columbia, SC: The University of South Carolina Press.
Coşkun, Feray. 2011. "An Ottoman Preacher's Perception of a Medieval Cosmography: Mahmud al-Hatib's Translation of Kharidat al-Aja'ib wa Faridat al-Ghara'ib." *Al-Masaq* 23 (1): 53–66.

Coşkun, Şevki. 2006. "Sağa Yatarak Uyuma." *Sızıntı* 28 (327).
Çağatay, Neşet. 1968. "The Tradition of Mavlid Recitations in Islam Particularly in Turkey." *Studia Islamica* 28: 127–133.
Çaha, Ömer, Yasin Aktay, Ferhat Kentel, and Ramazan Yelken. 2011. *Türkiye Cemaatlerle Barışık*. Istanbul: Andy-ar Strateji Geliştirme ve Sosyal Araştırmalar Merkezi.
Çakır, Ruşen, and Semih Sakallı. 2014. *100 Soruda Erdoğan x Gülen Savaşı*. Istanbul: Metis Yayıncılık.
Çelik, Gürkan, Johan Leman, and Karel Steenbrink, eds. 2015. *Gülen-Inspired Hizmet in Europe: The Western Journey of a Turkish Muslim Movement*. Brussels: Peter Lang.
Çepni, Ozan. 2018. "Güneydoğu Nurculara Kaldı." *Cumhuriyet*, February 13, 2018. Accessed July 17, 2018. http://www.cumhuriyet.com.tr/haber/egitim/925998/Guneydogu_Nurculara_kaldi.html.
Çınar, Alev. 2005. *Modernity, Islam, and Secularism in Turkey: Bodies, Places, and Time*. Minneapolis: University of Minnesota Press.
Danielson, Michael N., and Ruşen Keleş. 1985. *Politics of Rapid Urbanization: Government and Growth in Modern Turkey*. New York and London: Holmes and Meier.
Daston, Lorraine, and Katharine Park. 1998. *Wonders and the Order of Nature, 1150–1750*. New York: Zone Books.
Davison, Andrew. 2003. "Turkey, a 'Secular' State? The Challenge of Description." *South Atlantic Quarterly* 102 (2–3): 333–350.
Deeb, Lara. 2006. *An Enchanted Modern: Gender and Public Piety in Shi'i Lebanon*. Princeton: Princeton University Press.
Deeb, Lara. 2015. "Thinking Piety and the Everyday Together: A Response to Fadil and Fernando." *HAU: Journal of Ethnographic Theory* 5 (2): 93–96.
Delibaş, Kayhan. 2014. *The Rise of Political Islam in Turkey: Urban Poverty, Grassroots Activism and Islamic Fundamentalism*. London and New York: I.B. Tauris.
Dohrn, Kristina. 2014. "Translocal Ethics: Hizmet Teachers and the Formation of Gülen-Inspired Schools in Urban Tanzania." *Sociology of Islam* 1 (3–4): 233–256.
Dohrn, Kristina. 2018. "Navigating the Future of the Gülen Movement in Tanzania." In *Turkey's July 15th Coup: What Happened and Why*, edited by Hakan M. Yavuz and Bayram Balci. Salt Lake City: Utah University Press.
Donzel, Emeri J. van. 2011. "Mudjaddid." In *Encyclopedia of Islam*, 2nd Edition, edited by P. Bearman, Th. Bianquis, C. E. Bosworth, E. van Donzel and W. P. Heinrichs. Leiden: Brill.
Dumovich, Liza. 2018. "Pious Creativity: Negotiating Hizmet in South America after July 2016." *Politics, Religion & Ideology* 19 (1): 81–94.
Dupret, Baudouin. 2004. "The Person and the Law: Contingency, Individuation and the Subject of the Law." In *Standing Trial: Law and the Person in the Modern Middle East*, edited by Baudouin Dupret, 9–38. London and New York: I.B. Tauris.

Ebaugh, Helen R. F. 2010. *The Gülen Movement: A Sociological Analysis of a Civic Movement Rooted in Moderate Islam*. Dordrecht, London and New York: Springer.

Eickelman, Dale F. 1978. "The Art of Memory: Islamic Education and its Social Reproduction." *Comparative Studies in Society and History* 20 (4): 485–516.

Eickelman, Dale F. 1992. "Mass Higher Education and the Religious Imagination in Contemporary Arab Societies." *American Ethnologist* 19 (4): 643–655.

Eickelman, Dale F. 2003. "Qur'anic Commentary, Public Space, and Religious Intellectuals in the Writings of Said Nursi." In *Islam at the Crossroads: On the Life and Thought of Bediuzzaman Said Nursi*, edited by Ibrahim M. Abu-Rabi, 51–60. Albany, NY: SUNY Press.

Eickelman, Dale F., and Jon W. Anderson, eds. 2003. *New Media in the Muslim World: The Emerging Public Sphere*. Bloomington, IN: Indiana University Press.

Eickelman, Dale F., and James Piscatori. 1996. *Muslim Politics*. Princeton: Princeton University Press.

Eickelman, Dale F., and Armando Salvatore. 2006. "Muslim Publics." In *Public Islam and the Common Good*, edited by Armando Salvatore and Dale F. Eickelman, 3–27. Leiden and Boston: Brill.

El-Zein, Abdul Hamid. 1977. "Beyond Ideology and Theology: The Search for the Anthropology of Islam." *Annual Review of Anthropology* 6: 227–254.

Elliot, Alice. 2016. "The Makeup of Destiny: Predestination and the Labor of Hope in a Moroccan Emigrant Town." *American Ethnologist* 43 (3): 488–499.

Erder, Sema. 1996. *İstanbul'da Bir Kent Kondu: Ümraniye*. Istanbul: İletişim Yayınları.

Erdoğan, Latif. 2006 [1995]. *Fethullah Gülen Hocaefendi: Küçük Dünyam*. Istanbul: Ufuk Kitapları.

Es-Suyuti, Celaleddin. 1994. *Peygamberimizin Mucizeleri ve Büyük Özellikleri*. Konya: Uysal Kitabevi.

Euben, Roxanne L. 2001. *Enemy in the Mirror: Islamic Fundamentalism and the Limits of Modern Rationalism*. Princeton: Princeton University Press.

Ewing, Katherine P. 1997. *Arguing Sainthood: Modernity, Psychoanalysis, and Islam*. Durham, NC: Duke University Press.

Fadil, Nadia. 2011. "Not-/unveiling as an Ethical Practice." *Feminist Review* 98 (July): 83–109.

Fadil, Nadia, and Mayanthi Fernando. 2015. "Rediscovering the 'Everyday' Muslim: Notes on an Anthropological Divide." *HAU: Journal of Ethnographic Theory* 5 (2): 59–88.

Farag, Iman. 2001. "Private Life, Public Affairs: The Uses of Adab." In *Muslim Traditions and Modern Techniques of Power*, Yearbook of the Sociology of Islam, Vol. III, edited by Armando Salvatore, 93–120. Hamburg: Lit/New Brunswick, NJ and London: Transaction.

Fassin, Didier. 2014. "The Ethical Turn in Anthropology: Promises and Uncertainties." *HAU: Journal of Ethnographic Theory* 4 (1): 429–435.
Faubion, James D. 2011. *An Anthropology of Ethics*. Cambridge: Cambridge University Press.
Findley, Carter V. 1980. *Bureaucratic Reform in the Ottoman Empire: The Sublime Porte, 1789–1922*. Princeton: Princeton University Press.
Fortna, Benjamin. 2002. *Imperial Classroom: Islam, Education and the State in Late Ottoman Empire*. Oxford: Oxford University Press.
Foucault, Michel. 1972. *The Archeology of Knowledge and the Discourse on Language*. New York: Pantheon Books.
Foucault, Michel. 1980. *Power/Knowledge: Selected Interviews and Other Writings 1972–1977*. New York: Pantheon Books.
Foucault, Michel. 1982. "Le Combat de la Chasteté." *Communications* 35: 15–25.
Foucault, Michel. 1991. "Governmentality." In *The Foucault Effect: Studies in Governmentality*, edited by G. Burchell, C. Gordon and P. Miller, 87–104. Chicago: The University of Chicago Press.
Foucault, Michel. 1997a. "Technologies of the Self." In *Ethics: Subjectivity and Truth, Essential Works of Foucault, 1954–1984*, Vol. 1, edited by Paul Rabinow, 223–252. New York: New Press.
Foucault, Michel. 1997b. "The Ethics of Concern of the Self as a Practice of Freedom." In *Ethics: Subjectivity and Truth, Essential Works of Foucault, 1954–1984*, Vol. 1, edited by Paul Rabinow, 253–280. New York: New Press.
Foucault, Michel. 1997c. "On the Genealogy of Ethics: An Overview of Work in Progress." In *Ethics: Subjectivity and Truth, Essential Works of Foucault, 1954–1984*, Vol. 1, edited by Paul Rabinow, 281–301. New York: New Press.
Fountain, Philip, and Sin Wen Lau. 2013. "Anthropological Theologies: Engagements and Encounters." *The Australian Journal of Anthropology* 24 (3): 227–234.
Franks, Tim. 2014. "Fethullah Gulen: Powerful but Reclusive Turkish Cleric." *BBC News*, January 27, 2014. Accessed July 20, 2018. https://www.bbc.com/news/world-europe-25885817.
Friedmann, Yohanan. 2008. "Shaykh Ahmad Sirhindi and Bediuzzaman Nursi: Some Comparative Considerations." In *Spiritual Dimensions of Bediuzzaman Said Nursi's Risale-i Nur*, edited by Ibrahim M. Abu-Rabi, 275–285. Albany, NY: SUNY Press.
Gabrieli, Francesco. 2011. "Adab." In *Encyclopedia of Islam*, 2nd Edition, edited by P. Bearman, Th. Bianquis, C. E. Bosworth, E. van Donzel and W. P. Heinrichs. Leiden: Brill.
Gaibazzi, Paolo. 2015. "The Quest for Luck: Fate, Fortune, Work and the Unexpected Among Gambian Soninke Hustlers." *Critical African Studies* 7 (3): 227–242.
Gardet, Louis. 2011a. "Fikr." In *Encyclopedia of Islam*, 2nd Edition, edited by P. Bearman, Th. Bianquis, C. E. Bosworth, E. van Donzel and W. P. Heinrichs. Leiden: Brill.

Gardet, Louis. 2011b. "Ikhlas." In *Encyclopedia of Islam*, 2nd Edition, edited by P. Bearman, Th. Bianquis, C. E. Bosworth, E. van Donzel and W. P. Heinrichs. Leiden: Brill.

Gaskins, Suzanne, and Ruth Paradise. 2009. "Learning Through Observation in Daily Life." In *The Anthropology of Learning in Childhood*, edited by David F. Lancy, John Bock, Susanne Gaskins and Walnut Creek, 85–117. Lanham, MD: AltaMira Press.

Geertz, Clifford. 1968. *Islam Observed: Religious Development in Morocco and Indonesia*. New Haven: Yale University Press.

Gellner, Ernest. 1983. *Muslim Society*. Cambridge: Cambridge University Press.

Gerber, Haim. 2002. "The Public Sphere and Civil Society in the Ottoman Empire." In *The Public Sphere in Muslim Societies*, edited by Miriam Hoexter, Shmuel N. Eisenstadt and Nehemia Levtzion, 65–82. Albany, NY: SUNY Press.

Giladi, Avner. 1989. "Concepts of Childhood and Attitudes Towards Children in Medieval Islam: A Preliminary Study with Special Reference to Reaction to Infant and Child Morality." *Journal of the Economic and Social History of the Orient* 32 (2): 121–152.

Gilsenan, Michael. 1973. *Saint and Sufi in Modern Egypt: An Essay in the Sociology of Religion*. Oxford: Clarendon Press.

Gilsenan, Michael. 2005 [1982]. *Recognizing Islam: Religion and Society in the Modern Middle East*. London and New York: I.B. Tauris.

Gökalp, Ziya. 1959. "Islam and Modern Civilization." In *Turkish Nationalism and Western Civilization*, edited by Niyazi Berkes, 214–223. London: George Allen and Unwin.

Göle, Nilüfer. 1996. *The Forbidden Modern: Civilization and Veiling*. Ann Arbor: University of Michigan Press.

Göle, Nilüfer. 1997. "The Quest for the Islamic Self Within the Context of Modernity." In *Rethinking Modernity and National Identity in Turkey*, edited by Sibel Bozdoğan and Reşat Kasaba, 81–94. Seattle, WA: University of Washington Press.

Göle, Nilüfer. 2002. "Islam in Public: New Visibilities and New Imaginaries." *Public Culture* 14 (1): 173–190.

Gräf, Bettina, and Jakob Skovgaard-Petersen. 2009. *Global Mufti: The Phenomenon of Yusuf al-Qaradawi*. New York: Columbia University Press.

Green, Nile. 2012. *Sufism: A Global History*. Oxford: Wiley-Blackwell.

Guida, Michelangelo. 2008. "The Sèvres Syndrome and 'Komplo' Theories in the Islamist and Secular Press." *Turkish Studies* 9 (1): 37–52.

Guida, Michelangelo. 2010. "The New Islamists' Understanding of Democracy in Turkey: The Examples of Ali Bulaç and Hayreddin Karaman." *Turkish Studies* 11 (3): 347–370.

Guida, Michelangelo. 2012. "Founders of Islamism in Republican Turkey: Kısakürek and Topçu." In *Intellectuals and Civil Society in the Middle East: Liberalism, Modernity* and Political Discourse, edited by Mohammed A. Bamyeh, 111–133. London and New York: I.B. Tauris.

Guida, Michelangelo. 2014. "Nurettin Topçu and Necip Fazıl Kısakürek: Stories of 'Conversion' and Activism in Republican Turkey." *Journal for Islamic Studies* 34 (1): 98–117.

Guyer, Paul. 2010. *Kant on Freedom, Law, and Happiness*. Cambridge: Cambridge University Press.

Gülen, Fethullah. 1990. "Beklenen Gençlik." *Sızıntı* 135 (April).

Gülen, Fethullah. 1996. *I'lâ-yi Kelimetullah veya Cihad*. Izmir: Nil Yayınları.

Gülen, Fethullah. 1997. "Kaos İçindeki Işık." *Sızıntı* 218 (March).

Gülen, Fethullah. 1998a. "Claims and Answers." *Aksiyon*, June 6, 1998.

Gülen, Fethullah. 1998b. *İrşad Ekseni*. Izmir: Nil Yayınları.

Gülen, Fethullah. 1998c. *Ruhumuzun Heykelini Dikerken*. Istanbul: Nil Yayınları.

Gülen, Fethullah. 1998d. *Towards the Lost Paradise*. Izmir: Kaynak.

Gülen, Fethullah. 1999. *Sonsuz Nur*. Izmir: Nil Yayınları.

Gülen, Fethullah. 2005. "İsyan Ahlakı Değil İnat Ahlaksızlığı." *Herkül.org*, June 12, 2005. Accessed May 15, 2016. www.herkul.org/kirik-testi/isyan-ahlaki-degil-inat-ahlaksizligi.

Gülen, Fethullah. 2008. *Prizma 2*. Izmir: Nil Yayınları.

Gülen, Fethullah. 2010a. "Gıybet Eden Yanınızda Konuşturmayın." *Zaman Gazetesi*, March 12, 2010.

Gülen, Fethullah. 2010b. "Gıybet ve Fitnenin Olduğu bir Börüşme Kısırdır." *Zaman Gazetesi*, March 5, 2010.

Gülen, Fethullah. 2010c. "İhtilaf Ne Zaman Rahmet Olur?", April 9, 2010. Accessed August 7, 2012. http://tr.fgulen.com/content/view/18377/18/.

Gülen, Ramiz B. (penname of Gülen, Fethullah). 1981a. "Gençliğin Problemlerine Doğru." *Sızıntı* 3 (26).

Gülen, Ramiz B. (penname of Gülen, Fethullah). 1981b. "Gençliğin Problemlerine Doğru: Yuva." *Sızıntı* 3 (28).

Gülen, Ramiz B. (penname of Gülen, Fethullah). 1981c. "Gençlik: Gençliğin Problemleri." *Sızıntı* 3 (35).

Gülen, Ramiz B. (penname of Gülen, Fethullah). 1990. "Beklenen Gençlik." *Sızıntı* 12 (135).

Gülen, Ramiz B. (penname of Gülen, Fethullah). 1992a. "Işık Evler (1)." *Sızıntı* 14 (156).

Gülen, Ramiz B. (penname of Gülen, Fethullah). 1992b. "Işık Evler (2)." *Sızıntı* 14 (157).

Güneş-Ayata, Ayşe. 1991. "Pluralism Versus Authoritarianism: Political Ideas in Two Islamic Publications." In *Islam in Modern Turkey: Religion, Politics and Literature in a Secular State*, edited by Richard Tapper, 254–279. London and New York: I.B. Tauris.

Güven, Yusuf M. 2010. *Gözümü Haramdan Nasıl Kururum*. Istanbul: Işık Yayınları.

Habermas, Jürgen. 1989. *The Structural Transformation of the Public Sphere: An Inquiry Into a Category of Bourgeois Society*. Cambridge: Polity Press.

Hadot, Pierre. 1995. *Philosophy as a Way of Life: Spiritual Exercises From Socrates to Foucault*. Malden, MA: Blackwell.

Hadot, Pierre. 2004. *What is Ancient Philosophy?* Cambridge, MA: Harvard University Press.

Hallaq, Wael B. 2009. *Shari'a: Theory, Practice, Transformations*. Cambridge: Cambridge University Press.

Hallaq, Wael B. 2013. *The Impossible State: Islam, Politics, and Modernity's Moral Predicament*. New York: Columbia University Press.

Halstead, Mark J. 2004. "An Islamic Concept of Education." *Comparative Education* 40 (4): 517–529.

Hart, Kimberly. 2013. *And Then We Work for God: Rural Sunni Islam in Western Turkey*. Stanford: Stanford University Press.

Hatina, Meir. 2006. "Restoring a Lost Identity: Models of Education in Modern Islamic Thought." *British Journal of Middle Eastern Studies* 33 (2): 179–197.

Hefner, Robert W. 2000. *Civil Islam: Muslims and Democratization in Indonesia*. Princeton: Princeton University Press.

Hefner, Robert W. 2007. "Introduction: The Culture, Politics, and Future of Muslim Education." In *Schooling Islam: The Culture and Politics of Modern Muslim Education*, edited by Robert W. Hefner and Qasim Muhammad Zaman, 1–39. Princeton: Princeton University Press.

Hendrick, Joshua D. 2010. "Globalization, Islamic Activism, and Passive Revolution in Turkey: The Case of Fethullah Gülen." *Journal of Power* 2 (3): 343–368.

Hendrick, Joshua D. 2013. *Gülen: The Ambiguous Politics of Market Islam in Turkey and the World*. New York: New York University Press.

Hendrick, Joshua D. 2018. "A Turkish Red Herring? The Production and Consumption of Fethullah Gülen as 'Good Islam'." In *Turkey's July 15th Coup: What Happened and Why*, edited by Hakan M. Yavuz and Bayram Balci, 287–308. Salt Lake City: University of Utah Press.

Henkel, Heiko. 2007. "The Location of Islam: Inhabiting Istanbul in a Muslim Way." *American Ethnologist* 34 (1): 57–70.

Hermansen, Marcia. 2007. "The Cultivation of Memory in the Gülen Community." In *Proceedings of the International Conference on the Muslim World in Transition*, 60–76. Leeds: Metropolitan University Press.

Heyd, Uriel. 1961. "The Ottoman Ulema and Westernization in the Time of Selim III and Mahmud II." In *Scripta Hierosolymitana: Studies in Islamic History and Civilization*, Vol. IX, 63–96. Jerusalem: Magnes Press.

Hirschkind, Charles. 2006. *The Ethical Soundscape: Cassette Sermons and Islamic Counterpublics*. New York: Columbia University Press.

Hodgson, Marshall G. S. 1970. "The Role of Islam in World History." *International Journal of Middle East Studies* 1 (2): 99–123.
Hodgson, Marshall G. S. 1974. *The Venture of Islam: Conscience and History in a World Civilization*, Vol. I. Chicago: The University of Chicago Press.
Hodgson, Marshall G. S. 1977. *The Venture of Islam: Conscience and History in a World Civilization*, Vol. II. Chicago: The University of Chicago Press.
Hourani, Albert. 1981. "Sufism and Modern Islam: Shaikh Khalid and the Naqshbandi Order." In *The Emergence of the Modern Middle East*, edited by Albert Hourani, 75–89. Berkeley: University of California Press.
Hürriyet Daily News. 2013. "Turkish Government Determined to Close Private Tutoring Schools." *Hürriyet Daily News*, November 5, 2013. Accessed May 5, 2017. http://www.hurriyetdailynews.com/turkish-government-determined-to-close-private-tutoring-schools-57375.
Hürriyet Daily News. 2016. "Hundreds of Companies Seized in Probe Into Turkey's Failed Coup Attempt." *Hürriyet Daily News*, August 28, 2016. Accessed July 17, 2018. http://www.hurriyetdailynews.com/hundreds-of-companies-seized-in-probe-into-turkeys-failed-coup-attempt--103324.
Idris, Jafaar Sheikh. 1990. "Is Man the Vicegerent of God?" *Journal of Islamic Studies* 1 (1): 99–110.
Irfan, Omar. 1993. "Khidr in the Islamic Tradition." *The Muslim World* 83 (3–4): 279–294.
İnsel, Ahmet. 1997. "Altın Nesil, Yeni Muhafazakarlık ve Fethullah Gülen." *Birikim* 99 (July): 67–76.
Johnson, William A. 2000. "Toward a Sociology of Reading in Classical Antiquity." *The American Journal of Philology* 121 (4): 593–627.
Kahn, Joel S. 2011. "Understanding: Between Belief and Unbelief." *The Australian Journal of Anthropology* 22 (1): 76–88.
Kahn, Joel S. 2016. *Asia, Modernity, and the Pursuit of the Sacred: Gnostics, Scholars, Mystics, and Reformers*. New York: Palgrave Macmillan.
Kandil, Hazem. 2016. *Inside the Brotherhood*. Cambridge: Polity Press.
Kant, Immanuel. 2009. *An Answer to the Question: 'What is Enlightenment'?* London: Penguin.
Kaplan, Samuel. 2006. *The Pedagogical State*. Stanford: Stanford University Press.
Kara, Ismail. 1998 [1990]. *Türkiye'de İslamcılık Düşüncesi*, Vol. I–III. Istanbul: Kitabevi Yayınları.
Karabaşoğlu, Metin. 2003. "Text and Community: An Analysis of the Risale-i Nur Movement." In *Islam at the Crossroads: On the Life and Thought of Bediuzzaman Said Nursi*, edited by Ibrahim M. Abu-Rabi, 263–296. Albany, NY: SUNY Press.
Karamustafa, Ahmet T. 2007. *Sufism: The Formative Period*. Edinburgh: Edinburgh University Press.

Kasaba, Reşat. 1997. "Kemalist Certainties and Modern Ambiguities." In *Rethinking Modernity and National Identity in Turkey*, edited by Sibel Bozdoğan and Reşat Kasaba. Seattle, WA: University of Washington Press.

Koru, Fehmi. 2016. *Ben Böyle Gördüm: Cemaat'in Siyasetle Sınavı*. Istanbul: Alfa Yayınları.

Kosky, Jeffrey L. 2004. "The Birth of the Modern Philosophy of Religion and the Death of Transcendence." In *Transcendence: Philosophy, Literature, and Theology Approach the Beyond*, edited by Regina Schwartz, 13–29. London and New York: Routledge.

Koyuncu-Lorasdağı, Berrin. 2010. "The Prospects and Pitfalls of the Religious Nationalist Movement in Turkey: The Case of the Gülen Movement." *Middle Eastern Studies* 46 (2): 221–234.

Köksal, Asım M. 2013. *Hazreti Muhammed ve İslamiyet*. Istanbul: Işık Yayınları.

Kuhn, Thomas. 1962. *The Structure of Scientific Revolutions*. Chicago: The University of Chicago Press.

Kuşpınar, Bilal. 1996. "Said Nursi's Evaluation of Sufism." In *Proceedings of the International Symposium on Bediuzzaman* Vol. III, 452–462. Istanbul: Nesil Matbaacılık.

Kuşpınar, Bilal. 2010. "Death in Nursi's Thought." In *Theodicy and Justice in Modern Islamic Thought: The Case of Said Nursi*, edited by Ibrahim M. Abu-Rabi, 53–68. Farham and Burlington: Ashgate.

Laidlaw, James. 2002. "For an Anthropology of Ethics and Freedom." *The Journal of the Royal Anthropological Institute* 8 (2): 311–332.

Laidlaw, James. 2014. *The Subject of Virtue: An Anthropology of Ethics and Freedom*. Cambridge: Cambridge University Press.

Lambek, Michael. 1993. *Knowledge and Practice in Mayotte: Local Discourses of Islam, Sorcery and Spirit Possession*. Toronto: University of Toronto Press.

Lambek, Michael. 2000. "The Anthropology of Religion and the Quarrel Between Poetry and Philosophy." *Current Anthropology* 41 (3): 309–320.

Lambek, Michael. 2010. "Toward an Ethics of the Act." In *Ordinary Ethics: Anthropology, Language, and Action*, 39–63. New York: Fordham University Press.

Lapidus, Ira M. 1975. "The Separation of State and Religion in the Development of Early Islamic Society." *International Journal of Middle East Studies* 6 (4): 363–385.

Lapidus, Ira M. 1984. "Knowledge, Virtue, and Action: The Classical Muslim Conception of Adab and the Nature of Religious Fulfillment in Islam." In *Moral Conduct and Authority: The Place of Adab in South Asian Islam*, edited by Barbara D. Metcalf, 39–61. Berkeley: University of California Press.

Lapidus, Ira M. 1996. "State and Religion in Islamic Societies." *Past and Present* 151 (1): 363–85.

Lave, Jean, and Etienne Wenger. 1991. *Situated Learning: Legitimate Peripheral Participation*. Cambridge: Cambridge University Press.

Lemons, J. Derrick. 2018. "Introduction: Theologically Engaged Anthropology." In *Theologically Engaged Anthropology*, edited by J. Derrick Lemons, 1–17. Oxford: Oxford University Press.

REFERENCES

Lerner, Daniel. 1958. *The Passing of Traditional Society: Modernizing the Middle East.* New York: Free Press.

LeVine, Mark, and Armando Salvatore. 2009. "Religious Mobilization and the Public Sphere: Reflections on Alternative Genealogies." In *Publics, Politics and Participation: Locating the Public Sphere in the Middle East and North Africa*, edited by Seteney Shami, 65–90. New York: Social Science Research Council.

Lewis, Bernard. 1968 [1961]. *The Emergence of Modern Turkey*, 2nd Edition. Oxford: Oxford University Press.

Lewis, Geoffrey. 1999. *The Turkish Language Reform: A Catastrophic Success.* Oxford: Oxford University Press.

MacIntyre, Alasdair. 1984 [1981]. *After Virtue.* Notre Dame, IN: University of Notre Dame Press.

MacIntyre, Alasdair. 1988. *Whose Justice? Which Rationality?* London: Duckworth.

MacIntyre, Alasdair. 1991. *Three Rival Versions of Moral Enquiry: Encyclopaedia, Genealogy, and Tradition.* Notre Dame, IN: University of Notre Dame Press.

Mahmood, Saba. 2005. *Politics of Piety: The Islamic Revival and the Feminist Subject.* Princeton: Princeton University Press.

Malik, Jamal. 2018. "The Sociopolitical Entanglements of Sufism." In *The Wiley Blackwell History of Islam*, edited by Armando Salvatore, Roberto Tottoli and Babak Rahimi, 585–606. Oxford: Wiley-Blackwell.

Mamdani, Mahmood. 2002. "Good Muslim, Bad Muslim: A Political Perspective on Culture and Terrorism " *American Anthropologist* 104 (3): 766–775.

Mardin, Şerif. 1969. "Power, Civil Society and Culture in the Ottoman Empire." *Comparative Studies in Society and History* 11 (3): 258–281.

Mardin, Şerif. 1971. "Ideology and Religion in the Turkish Revolution." *International Journal of Middle East Studies* 2 (3): 197–211.

Mardin, Şerif. 1973. "Center-Periphery Relations: A Key to Turkish Politics?" *Daedalus* 102 (1): 169–190.

Mardin, Şerif. 1989. *Religion and Social Change in Modern Turkey: The Case of Bediuzzaman Said Nursi.* Albany, NY: SUNY Press.

Mardin, Şerif. 1991a. "The Just and the Unjust." *Daedalus* 120 (3): 113–129.

Mardin, Şerif. 1991b. "The Nakşibendi Order in Turkish History." In *Islam in Modern Turkey: Religion, Politics and Literature in a Secular State*, edited by Richard Tapper, 121–142. London and New York: I.B. Tauris.

Mardin, Şerif. 1997. "Projects as Methodology: Some Thoughts on Modern Turkish Social Science." In *Rethinking Modernity and National Identity in Turkey*, edited by Sibel Bozdoğan and Reşat Kasaba, 64–80. Seattle, WA: University of Washington Press.

Mardin, Şerif. 2000 [1962]. *The Genesis of Young Ottoman Thought: A Study in the Modernization of Turkish Political Ideas.* Syracuse, NY: Syracuse University Press.

Mardin, Şerif. 2005. "Turkish Islamic Exceptionalism Yesterday and Today: Continuity, Rupture and Reconstruction in Operational Codes." *Turkish Studies* 6 (2): 145–165.

Mardin, Şerif. 2006. "Islam in Nineteenth- and Twentieth-Century Turkey." In *Religion, Society and Modernity in Turkey*, edited by Şerif Mardin, 260–297. Syracuse, NY: Syracuse University Press.

Marranci, Gabriele. 2008. *The Anthropology of Islam*. Oxford: Berg.

Marsden, Magnus. 2005. *Living Islam: Muslim Religious Experience in Pakistan's North-West Frontier*. Cambridge: Cambridge University Press.

Martensson, Ulrika. 2007. "The Power of Subject: Weber, Foucault and Islam." *Critique: Critical Middle Eastern Studies* 16 (2): 97–136.

Marty, Martin E., ed. 2015. *Hizmet Means Service: Perspectives on an Alternative Path Within Islam*. Berkeley: University of California Press.

Mattingly, Cheryl. 2014. "Moral Deliberation and the Agentive Self in Laidlaw's Ethics." *HAU: Journal of Ethnographic Theory* 4 (1): 473–486.

Mauss, Marcel. 1985. "A Category of the Human Mind: The Notion of Person; the Notion of Self." In *The Category of the Person: Anthropology, Philosophy, History*, edited by Michael Carrithers, Steven Collins and Steven Lukes, 1–25. Cambridge: Cambridge University Press.

Meeker, Michael. 1991. "The New Muslim Intellectuals in the Republic of Turkey." In *Islam in Modern Turkey: Religion, Politics and Literature in a Secular State*, edited by Richard Tapper, 189–219. London and New York: I.B. Tauris.

Menin, Laura. 2015. "The Impasse of Modernity: Personal Agency, Divine Destiny, and the Unpredictability of Intimate Relationships in Morocco." *Journal of the Royal Anthropological Institute* 21 (4): 892–910.

Merriam, Charles Edward. 1999 [1900]. *History of the Theory of Sovereignty Since Rousseau*. Clark, NJ: The Lawbook Exchange, Ltd.

Messick, Brinkley. 1993. *The Calligraphic State: Textual Domination and History in a Muslim Society*. Berkeley: University of California Press.

Messick, Brinkley. 1997. "Genealogies of Reading and the Scholarly Cultures of Islam." In *Cultures of Scholarship*, edited by S. C. Humphreys. Ann Arbor: The University of Michigan Press.

Meyer, Brigit. 2008. "Religious Sensations: Why Media, Aesthetics and Power Matter in the Study of Contemporary Religion." In *Religion: Beyond a Concept*, edited by Hent de Vries, 704–723. New York: Fordham University Press.

Milbank, John. 2004. "Sublimity: The Modern Transcendent." In *Transcendence: Philosophy, Literature, and Theology Approach the Beyond*, edited by Regina Schwartz, 211–234. New York and London: Routledge.

Milbank, John. 2006 [1990]. *Theology and Social Theory: Beyond Secular Reason*. Oxford: Wiley-Blackwell.

Mitchell, Timothy. 1988. *Colonizing Egypt*. Berkeley: University of California Press.
Mittermaier, Amira. 2011. *Dreams That Matter: Egyptian Landscapes of the Imagination*. Berkeley: University of California Press.
Mittermaier, Amira. 2012. "Dreams From Elsewhere: Muslim Subjectivities Beyond the Trope of Self-Cultivation." *Journal of the Royal Anthropological Institute* 18 (2): 247–265.
Moosa, Ebrahim. 2005. *Ghazali and the Poetics of Imagination*. Chapel Hill, NC: The University of North Carolina Press.
Nakissa, Aria. 2014. "An Epistemic Shift in Islamic Law: Educational Reform at al-Azhar and Dar al-Ulum." *Islamic Law and Society* 21 (3): 209–251.
Navaro-Yashin, Yael. 2002a. *Faces of the State: Secularism and Public Life in Turkey*. Princeton: Princeton University Press.
Navaro-Yashin, Yael. 2002b. "The Market for Identities: Secularism, Islamism, Commodities." In *Fragments of Culture: The Everyday of Modern Turkey*, edited by Deniz Kandiyoti and Ayşe Saktanber, 221–253. New Brunswick, NJ: Rutgers University Press.
Netton, Richard. 2000. *Sufi Ritual: The Parallel Universe*. Surrey: Curzon Press.
Neyzi, Leyla. 2001. "Object or Subject? The Paradox of 'Youth' in Turkey." *International Journal of Middle East Studies* 33 (3): 411–432.
Noddings, Nel. 1984. *Caring: A Relational Approach to Ethics and Moral Education*. Berkeley: University of California Press.
Noddings, Nel. 2002. *Educating Moral People: A Caring Alternative to Character Education*. New York: Teachers College Press.
Noor, Farish A. 2012. *Islam on the Move: The Tablighi Jama'at in Southeast Asia*. Amsterdam: Amsterdam University Press.
Norden, Eduard. 1923 [1989]. *Die Antike Kunstprosa*, Vol. I, 4th Edition. Leipzig and Berlin: Teubner.
Norton, Jenny, and Cagli Kasapoglu. 2016. "Turkey's Post-Coup Crackdown Hits 'Gulen Schools' Worldwide." *BBC News*, September 23, 2016. Accessed July 17, 2018. https://www.bbc.com/news/world-europe-37422822.
NTV. 2009. "YÖK, Katsayı Uygulamasını Kaldırdı." *NTV.com.tr*, July 20, 2009. Accessed May 5, 2017. http://www.ntv.com.tr/turkiye/yok-katsayi-uygulamasini-kaldirdi,ywcOPJKV7ESa6iJsaP4pcw.
Nursi, Said. 1993a. *The Rays Collection*. Translated by Şükran Vahide. Istanbul: Sözler Publications.
Nursi, Said. 1993b. *The Words*. Translated by Şükran Vahide. Istanbul: Sözler Publications.
Nursi, Said. 1995a. *Asa-yı Musa*. Istanbul: Envar Neşriyat.
Nursi, Said. 1995b. *The Flashes Collection*. Translated by Şükran Vahide. Istanbul: Sözler Publications.

Nursi, Said. 1995c. *İşaratü'l İ'caz*. Istanbul: Envar Neşriyat.
Nursi, Said. 1995d. *Tarihçe-i Hayat*. Istanbul: Envar Neşriyat.
Nursi, Said. 1997. *The Letters*. Translated by Şükran Vahide. Istanbul: Sözler Publications.
Ochs, Elinor, and Merav Shohet. 2006. "The Cultural Structuring of Mealtime Socialization." *New Directions for Child and Adolescent Development* 111: 35–49.
Ortner, Sherry B. 1984. "Theory in Anthropology Since the Sixties." *Comparative Studies in Society and History* 26 (1): 126–166.
Özbek, Nadir. 2005. "Philanthropic Activity, Ottoman Patriotism, and the Hamidian Regime, 1876–1909." *International Journal of Middle East Studies* 1 (37): 59–81.
Özdalga, Elisabeth. 2003. "Secularizing Trends in Fethullah Gülen's Movement: Impasse or Opportunity for Further Renewal?" *Critique: Critical Middle Eastern Studies* 12 (1): 61–73.
Özdalga, Elisabeth. 2006. "The Hidden Arab: A Critical Reading of the Notion of 'Turkish Islam'." *Middle Eastern Studies* 42 (4): 551–570.
Özyürek, Esra. 1997. "'Feeling Tells Better Than Language:' Emotional Expression and Gender Hierarchy in the Sermons of Fethullah Gülen Hocaefendi." *New Perspectives on Turkey* 16 (Spring): 41–51.
Özyürek, Esra. 2006. *Nostalgia for the Modern: State Secularism and Everyday Politics in Turkey*. Durham, NC: Duke University Press.
Pandian, Anand. 2008. "Tradition in Fragments: Inherited Forms and Fractures in the Ethics of South India." *American Ethnologist* 35 (3): 466–480.
Pandya, Sophia, and Nancy Elizabeth Gallagher. 2012. *The Gülen Hizmet Movement and its Transnational Activities: Case Studies of Altruistic Activism in Contemporary Islam*. Boca Raton, FL: BrownWalker Press.
Paradise, Ruth, and Barbara Rogoff. 2009. "Side by Side: Learning by Observing and Pitching In." *Ethos* 37 (1): 102–138.
Paul, Jürgen. 2014. "*Khidma* in the Social History of Pre-Mongol Iran." *Journal of the Economic and Social History of the Orient* 3 (57): 392–422.
Rahman, Fazlur. 1966. "The Status of the Individual in Islam." *Islamic Studies* 5 (4): 319–330.
Rahman, Fazlur. 1979 [1966]. *Islam*. Chicago: The University of Chicago Press.
Rahman, Taha Abdel. 2003. "The Separation of Human Philosophy From the Wisdom of the Qur'an in Said Nursi's Work." In *Islam at the Crossroads: On the Life and Thought of Bediuzzaman Said Nursi*, edited by Ibrahim M. Abu-Rabi, 199–214. Albany, NY: SUNY Press.
Rasanayagam, Johan. 2010. *Islam in Post-Soviet Uzbekistan: The Morality of Experience*. Cambridge: Cambridge University Press.
Renard, John. 1988. "Al-Jihad al-Akbar: Notes on a Theme in Islamic Spirituality." *Muslim World* 78 (3–4): 225–242.

Risale Haber. 2016. "Fethullah Gülen Said Nursi'nin her Şeyini Çaldı." *Risale Haber*, July 29, 2016. Accessed July 17, 2018. https://www.risalehaber.com/fethullah-gulen-said-nursinin-her-seyini-caldi-279025h.htm.

Robbins, Joel. 2006. "Anthropology and Theology: An Awkward Relationship?" *Anthropological Quarterly* 79 (2): 285–294.

Robbins, Joel. 2016. "What is the Matter with Transcendence? On the Place of Religion in the New Anthropology of Ethics." *Journal of the Royal Anthropological Institute* 22 (4): 767–808.

Robinson, Francis. 2004. "Other-Worldly and This-Worldly Islam and the Islamic Revival: A Memorial Lecture for Wilfred Cantwell Smith Delivered at the Royal Asiatic Society on 10 April 2003." *Journal of the Royal Asiatic Society* 14 (1): 47–58.

Saenger, Paul. 1997. *Space Between Words: The Origins of Silent Reading*. Stanford: Stanford University Press.

Saktanber, Ayşe. 1991. "Muslim Identity in Children's Picture-Books." In *Islam in Modern Turkey: Religion, Politics and Literature in a Secular State*, edited by Richard Tapper, 171–188. London and New York: I.B. Tauris.

Saktanber, Ayşe. 2002a. *Living Islam: Women and Islamic Politics in Turkey*. London and New York: I.B. Tauris.

Saktanber, Ayşe. 2002b. "'We Pray Like You Have Fun:' New Islamic Youth in Turkey Between Intellectualism and Popular Culture." In *Fragments of Culture: The Everyday of Modern Turkey*, edited by Deniz Kandiyoti and Ayşe Saktanber, 254–276. New Brunswick, NJ: Rutgers University Press.

Salvatore, Armando. 2001a. "Introduction: The Problem of the Ingraining of Civilizing Traditions Into Social Governance." In *Muslim Traditions and Modern Techniques of Power*, Yearbook of the Sociology of Islam, Vol. III, edited by Armando Salvatore, 9–42. Hamburg: Lit/New Brunswick, NJ and London: Transaction.

Salvatore, Armando. 2001b. "After the State: Islamic Reform and the 'Implosion' of Shari'a." In *Muslim Traditions and Modern Techniques of Power*, Yearbook of the Sociology of Islam, Vol. III, edited by Armando Salvatore, 123–140. Hamburg: Lit/New Brunswick, NJ and London: Transaction.

Salvatore, Armando. 2004. "The 'Implosion' of Shari'a within the Emergence of Public Normativity: The Impact on Personal Responsibility and the Impersonality of Law." In *Standing Trial: Law and the Person in the Modern Middle East*, edited by Baudouin Dupret, 116–139. London: I.B. Tauris.

Salvatore, Armando. 2007. *The Public Sphere: Liberal Modernity, Catholicism, Islam*. New York: Palgrave Macmillan.

Salvatore, Armando. 2011. "Civility: Between Disciplined Interaction and Local/Translocal Connectedness." *Third World Quarterly* 32 (5): 807–825.

Salvatore, Armando. 2016. *The Sociology of Islam: Knowledge, Power and Civility*. Oxford: Wiley-Blackwell.

Salvatore, Armando, and Dale F. Eickelman. 2002. "The Public Sphere and Muslim Identities." *European Journal of Sociology* 43 (1): 92–115.

Salvatore, Armando, and Dale F. Eickelman. 2006. *Public Islam and the Common Good*. Leiden: Brill.

Salvatore, Armando, and Babak Rahimi. 2018. "The Crystallization and Expansiveness of Sufi Networks Within the Urban-Rural-Nomadic Nexus of the Islamic Ecumene." In *The Wiley Blackwell History of Islam*, edited by Armando Salvatore, Roberto Tottoli and Babak Rahimi, 253–271. Oxford: Wiley-Blackwell.

Sarıçam, İbrahim. 2004. *Hz. Muhammed ve Evrensel Mesajı*. Ankara: Diyanet İşleri Başkanlığı Yayınları.

Saul, Stephanie. 2011. "Charter Schools Tied to Turkey Grow in Texas." *The New York Times*, June 6, 2011. Accessed April 15, 2019. https://www.nytimes.com/2011/06/07/education/07charter.html.

Schielke, Samuli. 2007. "Hegemonic Encounters: Criticism of Saints-day Festivals and the Formation of Modern Islam in Late 19th and Early 20th-Century Egypt." *Die Welt des Islams* 47 (3–4): 319–355.

Schielke, Samuli. 2009. "Ambivalent Commitments: Troubles of Morality, Religiosity and Aspiration Among Young Egyptians." *Journal of Religion in Africa* 39 (2): 158–185.

Schielke, Samuli. 2010. "Second Thoughts About the Anthropology of Islam, or How to Make Sense of Grand Schemes in Everyday Life." *ZMO Working Papers*, No. 2: 1–16.

Schielke, Samuli. 2019. "The Power of God: Four Proposals for an Anthropological Engagement." *Leibniz-Zentrum Moderner Orient*, No. 13: 1–20.

Schielke, Samuli, and Liza Debevec. 2012. *Ordinary Lives and Grand Schemes: An Anthropology of Everyday Religion*. New York: Berghahn.

Schimmel, Annemarie. 1994. *Deciphering the Signs of God: A Phenomenological Approach to Islam*. Albany, NY: SUNY Press.

Schimmel, Annemarie. 2011 [1975]. *Mystical Dimensions of Islam*. Chapel Hill, NC: The University of North Carolina Press.

Schwartz, Regina. 2004. "Introduction: Transcendence: Beyond." In *Transcendence: Philosophy, Literature, and Theology Approach the Beyond*, edited by Regina Schwartz, vii–xii. New York and London: Routledge.

Shively, Kim. 2005. "Religious Bodies and the Secular State: The Merve Kavakçı Affair." *Journal of Middle East Women's Studies* 1 (3): 46–72.

Shively, Kim. 2008. "Taming Islam: Studying Religion in Secular Turkey." *Anthropological Quarterly* 81 (3): 683–711.

Silverstein, Brian E. 2007. "Sufism and Modernity in Turkey: From the Authenticity of Experience to the Practice of Discipline." In *Sufism and the "Modern" in Islam*, edited by Martin van Bruinessen and Julia D. Howell, 39–60. London and New York: I.B. Tauris.

Silverstein, Brian E. 2008. "Disciplines of Presence in Modern Turkey: Discourse, Companionship and the Mass Mediation of Islamic Practice." *Cultural Anthropology* 23 (1): 118–153.
Silverstein, Brian E. 2011. *Islam and Modernity in Turkey*. New York: Palgrave Macmillan.
Sirriyeh, Elizabeth. 1999. *Sufis and Anti-Sufis: The Defence, Rethinking and Rejection of Sufism in the Modern World*. London: Curzon Press.
Smith, Wilfred Cantwell. 1977. *Islam in Modern History*. Princeton: Princeton University Press.
Soares, Benjamin, and Filippo Osella. 2010. "Islam, Politics, Anthropology." In *Islam, Politics, Anthropology*, edited by Benjamin Soares and Filippo Osella, 1–22. Malden and Oxford: Wiley-Blackwell and Royal Anthropological Institute.
Spadola, Emilio. 2014. *The Calls of Islam: Sufis, Islamists, and Mass Mediation in Urban Morocco*. Bloomington, IN: Indiana University Press.
Starrett, Gregory. 1995. "The Hexis of Interpretation: Islam and the Body in the Egyptian Popular School." *American Ethnologist* 22 (4): 953–969.
Starrett, Gregory. 1998. *Putting Islam to Work: Education, Politics, and Religious Transformation in Egypt*. Berkeley: University of California Press.
Stroumsa, Guy G. 2015. "The New Self and Reading Practices in Late Antique Christianity." *Church History and Religious Culture* 95 (1): 1–18.
Suffa Vakfı. 2016. "Tarihinde Erzurum'da Yapılan Umumi İstişarenin tam Metnidir." *Suffavakfi.org.tr*, July 30, 2016. Accessed July 4, 2018. http://suffavakfi.org.tr/sayfa/30072016-tarihinde-erzurumda-yapilan-umumi-istisarenin-tam-metnidir.
Sunier, Thijl. 2014. "Cosmopolitan Theology: Fethullah Gülen and the Making of a 'Golden Generation.'" *Ethnic and Racial Studies* 37 (12): 2193–2208.
Sunier, Thijl, and Mehmet Sahin. 2015. "The Weeping Sermon: Persuasion, Binding and Authority Within the Gülen Movement." *Culture and Religion* 16 (2): 228–241.
Sviri, Sara. 2002. "The Self and its Transformation in Sufism: With Special Reference to Early Literature." In *Self and Self-Transformation in the History of Religions*, edited by David Shulman and Guy S. Stroumsa, 195–215. Oxford: Oxford University Press.
Şahiner, Necmeddin. 1979. *Said Nursi ve Nurculuk Hakkında Aydınlar Konuşuyor*. Istanbul: Yeni Asya Yayınları.
T24. 2010. "Erdoğan: Bizim Kitabımızda Ayrımcılık Yok Çine." *T24*, October 10, 2010. Accessed February 27, 2018. http://t24.com.tr/haber/erdogan-bizim-kitabimizda-ayrimcilik-yok-cine-aa,104221.
T24. 2016. "Star Yazarı, 'Cemaat Abilerinin Gülen'e Yazdığı' İddia Edilen Mektubu Yayımladı." *T24*, August 3, 2016. Accessed July 17, 2018. http://t24.com.tr/haber/star-yazari-cemaat-abilerinin-gulene-yazdigi-iddia-edilen-mektubu-yayimladi,353175.
Tanrıkulu, Nurbanu. 2014. "Disturbing Mavi Marmara Remarks Add to Gülen's Deteriorating Reputation." *Daily Sabah*, February 6, 2014. Accessed June 14, 2018. https://

www.dailysabah.com/turkey/2014/02/06/disturbing-mavi-marmara-remarks-add-to-gulens-deteriorating-reputation.

Tapper, Nancy, and Richard Tapper. 1991. "Religion, Education and Continuity in a Provincial Town." In *Islam in Modern Turkey: Religion, Politics and Literature in a Secular State*, edited by Richard Tapper, 56–83. London and New York: I.B. Tauris.

Tapper, Richard, and Nancy Tapper. 1987. "The Birth of the Prophet: Ritual and Gender in Turkish Islam." *Man*, New Series, 22 (1): 69–92.

Tavernise, Sabrina. 2008. "Turkish Schools Offer Pakistan a Gentler Vision of Islam." *New York Times*, May 4, 2008. Accessed April 16, 2019. https://www.nytimes.com/2008/05/04/world/asia/04islam.html.

Taylor, Charles. 1989. *Sources of the Self: The Making of the Modern Identity*. Cambridge, MA: Harvard University Press.

Taylor, Charles. 2004. "A Place for Transcendence?" In *Transcendence: Philosophy, Literature, and Theology Approach the Beyond*, edited by Regina Schwartz, 1–11. New York and London: Routledge.

Tee, Caroline. 2016. *The Gülen Movement in Turkey: The Politics of Islam and Modernity*. London and New York: I.B. Tauris.

Tee, Caroline. 2018. "The Gülen Movement in London and the Politics of Public Engagement: Producing 'Good Islam' Before and After 15 July." *Politics, Religion & Ideology* 19 (1): 109–122.

Tittensor, David. 2014. *The House of Service: The Gülen Movement and Islam's Third Way*. New York: Oxford University Press.

Topbaş, Osman Nuri. 2006. *Hazret-i Muhammed Mustafa: Sallallahu Aleyhi ve Sellem*. Istanbul: Erkam Yayınları.

Topçu, Nurettin. 1997. *Türkiye'nin Maarif Davası*. Istanbul: Dergah Yayınları.

Toprak, Binnaz. 1981. *Islam and Political Development in Turkey*. Leiden: Brill.

Trimingham, J. Spencer. 1971. *The Sufi Orders in Islam*. Oxford: Clarendon Press.

Tuğal, Cihan. 2009. *Passive Revolution: Absorbing the Islamic Challenge to Capitalism*. Stanford: Stanford University Press.

Turam, Berna. 2007. *Between Islam and the State: The Politics of Engagement*. Stanford: Stanford University Press.

Turner, Colin. 2013. *The Qur'an Revealed: Analysis of Said Nursi's Epistles of Light*. Berlin: Gerlach Press.

Uludağ, Süleyman. 1997. "Hadim." In *TDV İslam Ansiklopedisi*, 23–24. Istanbul: İslam Araştırma Merkezi.

Ünal, Ali. 2008. *The Qur'an, With Annotated Interpretation in Modern English*. Somerset, NJ: Tughra Books.

Ünal, Ali, and Alphonse Williams. 2000. *The Advocate of Dialogue: Fethullah Gülen*. Fairfax, VA: The Fountain.

Vahide, Şükran. 2005. *Islam in Modern Turkey: An Intellectual Biography of Bediuzzaman Said Nursi*. Albany, NY: SUNY Press.

Valkenberg, Pim. 2015. *Renewing Islam by Service: A Christian View of Fethullah Gülen and the Hizmet Movement*. Washington, DC: The Catholic University of America Press.

Vicini, Fabio. 2013. "Pedagogies of Affection: The Role of Emulation in Learning Processes—Extracurricular Islamic Education in the Fethullah Gülen Community in Istanbul." *Anthropology & Education Quarterly* 44 (4): 381–398.

Vicini, Fabio. 2014a. "'Do Not Cross Your Legs:' Islamic Sociability Reciprocity and Brotherhood in Turkey." *La Ricerca Folklorica* 69: 93–104.

Vicini, Fabio. 2014b. "The Irrepressible Charm of the State: Dershane Closures and the Domestic War for Power in Turkey." *Jadaliyya*, March 24, 2014. Accessed June 26, 2018. http://www.jadaliyya.com/Details/30437/The-Irrepressible-Charm-of-the-State-Dershane-Closures-and-the-Domestic-War-for-Power-in-Turkey.

Vicini, Fabio. 2015. "Representing Islam: Cinematographic Productions of the Gülen Movement." In *The Gülen Media Empire*, edited by Lea Nocera, 93–101. Rome: Reset.

Vicini, Fabio. 2016. "Post-Islamism or Veering Toward Political Modernity? State, Ideology and Islam in Turkey." *Sociology of Islam* 4 (3): 261–279.

Vicini, Fabio. 2017. "Thinking Through the Heart: Islam, Reflection and the Search for Transcendence." *Culture and Religion* 18 (2): 110–128.

Vicini, Fabio. 2018. "Turkish Islamism, Conservatism and Human Rights Before and After Gezi: The Case of *Mazlumder*." *British Journal of Middle Eastern Studies* 45 (5): 760–775.

Villelabeitia, Ibon. 2009. "Ex-Turkish Army Chief Says 'E-coup' Justified." *Reuters*, May 8, 2009. Accessed June 14, 2018. https://www.reuters.com/article/us-turkey-military-general/ex-turkish-army-chief-says-e-coup-justified-idUSTRE5471UQ20090508.

Waley, Muhammad Isa. 1999 [1993]. "Contemplative Disciplines in Early Persian Sufism." In *The Heritage of Sufism*, Vol. I, edited by Leonard Lewisohn, 497–548. Oxford: Oneworld Publications.

Walton, Jeremy F. 2017. *Muslim Civil Society and the Politics of Religious Freedom in Turkey*. New York: Oxford University Press.

Weber, Max. 1978. *Economy and Society*. Berkeley: University of California Press.

Weber, Max. 2005 [1930]. *The Protestant Ethic and the Spirit of Capitalism*. Oxon and New York: Routledge.

Weismann, Itzchak. 2007. *The Naqshbandiyya: Orthodoxy and Activism in a Worldwide Sufi Tradition*. Oxon and New York: Routledge.

Weismann, Itzchak. 2011. "Modernity From Within: Islamic Fundamentalism and Sufism." *Der Islam* 86 (1): 142–170.

Werbner, Pnina. 2017. "The Abstraction of Love: Personal Emotion and Mystical Spirituality in the Life Narrative of a Sufi Devotee." *Culture and Religion* 18 (2): 165–180.

White, Jenny B. 2002. *Islamist Mobilization in Turkey: A Study in Vernacular Politics*. Seattle, WA: University of Washington Press.

White, Jenny B. 2012. *Muslim Nationalism and the New Turks*. Princeton: Princeton University Press.

Williams, Bernard. 2011 [1985]. *Ethics and the Limits of Philosophy*. Oxon: Routledge.

Wittgenstein, Ludwig. 1986 [1958]. *Philosophical Investigations*. Translated by G. E. M. Anscombe. Oxford: Basil Blackwell.

Woodall, Martha, and Claudio Gatti. 2011. "U.S. Charter-School Network With Turkish Link Draws Federal Attention." *The Inquirer*, March 20, 2011. Accessed April 16, 2019. https://www.philly.com/philly/news/homepage/20110320_U_S__charter-school_network_with_Turkish_link_draws_federal_attention.html.

Yavuz, M. Hakan. 2003a. *Islamic Political Identity in Turkey*. New York: Oxford University Press.

Yavuz, M. Hakan. 2003b. "Islam in the Public Sphere: The Case of the Nur Movement." In *Turkish Islam and the Secular State: The Gülen Movement*, edited by M. Hakan Yavuz and John L. Esposito, 1–18. Syracuse, NY: Syracuse University Press.

Yavuz, M. Hakan. 2003c. "The Gülen Movement: The Turkish Puritans." In *Turkish Islam and the Secular State: The Gülen Movement*, edited by M. Hakan Yavuz and John L. Esposito, 19–47. Syracuse, NY: Syracuse University Press.

Yavuz, M. Hakan. 2013. *Toward an Islamic Enlightenment: The Gülen Movement*. New York: Oxford University Press.

Yavuz, M. Hakan, and Bayram Balci, eds. 2018. *Turkey's July 15th Coup: What Happened and Why*. Salt Lake City: Utah University Press.

Yeğin, Abdullah. 2005. *Yeni Lugat: Islami, İlmi, Edebi, Felsefi*. Istanbul: Hizmet Vakfı Yayınları.

Yeni Şafak. 2018. "İki Yılda Büyük Temizlik." *Yeni Şafak*, July 9, 2018. Accessed July 10, 2018. https://www.yenisafak.com/gundem/iki-yilda-buyuk-temizlik-3382884.

Yilmaz, Hale. 2016. *Becoming Turkish: Nationalist Reforms and Cultural Negotiations in Early Republican Turkey 1923–1945*. Syracuse, NY: Syracuse University Press.

Yinanç, Barçın. 2017. "Ample Evidence to Prove That Gülenists Were Behind Turkey's Coup Attempt: Journalist Sedat Ergin." *Hurriyet Daily News*, August 28, 2017. Accessed April 16, 2019. http://www.hurriyetdailynews.com/ample-evidence-to-prove-that-gulenists-were-behind-turkeys-coup-attempt-journalist-sedat-ergin-117241.

Zachs, Fruma. 2014. "Growing Consciousness of the Child in Ottoman Syria in the 19th Century: Modes of Parenting and Education in the Middle Class." In *The Ottoman Middle East: Studies in Honor of Amnon Cohen*, edited by Eyal Ginio and Elie Podeh, 113–128. Leiden: Brill.

Zaman, Muhammad Qasim. 2002. *The Ulama in Contemporary Islam: Custodians of Change*. Princeton: Princeton University Press.

Zamboni, Lodovico. 2005. *La Sura della Famiglia di Imran Nella Sapienza Islamica*. Reggio Emilia: Edizioni Orientamento Al Qibla.

Zengin Arslan, Berna. 2009. *Pious Science: The Gülen Community and The Making of a Conservative Modernity in Turkey*, PhD thesis, University of California Santa Cruz, Santa Cruz.

Zigon, Jarrett. 2009. "Morality and Personal Experience: The Moral Conceptions of a Muscovite Man." *Ethos* 37 (1): 78–101.

Zizek, Slavoj. 2004. "The Descent of Transcendence Into Immanence or, Deleuze as a Hegelian." In *Transcendence: Philosophy, Literature, and Theology Approach the Beyond*, edited by Regina Schwartz, 235–248. New York and London: Routledge.

Zürcher, Erik J. A. 1993. *Turkey: A Modern History*. London and New York: I.B. Tauris.

Index

1980 military coup   56, 60, 139

Abduh, Muhammad   185
Abdüllahmid II, Sultan   134–136
Abrahamic traditions   177
accountability   180
　personal   182, 185
adab (norms of virtuous behavior)   76
Agamben, Giorgio   78
agency   12–14
　and person   178
　and social structure   201
　human   9, 194
　modern liberal view of   169, 176
　moral   180–183
　non-human   5
　secular liberal view of   14, 179–180
AKP   17, 19, 27–30, 36, 42–46, 59, 62, 135, 141–142, 205
al-Afghani, Jamal al-Din   116
al-alam al-mithal (world of images) (*see also* cosmology *under* Ibn Arabi)   121
al-Ansari, Khwajah Abdullah   89
al-Banna, Hasan   185
al-Ghazali, Abu Hamid   89, 111, 115, 123
Ali ibn Abi Talib   185
al-Jilani, Abd al-Qadir   47
al-Qadarawi, Shaykh Yusuf   41
al-Shahrazuri, Mawlana Khalid   47
Ambrose, St.   98
Anderson, Benedict   8, 98, 135
angel(s)   46, 121, 124, 184–185
Aquinas, Thomas   91–92, 180
Aristotle/Aristotelian   12–14, 81, 90–91, 152, 177, 180
Arnason, Johann P.   176
Asad, Talal   11, 13–16, 69, 78, 180–183, 200
　form of life in   78
　(secular) moral self   179
Augustine of Hippo, St.   98, 114
authority/authoritative   95, 163
　discourse (*see also* religious *under* discourse(s))   14, 67, 201
　discursive   110
　ecclesiastic   98

Enlightenment   175
　fragmentation of traditional   54
　higher goods   190
　in modern education   149
　in reading   97–98
　in the Ottoman Empire   50
　judicial   52
　knowledge   81
　legislative   52
　modern political   50, 97
　new media   99
　non-human   131
　of Said Nursi   47
　pedagogies of the Gülen community   132, 160
　prescriptions   16
　religious   99, 198
　text   7
　tradition   9, 13
　within brotherhood   26, 73, 77, 80–83
awareness
　Enlightenment   113
　lack of Islamic   68
　Muslim   105, 109
　of cosmic order   123
　of death   128
　of God   17
　of the transitory nature of this world   131, 204
　of world's problems   45
　religious   10, 38, 108, 119
　sense of the wondrous   114
　spiritual   3, 71, 109
　spiritual growth   70
　tefekkür   128
axial/Axial
　Age theory   181
　breakthrough   87, 189
　salvation religions   87, 189, 192
　traditions   176–177, 181

Baghdad   47, 118
Balkans   44, 61
Bellah, Robert N.   189, 192
Bergson, Henri   42, 139

Blondel, Maurice   139
Bourdieu, Pierre   13–14, 201
brotherhood (*uhuvvet, kardeşlik*)
   and secular ethics   193
   as civility pattern   79, 189
   as corporate personality (*şahsı*
      manevi)   86–88
   as ethics   189–193
Bulaç, Ali   42, 60

Caliph/Caliphate   51, 185
caritas (virtue of charity)   91–92
cemaat (religious community)   17–18, 58
   self-enclosure   87
   urbanization   58–59
Central Asia   44, 61
charisma
   as knowledge   82
   of Islamic tradition   35
   of Said Nursi   106
Chittick, William   120
Christianity   5, 24, 34, 78–79, 89, 124, 131,
      176–178
citizen(s)/citizenship   102, 149
   good Muslim   140
   national education of   54, 133
   of the Ottoman nation   134, 186
   of the Republic   55
civic engagement   20–22, 26, 32, 36,
      131, 169–170, 190, 194–195, 198,
      203, 205
   and world-renouncing philosophy   204
civility (*see also* as civility pattern *under*
      brotherhood)   88, 96, 205
   Islamic/Muslim   20–22, 36, 76, 79,
      169–170, 172, 204, 206
civilization(s)
   human   176
   Islamic   21, 50, 66, 103, 139, 173, 185
   modern   10, 179
   Turkish   139
   Western technical   54
   world   46, 177
civilizing
   mission   31, 40, 186
civil society   20–21, 61
class(es)   37, 103, 142, 192
   conservative bourgeois   19, 141
   literati   76

   middle-high   45, 142
   of religious scholars   98
   secular elite   17, 141
   ulema (scholars of Islam)   33, 51, 55, 135
code(s)
   civil   51
   ethical   79
   European-like   52, 54
   of comportment   58
   of conduct   65
colonial/colonialism   52, 79
common good   53, 103, 181, 204
connectedness   92
   and love   84
   in brotherhood   64, 89, 95
constitution/constitutional
   in the Ottoman Empire   136, 174
   of *hizmet*   84
   referendum   27
   reform   56
contract/contractual
   social   51, 86, 90, 103
   solidarity   86
Corbin, Henri   121
culture(s)   12, 19, 24, 35, 37, 50–51, 57, 72, 76,
      102, 124, 138, 171

Darwin, Charles   163
death   68, 118, 123, 166
   as transitory character of worldly life   120
   contemplation of   125–129
Deeb, Lara   9, 15
Deleuze, Gilles   90
Demirci, Osman   36
Democratic Party (*Demokrat Parti*)   57
dershane
   as Nur house   63
   as preparatory schools run by the Gülen
      community   44, 142
devotion   33–34, 56, 93–94, 156
dhikr (remembrance or invocation of
      God)   115–116, 126
discipline/disciplinary   64, 70, 77, 93, 137,
      146, 150, 152–154, 160, 165, 201–202
   practice   5, 13, 69, 78
discourse(s) (*see also* discourse *under*
      politics/political)
   areligious   38
   epistemological   129–130

discourse(s) (cont.)
　ethical　14
　humanitarian　49
　human rights　20
　Islamic　12, 62, 196
　modernist　9
　nationalist　46, 116, 138, 140
　on education　133
　prophetic　103
　public　135
　reformist　184–185
　religious　15, 201
　Republican　32, 148
　scientific　33, 112–113, 130
　speculative　103
disposition(s) (*see also* disposition *under* ethic(s)/ethical)　12–13, 78, 91, 98, 113, 124, 128, 134, 150, 152, 156, 159–160, 181–183, 199–200
Diyanet İşleri Başkanlığı (Directorate of Religious Affairs)　35, 58, 60
Durkheim, Emile　54, 69

economic liberalization (1980s)　43, 48, 60, 141
education　18, 35–37, 50–52, 60, 204
　among peers　26, 80, 143–144, 166–177
　and preaching　150
　as a contested object　133–135
　changes in　9
　educational facilities　132
　educational mission　18, 25, 48, 132
　exemplariness in　81
　Islamic　13, 26, 152
　Islamic ethic of (*see also* pedagogical philosophy *under* Gülen, Fethullah)　143
　late-Ottoman debates on　148
　mass　132
　mass higher　54
　modern　99
　national　54, 140
　of the children　148–149
　of the citizen　204
　of the *imams*　55
　public　141
　reform in Ottoman times　134–136
　sector　18, 30, 142, 205
　secularization of　55

ego-alter relationship　176, 181, 190
Eisenstadt, Shmuel N.　176
embodiment　13, 63, 78, 81–82, 87–89, 124, 151, 160, 181, 188, 201
emotion(s)/emotional　69, 78, 104, 124, 128, 155–156, 179–180, 189, 200–201
Enlightenment　3–4, 113, 148, 175
　Scottish　90, 179–180
Erbakan, Necmettin　59, 61
Erdoğan, Mustafa　42
Erdoğan, Recep Tayyip　30, 46, 59
Ergenekon trial　23, 27, 196
Ersoy, Mehmet Akif　41, 140
ethic(s)/ethical　35, 76, 103, 124, 131, 149, 174–176, 180, 199, 202
　Aristotelian　12–13, 91
　as different from morality　181
　conduct　3, 15, 70, 92
　deliberation　13, 90, 175
　disposition　70, 92, 179, 182, 200
　everyday life　5
　formation　13, 16, 87, 202
　Islamic (*see also* ethical tradition *under* Islam/Islamic)　18, 137, 143
　Kant　175
　life　5, 91, 131
　narrative　14–16
　of brotherliness　189, 203
　orientation　124
　reasoning　6
　system　60
　turn in anthropology　12–15
ethos　5, 20, 54, 133, 139–140, 167, 184

Fatih Mehmet, Sultan　42, 156
Fichte, Johann Gottlieb　4, 178
fiqh (*see* jurisprudence *under* Islam/Islamic)
Fırıncı, Mehmet　30
Fortna, Benjamin　134
Foucault, Michel　5, 9, 90
　governmentality　186
freedom　136, 169
　Islamic　173–175
　Kant on　175

Gilsenan, Michael　83
gıybet (sin of gossiping and talking behind one's back)　88
Gökalp, Ziya　54, 139

grace 85, 91–92
Gramsci, Antonio 19, 103
Gülen community
  access to 23
  activism/activist(s) in (*see also aksiyon insanı under* Gülen, Fethullah *and* civic engagement) 40, 44, 48, 139, 170, 193, 203
  and outside society 67–69
  businessmen/business associations 39, 43
  character formation in 150–152
  clash with the AKP 27–28, 44, 142, 205
  class composition 45
  coup attempt of July 15 28, 170
  distinctive elements 167
  dormitories 151–153
  editorial activities 41
  educational network 44
  eschatological project 186
  exemplary conduct 152, 157–159
  hizmet (religiously inspired service) 48
  ideologization within 196–197
  initial expansion 60
  inner-worldly asceticism 170
  investments in education (*see also dershane*) 44, 142
  media productions of 42
  meetings of (*sohbet*) 67, 153, 156, 191
  narratives of 42, 137
  narrative strategies 156–157
  national project 133
  neoliberalism 19
  party politics 59
  pedagogical methods 145–148, 155
  preaching mission 154
  reading 2
  recruitment 142
  reform project 18, 132
  responsibilization 162–167
  science 75, 136
  selection criteria for students 145
  self-enclosure of 87, 196–197
  Sızıntı (magazine) 41, 75, 112, 149–150, 159
  summer camps 137
  sunna in 75
  tension with secular order 193–195
  terrorist organization 28
  tutoring of young students 142–146, 151–154
  undermining secularists' grasp on power 27
  upward mobility 35, 144–145
  Zaman (newspaper) 42
Gülen, Fethullah 41
  "Age of Felicity" (*Saadet Asrı*) 138
  aksiyon insanı (people of action) (*see also* philosophy of action *under* Gülen, Fethullah) 48, 137
  as a motivator 40, 132
  critique of Kemalist modernization 149
  critique of the AKP 28
  during Özal's years 61
  European thinkers 42
  first experiences as educator 136–137
  golden generation (*altın nesil*) 40, 137–140
  image after July 15 29
  inter-faith dialogue 44
  Islam as ethos (*see also* ethos) 140
  migration to the US 61
  national project 140
  Nursi's teachings 36, 136
  on how to achieve social reform 19, 23
  on *ışık evleri* (houses of the Gülen community) (*see also ışık evleri*) 154
  on *jihad* 150
  on Ottoman past 156
  on responsibility. *See* of preaching Islam *under* responsibility
  pedagogical philosophy 149–151, 158–159
  philosophy of action 45, 48, 139
  preaching style 138, 155–157
  soft coup of 1997 61
  Sufism 138
  Turkish-Islamic synthesis 138–139

Habermas, Jürgen 8
habitus 13–14, 201
hadith (saying or deed of Muhammad) 19, 34, 88, 111, 117, 126, 138, 148, 156, 192
Hadot, Pierre 3, 124
hakiki/hakikat (true/Truth) 85, 121, 125–126
  faith 108
  Muslims 39, 187
  of death 127

Hart, Kimberly   72
Hegel, Georg Wilhelm Friedrich   4, 89
hegemony/hegemonic   19–20, 52, 103
hierarchy
   intra-community   83
   of goods   53, 163, 176, 180–183, 188
Hirschkind, Charles   124, 128, 200
hizmet (religiously inspired service)   40, 186
   genealogy of   46–48
   hizmet evleri (*see ışık evleri*)
   narratives of   171–172
   sacrifice/dedication   138
   social reform   169
   youth   165–167
Hobbes, Thomas   51, 90
Hodgson, Marshall   101, 103
Hume, David   179, 181

Ibn Arabi   41, 70, 116, 122–124, 126, 130
   cosmology   117, 120–121
   imagination (*khayal*)   118, 121
   on *tefekkür*   116
   spiritual growth   185
   wahdat al-wujud   121
Ibn Khaldun   148
Ibn Sina (Avicenna)   103
Ibn Taymiyyah   33, 121
ihlas/ikhlas (virtue of purity and sincerity)   64, 84–95, 125, 128, 152, 157, 188, 191
Ilyas, Muhammad   185
imagination (*see also* imagination *under* Ibn Arabi)   105
   poetic (*see* Vico, Giambattista)
   technique of (*tahayyül*)   125–126
   teleological   5
imam hatip lisesi (religious vocational schools)   58, 141
intellect/intellectual   12, 29, 33, 39, 60, 70, 76, 78, 100, 103, 109–110, 115, 117–118, 122, 129–131, 134, 172, 175, 179, 184, 189, 190, 196
   deliberation   13
   discernment   2, 8, 199–201
   engagement   6–7, 32, 100
   practice   3, 22, 105, 198, 202

   repertoire(s) (*see also* as intellectual repertoire(s) *under* tradition)   56
   speculation   10, 53, 118, 204, 126, 130
   virtue(s)   13, 152
intellectual(s)   43
   elites   50
   modernist   116
   Muslim   41–42, 60, 139–140, 148–149, 174, 184
   nationalist   41–42, 54
   public   53, 56
Iqbal, Muhammad   185
Islam/Islamic
   civilizing mission (*see also* mission *under* civilizing)   186
   ethical tradition   50–56
   jurisprudence (*fiqh*)   7, 52–53, 156
   knowledge   7, 97–99
   revival (1980s)   17–19, 46, 59–60, 65
   theodicy   107
   tradition (*see also* tradition(s))   7–12, 16, 21, 32, 39, 53, 78–79, 92, 99, 100, 109, 120, 129–130, 148, 168–170, 176–177, 184, 198–199, 203
ışık evleri (houses of the Gülen community). (*see* Nur houses *and* on *ışık evleri under* Gülen, Fethullah)

jihad (struggle)   188
   greater and lesser (*see on jihad under* Gülen, Fethullah)
Job, Prophet (*Eyüp*)   157–158
Joseph, Prophet   127
Judaism   124, 177
justice   5, 181
   administration of   51–52
   distributive   52
   God's   114
   Islamic   156, 173
   social   58
Justice and Development Party (*Adalet Kalkınma Partisi*) (see AKP)
Justice Party (*Adalet Partisi*)   57–59

Kahn, Joel S.   4–5, 203
Kant, Immanuel   4, 42, 175, 179, 194
Kantian   14, 175, 181

INDEX

Karabaşoglu, Metin   196
Karaman, Hayreddin   60
Kemalism
    as modernization project   135
    elites   55–56
    ideals   57
    reforms   54, 57
Kemal, Mustafa (Atatürk)   54, 56, 62, 102, 135, 205
Kemal, Namık   54, 86
Khalidi (Sufi order)   46–47, 49, 74
khalifa (vicegerent of God on earth)   185
Khan, Sayyid Ahmad   185
Khidr (the "Verdant")   127
Khorasan   89
Kırkıncı, Mehmet   36, 136
Kısakürek, Necip Fazıl   42, 139
knowledge
    and theology   3
    heart as the locus of (*see also* imagination *under* Ibn Arabi)   116, 118
    Islamic (*see* knowledge *under* Islam/Islamic)
    knowledge-power   21, 50, 80, 83, 95
    orally-transmitted   110
    religious   18, 99, 116, 133
Kosky, Jeffrey L.   4

Laidlaw, James   13–15, 91
Lapidus, Ira   129
Late Antiquity   89, 114
law(s)   58, 180
    impersonal   53
    Islamic   51–53, 156
    moral   181
    personal   51
    Roman   178
    secular   52
liberty/ies (*see also* freedom)   166, 173–177
    of conscience   178
Locke, John   179
love   5, 137
    brotherly   77, 153, 192–193
    connectedness   84
    disposition   92
    for the *shaykh*   47, 83
    in pedagogy   146–147, 150–151

self-love   180
sincere   84
world-denying   189, 192
Lutero, Martin   4

MacIntyre, Alasdair   10, 12–13, 15, 64, 90–91, 124, 176
    on apprenticeship   81–82
    on moral sense   180–183
Mahmood, Saba   14, 69, 71, 200–201
Malamati order   89
Mardin, Şerif   52, 54, 57
    Nur movement   102–103
Marx, Karl   89
Massignon, Louis   139
master   7
    annihilation in (*fena fi-ş şeyh*)   191
    authority   47–48, 149
    dedication to   47
    presence   97, 110
    relationship with the pupil   48
    Sufi   47, 64
Mattingly, Cheryl   15
Mauss, Marcel   178–179
Mawdudi, Abdul A'la   185
media
    debate   60
    modern   41, 54, 99, 130
    on Islam   124
meditative reflection (*see tefekkür*)
medrese/madrasa (traditional Muslim college)   7, 51–54, 101, 136, 150
Menderes, Adnan   42
Messick, Brinkley   53, 110
Meyer, Birgit   5, 202
Middle Ages   180
Middle East   22, 130, 184, 206
Milbank, John   4, 82, 89–92, 188, 203
Mittermaier, Amira   5–6, 200, 202
modernization   7, 18, 22, 50, 109, 130, 134–135, 140, 149, 192, 194, 196, 205
    alternative   18
    and "disenchantment"   113
    European-style   56
    theory   17
modern/modernity
    European   179

modern/modernity (cont.)
  forms of communication 99
  schooling 7, 55, 99
monastic
  rule 78
morality/moral(s) 14, 33, 39, 52, 93, 95, 114,
    124, 133, 139–140, 152–153, 174, 178, 182
  advancement 204
  agency 180–183
  and collective body 86
  and social cohesion 54
  commitment 59
  conduct 77, 162
  deliberation (*see also* deliberation *under*
    ethic(s)/ethical) 12–15
  ethos (*see* ethos)
  Islamic 40, 60, 135, 139, 153
  law 175–176, 181
  person 178
  philosophy 12
  reasoning 22, 179–181
  reform 12, 150
  responsibility 182
  self (*see* (secular) moral self *under* Asad,
    Talal)
  sense 180–181, 189
Motahhari, Ayatollah Morteza 186
Motherland Party (*Anavatan
  Partisi-ANAP*) 59
movement(s)
  Islamic 1, 9, 22, 194, 199
  reformist 74, 184–186
  religious 17, 31, 196
müceddit (renewer of Islam) 33, 105
Muhammad, Prophet 7, 42, 47, 64, 74–77,
    88, 103, 111, 115, 127, 138, 152, 154–155, 158,
    164–165, 185, 192
  biographical accounts (*siyer*) of 156
  companions 121, 138
  prophecy 89
Muslim Brotherhood 133, 184

namaz (daily prayer) (*see* prayer)
Naqshbandi (Sufi order) 30, 47, 49, 59, 65,
    74, 89, 103–104, 116, 121, 125–126
nation 9, 35, 54, 60, 135, 137–138, 140, 156, 194
  nation-state 35, 52, 55, 133, 168, 172
nationalism 8, 36, 205
Nationalist Movement Party (*Milliyetçi
  Hareket Partisi*, MHP) 30

nefs (lower self) 69–70, 87, 89, 95, 125, 189
  and *ruh* 70
  disciplining the 69
Neoplatonism 122
network(s) 23, 45, 60–61, 80, 87, 137,
    196, 204
  Islamic 17, 35, 57–59
  Nur 23, 35–36, 43
  political and economic 43
  school 167
  Sufi 59, 79
Nietzsche, Friedrich 90
niyet (intention) 68, 107
Nur houses
  authority in (*see* within brotherhood
    under authority/authoritative)
  leader of (*imam abi*) 80–81
  spaces 64–66
  visits (*ziyaret*) in 77
Nur movement 1, 33–34, 37
  as textual community 99
  branches of 36
  civic engagement (*see also* social reform
    under hizmet) 169
  critique of Gülen 30
  Islamic Reformism 8
  mission of 33, 102
  modernity 7
  pedagogy 83
  politics 59
  reading 72, 100
  role of the master 110
  Sufism 122
  sunna in 74–75
Nursi, Said 1, 88, 164
  and al-Ghazali 123
  and Ibn Arabi 121–123
  as a renewer of Islam (*müceddit*) 33
  biographic movie of 43
  concern for ordinary believers 97, 103
  critique of modernity 10
  critique of Sufism 116
  discontent with the state of Islam 33
  inspiration 106
  intellectual genealogy 116
  Islamic tradition 9–10
  late Ottoman Empire 34
  life 7, 56, 104, 166
  materialism 122
  "old" and "new" 56

on brotherhood (*see* as civility pattern *and* as corporate personality *and* as ethics *under* brotherhood)
on death 125
on education and science 18, 136
on ethics (*see* as ethics *under* brotherhood)
on freedom 173
on *hizmet* 47
on *tefekkür* 116–117
project for an Islamic university (*Medresetü'z-Zehra*) 136
reform in the Ottoman Empire 136
secularism 85
secularization 18
"social theology" 50, 55
students 30, 36, 117
Sufism 88, 101, 103
upbringing 103
wahdat al-wujud 121

Ortner, Sherry B. 201
Ottoman
citizens 135
court(s) 156
culture 52
education 148
elites 51, 134
Empire 9, 30, 33–35, 44, 50, 52–53, 55, 97
reform in (*see Tanzimat*)
epoch/times 17, 37, 57, 101, 135
history 42, 47
intellectuals 148, 174
language 8, 102, 114
poetry (*Divan*) 51
political system 50, 55
reformer(s) 1, 51, 134
sociopolotical model 60
state 50, 54
Özal, Turgut 43, 59–61
Özdenören, Rasim 60
Özel, İsmet 60

passion(s) 179–182
peasant(s)
Anatolian 51, 57
Persian/ate
court culture 76
Sufism 111, 115
Pestalozzi, Johann Heinrich 148

philosophers (Muslim) 105, 116
piety/pietistic 47, 89, 94, 156, 162, 185, 200
poetry (*see* Vico, Gianbattista)
politics/political 8, 17, 27, 29, 35, 43, 46, 51, 129, 131, 134, 169–170, 174, 179, 192–193, 195–196, 200, 203–205
action 21
argumentation 54
authority 50, 54, 97
contingency 169, 195
elites 20, 50
lobbying 44
micro 200
modern/modernity 22, 168, 186, 193
of brotherhood 203
party 17, 59
philosopher(s) 90
project 27, 133
rallies 46
scientist 200
success 19, 62
thought 54, 79
postmodern/ists 90
approaches 8
power 11, 15, 18–19, 21, 27, 29, 31, 36, 53, 82, 90, 170, 186, 195–196, 204–205
authority (*see* authority/authoritative)
discursive 9, 16
God's 16, 112, 114, 122–123
institutional 57
knowledge (*see also* knowledge-power *under* knowledge) 10
secular/modern 86, 179, 202
soft 43
state 30, 33
techniques/forms of 50, 97, 199
practice
Muslim life as 200–201
prayer (*namaz*) 1, 38–39, 64, 66, 69–73, 85, 93–94, 97, 143, 147, 152–155, 159, 162, 187, 192
and transcendence 71
beyond discipline 71
time 72–73
prophet(s)/prophetic (*see also* prophetic *under* discourse(s)) 32, 46, 66, 106, 155, 159
Protestant/Protestantism 4, 98, 178
prudentia 181
public 21, 41, 65, 103, 155

public (cont.)
    activity   43
    culture   99
    debate   50, 52–53
    discourse   44, 60, 199
    display of virtue   91–94
    employment   204
    expression   69
    institution(s)   30, 195
    intellectual(s)   53, 56
    interest   182
    issue(s)   42, 61
    life   186
    literate   8
    manifestation   17
    Muslim   60, 102, 112, 150, 156
    officer   170
    piety   89
    pious   36
    reading   97–98
    reasoning   179
    school   25
    space   35, 46, 56, 59, 63, 65, 205
    sphere   9, 19, 176
        transformation of   53–55
puritan/puritanism   8, 59, 194

Qadiri order   47
Qur'an/Qur'anic   2, 7, 8, 11, 46, 47, 48, 57, 66, 67, 68, 70, 73, 74, 75, 85, 88, 98, 101, 102–103, 104–107, 111, 115, 116–117, 119, 121, 123, 127, 136, 148–149, 154, 157, 158, 159, 161, 176, 184–185, 187
Qutb, Said   185

Rahman, Fazlur   184
rationalization   170
reading
    anthropology of   100, 109
    as key Nur practice   97
    common understanding of   105
    social history of   97–99
reciprocity   31
reform(s)/reformer(s)/reformist   1–2, 14, 19, 31, 34, 35, 39, 53, 56–57, 79, 103, 116, 129, 132–133, 136, 141, 149, 194
    Islamic   8, 34, 38, 74, 136, 150, 185–186, 204
    moral   12
    Nur movement   186–188
    Ottoman (*see also Tanzimat*)   51

protestant   98
scholar(s)   34, 38, 116
secular   50, 53–54
social   59, 140, 169, 171–172, 193, 198
religious
    knowledge (*see* tradition(s))
Republican People's Party (*Cumhuriyet Halk Partisi*, CHP)   56
responsibility (*see also* responsibilization *under* Gülen community)
    for religious mission   183, 188
    in Islam   184
    internalization of   186–188
    of preaching Islam (*tebliğ, irşad*)   188
    this-worldly engagement and   185
Rida, Rashid   116, 185
Risale-i Nur   7
    allegorical stories   104
    cultural specificity (*see* anthropology of *under* reading)
    cyclical reading of   105–109
    epistolary nature of   104
    semantic depth   105–107
    style   101–105
Robinson, Francis   185
Romans   50
Rousseau, Jean-Jacques   42, 148
Rumi, Mevlana Jalaluddin   104, 164

saint(s)   4, 33, 46, 57, 106, 108, 158
Salvatore, Armando   14, 21, 53, 79–80, 103, 176, 181–183, 203
Sassanids   50
Schielke, Samuli   16
secular/secularism (*see also* secular *under* agency *and* class(es) *and* law(s) *and* power *and* reform(s)/reformer(s)/reformist *and* self *and* sociability)   54–55, 62, 70, 78, 113, 124
    immanent approaches   5, 21
    logic   202
    modernity   22
    of social sciences   5
    ontology   90
    radical   44
    reason   21, 92, 96, 169, 188, 203
    schools   41, 83, 101–102
    Turkish (*laiklik*)   55
    view of religion   176
    worldview   185

INDEX 239

secular/secularism. *See also* secular *under* agency *and* class(es) *and* law(s) *and* power *and* reform(s)/reformer(s)/reformist *and* self *and* sociability
secularization 18, 21, 55, 135, 170, 192, 196, 205
self
   individual autonomous 6, 179
   secular formulations 179–183
   Western genealogy of 177–180
şeyhülislam (highest *ulema* office in the Ottoman Empire) 50
shari'a (Islamic normativity) 11, 51, 54, 79, 136, 176
Shariati, Ali 186
Shaykh Ahmad-i Jam 116
Sirhindi, Ahmad 41, 103–104, 121
sociability 24, 26, 76
   Muslim 31, 64, 95
   secular 65
social
   change 22, 102
   disunity 41
   divisions 193
   status 49
solidarity (*see also* solidarity *under* contract/contractual) 17, 20, 26, 32, 36, 52, 54, 57–58, 62, 76, 79, 86–87, 175, 182–183, 190, 192–193, 196, 202, 206
   modern 79
soul (*ruh*) (*see also nefs* (lower self)) 117
sovereignty 51, 86
   God's 194
Spinoza, Baruch 103
spiritual (*see also* spiritual *under* awareness) 33, 149–150, 161, 198
   atmosphere (*maneviyat*) 64, 66, 69, 72, 137
   guidance 154
   leader(s) 50, 61
   life 117
   maturation/advancement (*see also* spiritual growth *under* awareness) 47, 70–71, 94, 106–107, 118, 129, 154
   perfection (*al-insan al-kamil*) 70
   realm (*alam-i batin*) 116
Starrett, Gregory 132
subject(s)/subjectivity (*See also* agency) 5, 15, 53, 64, 177, 179, 190

autonomous 179
inter-subjective/inter-individual 31, 63–64, 75–77, 79–82, 87, 175, 181
passive 186
virtuous 202
Suffa community/foundation 1, 34, 36–39
   access to 24
   civic engagement in 171–173
   coup attempt of July 15 30
   difference from the Gülen community 40, 45, 132, 134
   houses of (*see also* Nur houses) 63, 65–66
   pedagogical path 106–108
   reading in 100, 129
   reflecting on nature (*see also tefekkür*) 111, 120
   reform project 172, 188
   responsibility 183
   tension with secular order 189, 193
Sufi(s)/Sufism 101, 104
   as non-elitist tradition 101
   barzakh 121
   contemplation of death (*rabıta-i mevt*) 125–126
   cosmology 103
   epistemology 106
   heart in (*See also* heart *under* transcendence *and* heart as the locus of *under* knowledge) 117
   leader (*şeyh*) 33–34
   lodge (*tekke*) 54, 101
   path (*tarikat*) 125
   sanctuary (*türbe*) 54
   scholars 103
   topos 108
Süleyman Chelebi 156
Sultan/Sultanate
   Ottoman 51
Sungur, Mustafa 101
sunna (Prophet Muhammad's exemplary conduct) 7, 11, 64, 74, 77, 79, 95, 160
   and *adab* 76
   norms of behavior 74–76
   scientific reliability of 75

Tablighi Jamaat 184
taklid/taklidi (imitation/imitative)
   faith 108
   Muslims by 38, 187

Tanzimat (period of reform in the Ottoman Empire)   51, 134–135
tefekkür (meditative reflection)   32, 100, 106, 110–114, 130, 175, 199
   cosmological framework   119–123
   genealogy of   115–118
   heart in   117
   on death   124–129
terbiye (character development in Islam) (*see* character formation in *under* Gülen community)
theologians (Muslim)   105, 118
Topçu, Nurettin   41–42, 139–140, 149
tradition(s) (*see also* tradition *under* Islam/Islamic)   7, 11–16
   as discourse   81
   as intellectual repertoire(s)   16
   continuity and change   100
   discursive   11–13, 16
transcendence   6, 202
   anthropology and theology   4
   as mediator of human relations   176
   as severed from tangible objects   4
   heart (*see also* heart as the locus of *under* knowledge)   117–118
   hierarchy of goods   181

ulema (scholars of Islam)   33–35, 51–53, 55, 135
Ünal, Ali   42

vakıf (pious endowment)   54, 58
Vico, Giambattista   102–103
virtue(s)   5, 63, 180
   ethicists (*see* MacIntyre, Alasdair)
   ethics (*see also* Aristotle/Aristotelian)   151
   non-heroic (*see also* Milbank, John)   90–92, 188
   self-sacrifice   159

Weber, Max   113, 169, 184, 192, 195
Welfare Party (*Refah Partisi*)   19, 46
White, Jenny B.   205
Williams, Bernard   15
Wittgenstein, Ludwig   78, 81

Yayla, Atilla   42
Young Ottomans   54, 56, 86, 136
youth (*see also* youth *under hizmet*)   135, 138, 140, 149, 166